HIGHER

Information Systems

Charlie Love

Hodder Gibson

A MEMBER OF THE HODDER HEADLINE GROUP

This book is dedicated to Vanessa Love,
the bravest person I know.
C x

Although every effort has been made to ensure that website addresses are correct at time of going to press, Hodder Gibson cannot be held responsible for the content of any website mentioned in this book. It is sometimes possible to find a relocated web page by typing in the address of a home page for a website in the URL window of your browser.

Hodder Headline's policy is to use papers that are natural, renewable and recyclable products and made from wood grown in sustainable forests. The logging and manufacturing processes are expected to conform to environmental regulations of the country of origin.

Orders: please contact Bookpoint Ltd, 130 Milton Park, Abingdon, Oxon OX14 4SB. Telephone: (44) 01235 827720. Fax: (44) 01235 400454. Lines are open from 9.00–6.00, Monday to Saturday, with a 24 hour message answering service. Visit our website at www.hoddereducation.co.uk. Hodder Gibson can be contacted direct on: Tel: 0141 848 1609; Fax 0141 889 6315; email: hoddergibson@hodder.co.uk

© Charlie Love 2005
First published in 2005 by
Hodder Gibson, an imprint of Hodder Education, a member of the Hodder Headline Group,
2a Christie Street,
Paisley PA1 1NB

Impression number   10   9   8   7   6   5   4   3   2

Year   2010   2009   2008   2007   2006   2005

Typeset in Usherwood Book 11½/12 pt by GreenGate Publishing Services, Tonbridge, Kent.

Printed and bound in Great Britain by Martins The Printers, Berwick-upon-Tweed.

A catalogue record for this title is available from the British Library

ISBN -10: 0 340 85045 0
ISBN -13: 978 0 340 85045 9

Contents

Foreword

Higher Information Systems by Charlie Love is an essential book for all students studying the Higher Information Systems course. It focuses on the two mandatory units of Relational Database Systems and Using Information. It covers all the content specified in the content statements for both these units in the arrangements documents published by SQA in 2004. The questions that are interspersed throughout the text reinforce the knowledge, understanding and problem solving skills that are necessary for students to deepen their understanding of the course content. The concepts that underpin the two mandatory units are very well explained through careful use of text, diagrams, graphics and screenshots from application packages. The combination of these features enhances the layout of the book, and make it extremely easy to read and understand.

This comes as no surprise as the author, Charlie Love, is renowned for the quality of his classroom support materials. Charlie has been involved with the subject of Information Systems since its inception in 1999. He has made a significant contribution to the subject, both in the support materials he has produced and in the advice he has given to the structure and content of the new Information Systems courses.

Having been a setter and examiner for Higher Information Systems with SQA, I believe this book will prove to be an invaluable resource for the subject. At a time when the subject has undergone a significant review with fundamental changes to all aspects of the course, I am confident that the profession will welcome this resource with open arms and indeed will use it as the main source on which they will base their teaching of Higher Information Systems.

Tom Liversedge
Principal Teacher of Computing, Portlethen Academy

Acknowledgements

The author wishes to thank the following for their help, assistance and guidance.

Karen Allardyce, David Bethune, James Bisset, Sheila Blakemore, Patricia Bruce, Joy Buchan, Colin Chisolm, Marie Craib, Bobby Elliott, Cathy Falconer, Fay Jaffray, Mike Jamieson, Tom Kelly, Tom Liversedge, Mary Love, Amber and Megan Love, David Mackie, George Mair, Lesley Mair, Alison Park, Ed Picksley, Morag Shaw, Ian Sorensen, Dot Tedman, All at Perfect Papers and John Mitchell (the world's most patient publisher).

Further information to support the study of Higher Information Systems may be found at **http://www.higherinformationsystems.com**.

The Publishers would like to thank the following for permission to use copyright material:

Amazon screenshot reproduced with permission. © 2005 Amazon.com. All rights reserved, p 274; British Computer Society logo reproduced with permission, p 197; Steve Connolly, photograph, p 273; Crown copyright material is reproduced with the permission of the Controller of HMSO, p 272; FileMaker is a trademark of FileMaker, Inc., registered in the U.S.and other countries. ScriptMaker and the file folder logo are trademarks of FileMaker, Inc., pp 142, 144; GreenGate Publishing, photographs, pp 6, 180, 182, 199, 210, 232, 266, 277; IBM Lotus Notes welcome screen reproduced courtesy of International Business Machines Corporation. Unauthorised use not permitted, p 260; Extract from Global CEO reprinted with permission from ICFAI Knowledge Center, pp 276-7; Screen shot from TSC2 help desk reprinted with permission from Servantix LLC, p 211; Kelkoo home page reproduced with permission, p 275; Macromedia and HomeSite are trademarks or registered trademarks of Macromedia, Inc. in the United States and/or other countries, pp 241, 243; John Mitchell, photographs, pp 7 (lower), 34, 166, 224; Navicat screenshot reproduced with permission, pp 119, 122; Nielsen/NetRatings Global Internet Trends table reproduced with permission, p 271; Screen shots reprinted by permission from Microsoft Corporation, pp 123, 210, 225, 236, 246; Global homepage for palmOne Inc. Image provided by palmOne, Inc, p 269; Extract from Said, A., Shawky, A., ElMasry, N., Ezzat, M. & Hassan, M. Proceedings of the 2nd Inter-Regional Conference on Environment– Water, ©1999, Presses polytechniques et universitaires romandes, reproduced with publisher's authorisation. All rights reserved, pp 169-70; Photo of Babbage's analytical engine from Science Museum/Science and Society Picture Library, p 7; Screenshot printed from thegreendoorsweetshop.co.uk with permission, p 275; Yahoo! avatars. Reproduced with permission of Yahoo! Inc. © 2005 by Yahoo! Inc. YAHOO! and the YAHOO! logo are trademarks of Yahoo! Inc, p 279.

Every effort has been made to trace copyright holders, but if any have been inadvertently overlooked the Publishers will be pleased to make the necessary arrangements at the first opportunity.

Information and Information Systems

Information, data and knowledge

Any book that deals with information systems must start by explaining what information is. Information is very difficult to describe because it can be interpreted in many different ways.

One concept of information is that it is the result of the processing of data. This definition might be correct, but it does not take account of *understanding* the data. This is where people come in. In order to understand properly what information is we need to define the terms **data**, **information** and **knowledge**, and the role of *people* in understanding the information presented to them.

Data

Data refers to facts. A single unit or item of data is called a **datum**. It is one or more symbols used to represent something. This might be the alphabetic characters used to spell your name, the numbers used to define your age or the vertical lines on a barcode to represent an item's product number. Collections of data can take a number of different forms.

In Figure 1.1 a number of different data items are shown. Each group of data items, whichever way it is organised, can be considered data. The terms **data item**, **data** and **datum** can be used interchangeably when referring to one single item of data. In this book we will use the term 'data' to refer to both collections of data items and to single data items.

> ### Data
>
> Data can be coded and structured for processing. This is usually done by a computer system. The symbols used to represent the data are meaningless until they are processed.
>
> Once data is placed in context, it becomes information. The subtle difference between data and information is that information is in context, data is not.

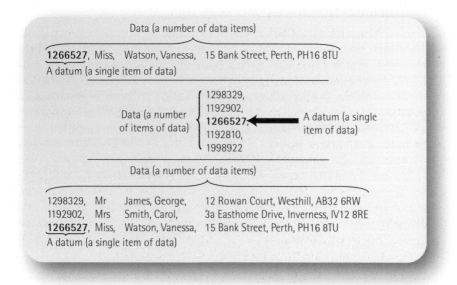

Figure 1.1 *Data and data items*

This barcode has data in machine-readable form

Information

Information is data that can be understood. If data is presented to a user in a way that the user can understand, then the data becomes information. Information is data placed within a meaningful context so that it can be interpreted by the user. If the user is unable to interpret the data then the context is not appropriate and the data does not become information.

A computer cannot understand the information that it stores. The computer can only store information in its memory as data. When a user enters data into a computer the user has an understanding of the context of the data, therefore, to that user, the data is information. To the computer the data is simply a collection of symbols, which it stores electronically in its memory and processes according to the instructions in its programs. The computer can output this data in a variety of forms. Whatever form it is in, when the appropriate context is applied to it and a human interprets it, the data becomes information (Figure 1.2).

> ### Information
>
> Information is data that is presented in context. Computers are not capable of understanding the data that they hold therefore a human is required to interpret the data by placing it in an appropriate context. When the data is interpreted it becomes information.

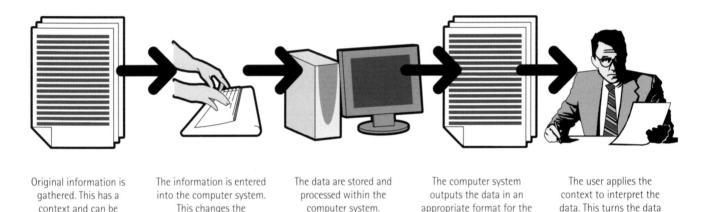

| Original information is gathered. This has a context and can be understood by the user. | The information is entered into the computer system. This changes the information into data as it is stored electronically in the computer's memory. | The data are stored and processed within the computer system. | The computer system outputs the data in an appropriate format for the user. | The user applies the context to interpret the data. This turns the data into information. |

Figure 1.2 Information, data and computer systems

Knowledge

Once information is understood, it becomes knowledge. Combining information with existing knowledge (what we already know) generates more knowledge. Whether something is information or not depends on how we perceive it; information is subjective. Information must always be set in a context that is meaningful to the person who requires it. Also, different people, depending on their existing knowledge, may interpret the same information in different ways.

It is easier to understand these ideas by looking at a couple of examples:

> ### Domain
>
> A domain is an area to which information can be assigned. For example, 'birds' is a domain containing information about birds. The size of this domain is large because there is a large amount of information about birds. The size of the domain would be reduced if an ornithologist decided to study one particular species of bird, say eagles. The domain of 'eagles' is smaller than 'birds' because there is less information within it.

Example 1

Take the string of symbols **827227**. Taken together these symbols form a data item, but by themselves they are meaningless. To turn these symbols into information a meaningful context must be applied to them. The user must interpret them. These symbols could be someone's telephone number, an employee's reference code or a personal identification number for a bank account. Information of this type will add to knowledge of a specific **domain**. For example, if the data item is an employee's reference code then it might contribute to our understanding of the number of people who work for a particular company. The domain in this case would be the company.

Example 2

A day trader is using a web browser and other specialised software to follow the trading of stocks and shares from home. The trader has very little experience of the business of share trading because she has only been trading for a matter of weeks. The trader sees that a new product for a company is selling well and has received several awards. She decides to buy shares in the company. In this case, the information about the particular product has caused the trader to buy shares.

An experienced stock market trader receives the same information about the sales of the product, but has the additional knowledge that the company is looking to take over a weaker rival. This possible takeover is seen as a risk and the trader therefore does not buy shares in the company.

This example shows how knowledge can influence the use of information. Both traders received the same information but the knowledge they possessed was different. This led them to make different decisions.

All information systems are designed to take in, store, process and then output data. Outside of the information system the data becomes information because it is understood by the user. The information is assigned to a domain and viewed within the context of that domain. When the information is interpreted it adds to the existing knowledge of the domain (Figure 1.3).

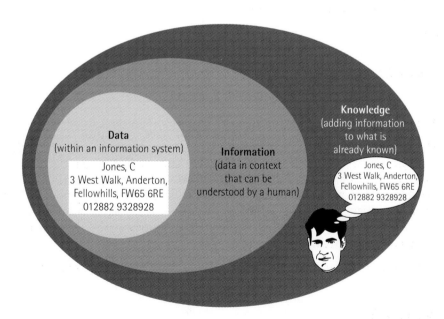

Figure 1.3 The relationship of data, information and knowledge

Questions

1. Explain the following terms:

a data

b datum

c information

d knowledge

e domain.

2. Why is *context* important in relation to data and information?

3. The telephone number 289389 is entered into a computer system. When held in the computer's memory, is this number data or information?

Explain your answer.

So, what is an information system?

Information systems are designed for processing information. Information systems collect, organise, store, process and display information in a variety of forms and formats (text, graphics, audio, etc.).

Often, information systems are described in terms of their inputs, processes and outputs, but this ignores the fact that every information system is designed to be part of some kind of human activity. All information systems are designed to reduce the amount of effort required by a human to complete an activity. This 'effort' might be physical effort, mental effort or a combination of both.

A paper-based diary is an information system. It reduces the requirement to remember appointments and important dates. A diary receives input from the user when an entry is made; it stores the entry and presents it in a suitable format for the user when required.

Any record-keeping system, for example an appointment book or a train timetable, can be regarded as an information system, however the term is most often used to describe computer-based systems.

Another example of a manual information system is a paper-based purchase order processing system (Example 3). In this manual system the storage consists of filing cabinets (using some kind of filing system, for example alphabetical or by date) and a card index. Details of the processes are described in written documents and by the working practices of the company.

In a computerised information system, the input, storage, processing and output of information are carried out using a computer. The computer requires a store of data and a number of processes (programs).

These modern information systems allow extremely fast, automated manipulation of data and have considerable advantages over manual systems, such as:

- the speed of accessing and processing data is vastly increased
- data can be organised in any way required

Information system

Any collection of processes and storage that allows data to be entered, manipulated and/or processed in some way and then output in an appropriate form for the user can be described as an information system. An information system can be manual or computer based.

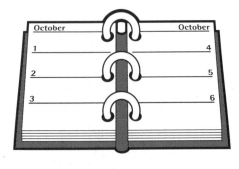

- data can be output in any required format
- physical storage is vastly reduced (from large paper files in manual systems to the hard disk of a computer system)
- processes can be changed easily by reprogramming the computer
- data can be shared between users (more than one person can view a customer's record at once because the data is stored electronically rather than on one piece of paper)
- data can be moved large distances extremely quickly (such as by e-mail).

Example 3

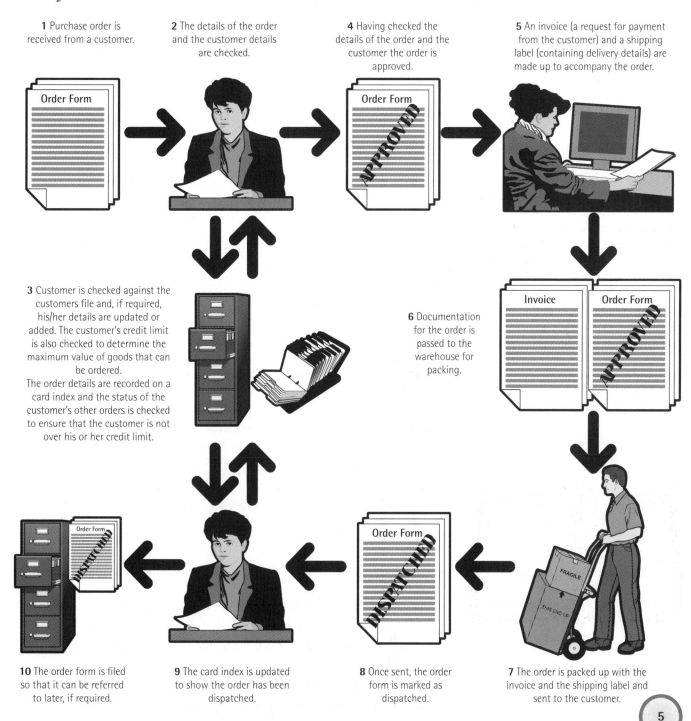

1 Purchase order is received from a customer.

2 The details of the order and the customer details are checked.

4 Having checked the details of the order and the customer the order is approved.

5 An invoice (a request for payment from the customer) and a shipping label (containing delivery details) are made up to accompany the order.

3 Customer is checked against the customers file and, if required, his/her details are updated or added. The customer's credit limit is also checked to determine the maximum value of goods that can be ordered.
The order details are recorded on a card index and the status of the customer's other orders is checked to ensure that the customer is not over his or her credit limit.

6 Documentation for the order is passed to the warehouse for packing.

10 The order form is filed so that it can be referred to later, if required.

9 The card index is updated to show the order has been dispatched.

8 Once sent, the order form is marked as dispatched.

7 The order is packed up with the invoice and the shipping label and sent to the customer.

These advantages over manual systems are some of the reasons why we have seen an exponential increase in the use of information systems in all areas of our lives. But have you ever thought about how much of a role information systems really play in your life?

Questions

1. What is an information system?

2. Why do computer-based information systems reduce the *physical storage requirements* of a system?

3. Give *three* other advantages (apart from those listed above) of a computer-based information system over a manual information system.

4. Describe an information system that you use each day or that has an influence on your life each day.

Where would we be without information systems?

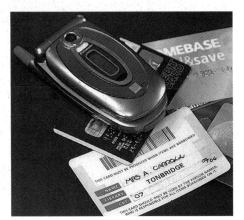

All of these involve the use of an information system

Information systems are used in every aspect of our lives; you might have a mobile phone with important numbers stored in its memory, you might use a debit or credit card to buy goods or you might borrow books from your local library. All these involve the use of an information system.

If you have milk delivered to your house each morning it would not be there if it wasn't for a number of information systems. The milk from the dairy farm is picked up each day because the farm's details are held in an information system that generates a document telling the tanker driver which farms are on his or her route. The tanker driver delivers the milk to the dairy and this is logged in an information system. The dairy uses an information system to monitor production, and each bottle of milk is coded according to the day and time of bottling – also done by an information system. An information system is also used to calculate sell-by and use-by dates.

Just think, without information systems you would not have fresh milk for your cornflakes each morning!

Information systems have a huge impact on our lives. Many people are concerned about this, and about people's dependence on information systems generally. Later in this book we will look at the social and ethical implications of information systems and how the law has been changed to take account of how information systems are used.

But how did we get to where we are today? Where did computer-based information systems come from?

A brief history of computers and information systems

Babbage and the early pioneers

The real beginnings of computers as we know them today lie with an English mathematics professor, Charles Babbage (1791–1871). Frustrated at the many errors he found while examining calculations for the Royal Astronomical Society, Babbage declared, 'I wish to God these calculations had been performed by steam!'. With those words, the automation of computers began. Babbage's first attempt at solving this problem was in 1822 when he proposed a machine to perform differential equations, called a Difference Engine. Powered by steam and as large as a locomotive, the machine had a stored program and could perform calculations and print the results automatically. After working on the Difference Engine for ten years, Babbage was suddenly inspired to begin work on the first general-purpose computer, which he called the Analytical Engine.

Figure 1.4 *Babbage's Analytical Engine*

Babbage's steam-powered engine, although ultimately never constructed, may seem primitive by today's standards. However, it included the basic elements of a modern general-purpose computer and was a breakthrough concept. Consisting of over 50,000 components, the basic design of the Analytical Engine included input devices in the form of perforated cards containing operating instructions and a 'store' for memory of 1000 numbers of up to 50 digits long.

It also contained a 'mill' with a control unit that allowed processing instructions in any sequence, and output devices to produce printed results. Babbage borrowed the idea of punch cards to encode the machine's instructions from the Jacquard loom. The loom, produced in 1820 and named after its inventor, Joseph-Marie Jacquard, used punched boards that controlled the patterns to be woven.

In 1889, an American inventor, Herman Hollerith (1860–1929), also applied the Jacquard loom concept to computing. His first task was to find a faster way to compute the results of the US census. The previous census, in 1880, had taken nearly seven years to count, and with an expanding population the bureau feared it would take ten years to count the latest census. Unlike Babbage's idea of using perforated cards to instruct the machine, Hollerith's method used cards to store data he fed into a machine that compiled the results mechanically. Instead of ten years, census takers compiled their results in just six weeks with Hollerith's machine. In addition to speeding up the processing, the punch cards served as a storage method for data and helped reduce errors. Hollerith's punch card reader became highly successful in the business world. Hollerith founded the Tabulating Machine Company in 1896, later to become International Business Machines (IBM) in 1924 after a series of mergers. Business, education and government used punch cards for data processing until the 1960s.

An efficient information system allows this store to keep track of thousands of DVDs and videos

In the ensuing years, several engineers made other significant advances. In 1931, Vannevar Bush (1890–1974) developed a calculator for solving differential equations. The machine could solve complex differential equations that had baffled scientists and mathematicians for many years. Also, what we now know as hypertext, and the concept of linking sections of documents together, have their origins in the ideas of Bush. In many ways he was the pioneer of hypermedia.

With the onset of the Second World War, governments sought to develop computers to exploit their potential strategic importance. By 1941 German engineer Konrad Zuse had developed a computer, the Z3, to design aeroplanes and missiles. The allied forces, however, made greater strides in developing powerful computers. In 1943, the British completed a secret code-breaking computer called Colossus to decode German messages, though the Colossus's impact on the development of the computer industry was rather limited for two important reasons. First, Colossus was not a general-purpose computer; it was only designed to decode secret messages. Second, the existence of the machine was kept secret until decades after the war.

Computers getting smaller

By 1948, the invention of the transistor greatly changed the course of computer development. The transistor replaced the large, cumbersome vacuum tube in televisions, radios and computers, and the size of electronic machinery has been shrinking ever since!

In the early 1960s, a number of commercially successful computers were used in businesses, universities and government. These second generation computers contained transistors in place of vacuum tubes. They also contained all the components we associate with the modern-day computer: printers, tape storage, disk storage, memory, operating systems and stored programs. By 1965, most large businesses routinely processed financial information using computers.

It was the stored program and programming languages that gave computers the flexibility needed to finally be cost effective and productive for business use. The instructions to run a computer for a specific function (known as a program) were held (stored) inside the computer's memory, and could quickly be replaced by a different set of instructions for a different function if required. A computer could print customer invoices, and minutes later design products or calculate employees' pay. New types of careers (programmers, analysts, computer systems experts, etc.) and the entire software industry began with second generation computers.

Though transistors were clearly an improvement over the vacuum tube, they still generated a great deal of heat, which damaged the computer's sensitive internal parts. In 1958, Jack Kilby, an engineer with Texas Instruments, developed the integrated circuit (IC) to solve this problem. The IC combined three electronic components onto a small silicon disc made from quartz called a semiconductor. This became known as a microchip, or 'chip' for short. Scientists later managed to fit even more components onto a single chip. As a result, computers became increasingly smaller as more and more components were squeezed onto a chip.

By the 1980s, very large-scale integration (VLSI) squeezed hundreds of thousands of components onto a chip. Ultra large-scale integration (ULSI) increased that number into the millions. The ability to fit so much onto an area about half the size of a five pence piece helped vastly diminish the size and price of computers.

It also increased their power, efficiency and reliability. In 1971, Intel developed the first microprocessor which took the integrated circuit one step further by locating all the components of a computer (central processing unit, memory and input and output controls) on one tiny chip.

Whereas previously the integrated circuit had to be manufactured to fit a special purpose, now one microprocessor could be manufactured and then programmed to meet any number of demands. Soon everyday household

Figure 1.5 *Many processing chips on one wafer of silicon. Courtesy of International Business Machines Corporation. Unauthorized use not permitted.*

items such as microwave ovens, television sets and cars with electronic fuel injection contained microprocessors.

Such condensed power allowed everyone the opportunity to harness a computer's power. Computers were no longer developed exclusively for large organisations and governments. By the mid-1970s computer manufacturers were seeking to make computers available to the general consumer.

When VisiCalc was introduced for the Apple II computer, many people suddenly saw a reason to buy a computer. VisiCalc, a spreadsheet program, allowed people to change one number in a budget and watch the effect it had on the entire budget. It was something new and valuable that could only be done with a computer. For thousands of people the computer was transformed into a device that could actually do something worthwhile.

The personal computer

In 1981, IBM introduced its personal computer (PC) for use in the home, office and school. The 1980s saw a huge expansion in computer use as clones of the IBM PC made the personal computer even more affordable. The number of personal computers in use worldwide more than doubled from 2 million in 1981 to 5.5 million in 1982. Ten years later, 65 million PCs were being used.

When IBM entered the market in 1981, software companies knew that writing IBM-compatible software would be profitable. New software produced in the 1980s included WordStar, Lotus 1-2-3, Microsoft Word and Word Perfect.

In direct competition with IBM's PC was Apple's Macintosh line, introduced in 1984. Notable for its user-friendly design, the Macintosh offered an operating system that allowed users to move screen icons instead of typing instructions.

During the 1980s Bill Gates, a founder of Microsoft, tried three times to interest IBM in Windows but was turned down each time. Although the Apple Mac operating system had changed the interface between users and their PCs, many DOS users continued to hang on to their command line-driven MS-DOS operating system, and it would be several more years before the Windows concept caught on.

The trend towards smaller and smaller computers has continued, working its way down from desktop to laptop computers (which can fit inside a briefcase) to palmtop (able to fit inside a pocket).

Information is everything

The availability of cheap and easy-to-use personal computers created a huge growth in the software industry. Businesses and other organisations of all sizes required software to process their data. Many of these organisations had software written specifically to meet their needs; others used off-the-shelf or customised programs. As companies moved to storing data digitally the speed and amount of data they could process increased greatly.

Companies began to change the way they worked in order to use the data they stored more efficiently. They began to link areas of their business together; processing customer orders was linked to stock control, shipping was linked to invoicing, etc. Information systems were capable of tracking each piece of data through a company. These information systems were able to provide management with detailed reports that presented a summary of the company's current state, such as stock levels, total sales, best-selling products, top customers, etc. Before computerisation reports of this type might have taken months to prepare. An information system was capable of producing one every day!

New ways have since been developed to store and manipulate data; database systems, expert systems, hypermedia systems, computer applications have all enjoyed significant development in recent years related to how computer systems store and manipulate data and provide information.

Information is now a major commodity. Companies sell and buy information about customers in order to reach new markets and generate revenue. Credit reference agencies hold records about the financial situations of millions of people and charge for others to access it. Direct marketing companies use consumer surveys and analyses of buying habits to profile individual people and then target them for advertising.

Information systems are the single most important factor in the increasing availability of information, and the vast majority of computing power in the world is dedicated to running them.

Developing an information system

The development of any information system has four key stages: **analysis**, **design**, **implementation** and **evaluation** (including testing and documentation). Each of these stages is vital to the successful development of the information system. All information systems development projects, large and small, involve each of these stages.

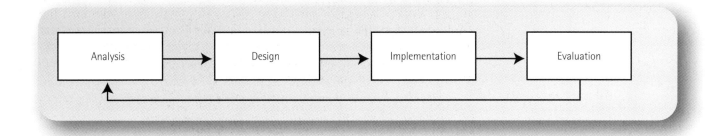

Figure 1.6 *The information systems development cycle*

Analysis

In medium- to large-scale projects, the analysis stage is carried out by a systems analyst. During this stage the analyst has to construct an exact specification for the work to be done. This specification is then agreed with the client who has requested the information system. For small-scale projects it might be one programmer, analyst, manager or other member of the workforce that carries out the analysis.

The purpose of the analysis stage is to produce a specification for development of the information system.

Example 4

An information system is required to replace an existing manual purchase order processing system (see Example 3). It is the job of the systems analyst to understand exactly how the existing manual system works so that he or she can create a specification for the new system.

The systems analyst will investigate the current system by examining existing company documents, interviewing employees and managers, observing the system in operation, studying the organisation of files and documents and so on.

Once satisfied, the analyst will produce a specification for the new system based on the current system. This specification will include improvements to the existing system such as computerisation, changes to the organisation of data and alterations to working practices that increase efficiency. The specification is normally agreed with the client to ensure the information system being proposed meets the client's needs.

Design

During the design phase the systems analyst or programmer uses the specification from the analysis phase to produce a design for the new system. The design will consist of written documentation stating, in detail, what is to be done during the implementation phase to create the information system described in the specification.

It is important, especially for medium- to large-scale projects, that the design can be broken into different pieces (i.e. that it is *modular*). This is so that implementation of the system can be carried out by a number of different programmers, all working at the same time. A modular design allows each programmer to work on his or her own component part of the system and then, once ready, the individual components can be brought together to produce the system.

Often at this stage a specific platform for the implementation is selected.

Example 4 (cont'd)

The systems analyst has created a detailed list of the inputs, processes and outputs required for the new information system. Also, the way data is stored in the system has been changed, so that it is more efficient and reduces the amount of duplicate data held. The systems analyst recommends a platform for implementing the design. This decision is based on the available resources (money, existing hardware/software, most appropriate platform for the system, etc.).

Implementation

During implementation the information system is created by following the details of the design and creating the programs required using the suggested platform. If an element of the design cannot be implemented due to weaknesses associated with the platform (such as the software not being able to carry out a required task) then there are two options: revise the specification to remove the need for this feature or select a different implementation platform which will allow the required task to be performed.

Example 4 (cont'd)

During the implementation two different programmers work to develop the system. The first programmer creates the new data structures and writes reports (invoices, shipping labels and management reports) that will extract data from the system and present it as information for the user. The other programmer writes the part of the software that will access the data and manipulate it.

Evaluation

Once the implementation of the information system is complete the process of evaluating the system begins. First, the product is thoroughly tested to ensure that it does what it is meant to do. Second, it is tested to see how robust it is and whether it will crash when erroneous data is entered.

Once the testing is completed documentation is created to accompany the information system. This documentation might describe how the system works, how areas of it might be improved and how and if the system meets the requirements of the specification.

The documentation from the evaluation phase can be used as the basis for future work on the system. It provides a useful source of information for any future analysis phase. This cycle of information systems development (analysis, design, implementation, evaluation) is called a *life cycle* because the final output from the cycle can be used as an input for a further cycle.

Example 4 (cont'd)

The system is tested by the programmers using real data supplied by the company. A few minor bugs in the software are identified and fixed by the programmers. The documentation is then created. The documentation contains a detailed user guide, a list of possible enhancements to the system in the future, a list of the few remaining bugs, and the specification and design from the analysis and design stages of the system's development.

This process of analysis, design, implementation and evaluation is common to all areas of information systems development. Whether the system is a database or a website, an expert system or custom application, each must be developed by following this cycle.

Questions

1. Name each of the stages in the development of an information system.

2. What is the role of a systems analyst in the development of an information system?

3. Give one reason why it is important to develop a *modular* design for an information system.

4. Why do you think it is important to test an information system?

5. Why is the development cycle called a *life cycle*?

Database Fundamentals

Understanding the database

A **database** is a store of data. We say it is data because it only becomes information when we apply a context to it! Any collection of data stored on paper or electronically is a database.

A manual database is very much like a filing cabinet, or more accurately, a series of filing cabinets. The database is a collection of **files** and each file, in turn, is a structured collection of data. In a manual system the files would be the folders hung inside the filing cabinet. Each file contains a collection of **records** and each record is divided into a series of areas known as **fields** (Figure 2.1).

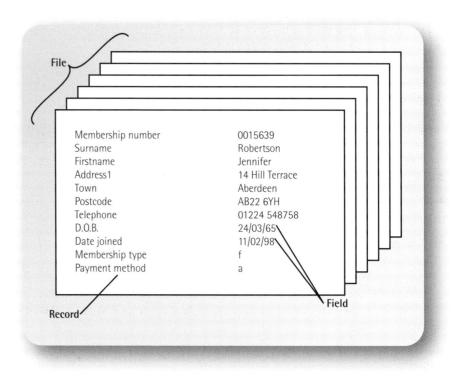

Figure 2.1 Structure of a simple database

When organisations first began to develop information systems they did so in small steps. Individual manual systems, such as payroll, stock control or accounts, would be analysed, redesigned and implemented as a computerised information system with little thought for the operation of the organisation as a whole. This approach clearly produced a number of different information systems, each with its own software platform, its own input and output requirements and its own files. This lead to a number of problems:

- Self-contained systems do not represent how an organisation works as a whole. All organisations are complex and require interacting and inter-dependent systems.

- The output from one system may have to be modified to provide the input for another system. This often involves data operators taking printouts of data from one system and re-entering this as the input for a second system. This requirement to re-enter data causes delays in the system.

- Information from a series of separate files is less valuable to an organisation because it does not present a complete picture. For example, a travel agent booking holidays would not get all the information he needs from the accommodation file; he may also need to look at the flights file and the transfers file in order to complete the holiday booking.

- Data may be duplicated in a number of files across the different information systems in an organisation. This creates problems when maintaining the data and introduces the risk of data being inconsistent within the organisation.

Because of these problems it is now desirable for organisations to have a single central pool of organisational data rather than a series of separate files. This central database is an organised store of data which, typically, can be used for more than one purpose and by more than one person at the same time.

This central database is integrated with a piece of software that controls all the access and manipulation of the data. This software is called a **database management system** or **DBMS**. We will look at a number of database management systems later in this book.

The relational data model

A data model is a plan for how a database is to be created. The data model details how the data is to be organised, how it can be accessed and how it can be manipulated. The relational data model is the most common data model currently in use and consists of three components:

- a data structure
- a set of data operators
- a set of data integrity rules.

Data structures

The relational data model has only one data structure. This is the **table** or **relation**.

student						
student_id	title	firstname	surname	date_of_birth	year_of_study	dept_code
9701111	Mr	Charlie	Burton	05/01/1975	4th	COMP
9802600	Miss	Susan	Low	12/09/1986	2nd	OENG
9802685	Mr	Alexander	Middleton	28/05/1980	2nd	MIS
9806666	Mr	Sandy	Ogston	14/12/1982	2nd	ENG
9807777	Mr	David	Wilson	21/10/1984	2nd	ENG
9891000	Mr	John	Smith	19/02/1986	1st	COMP

department

dept_code	dept_name	location	ext_no
COMP	School of Computer and Mathematical Sciences	Building A	1234
ENG	School of Electronic and Electrical Engineering	West Annex	2136
MIS	School of Management and Information	Building C	4101
OENG	School of Mechanical and Offshore Engineering	Building B	2134

Figure 2.2 Sample relations

The two tables in Figure 2.2, *student* and *department*, are relations because they adhere to a set of rules:

1 Every relation in a database must have a unique name.

2 Every column in a relation must have a unique name within that relation.

3 All entries in a column must be of the same kind.

4 The ordering of columns in a relation is not significant.

5 Each row in a relation must be unique. Duplicate rows are not allowed in a relation.

6 The order of the rows is not important in a relation.

7 Each cell in the relation (the intersection of a column and a row) must contain only one value. Multiple entries are not allowed in a cell.

Columns and column characteristics

Each column in a relation must have a unique name. Two or more relations within the same database may have columns with the same name and this, as you will see later, has a number of advantages.

When the same column name appears in more than one relation, and relations containing that column are referred to at the same time, then we use the relation name to distinguish between the two columns. For example, we would refer to the *dept_code* column in the above two relations as:

student.dept_code and *department.dept_code*

Each column in a relation must draw the data that it contains from the same domain. This means that each column must contain data of the same nature. This is easier to understand if we look at Figure 2.3, which is an incorrect snapshot of part of the student relation from the university example shown in Figure 2.2.

In this example the column is intended to store the surname of each student. However, the data entered for the third student is the student's phone number. Clearly, the data in this column is not all from the same domain (i.e. not all surnames) and, therefore, are invalid.

surname
Burton
Low
0821 928192
Ogston
Wilson
Smith

Figure 2.3 Column from student relation

Rows and row characteristics

Each row in a relation must be unique. This means that the combination of values in the columns of one row cannot be found elsewhere in the relation. Again, this is much easier to understand if we look at an example from the university database (Figure 2.4).

Here we see four rows from an incorrect snapshot of the student relation. Each cell (row/column intersection) of the first and fourth rows contains the

student_id	title	firstname	surname	date_of_birth	year_of_study	dept_code
9701111	Mr	Charlie	Burton	05/01/1975	4th	COMP
9802600	Miss	Susan	Low	12/09/1986	2th	OENG
9806666	Mr	Sandy	Ogston	14/12/1982	2th	ENG
9701111	Mr	Charlie	Burton	05/01/1975	4th	COMP

***Figure 2.4** Duplicate rows from the student relation*

same data. In fact, the fourth row is an exact duplicate of the first. The fourth row is not required because the data it stores is already held in the first row. If the fourth row were held in the relation then the relation would be invalid because each row would not then be unique. Now look at this other example (Figure 2.5).

student_id	title	firstname	surname	date_of_birth	year_of_study	dept_code
9701111	Mr	Charlie	Burton	05/01/1975	4th	COMP
9802600	Miss	Susan	Low	12/09/1986	2th	OENG
9806666	Mr	Sandy	Ogston	14/12/1982	2th	ENG
9701173	Mr	Charlie	Burton	05/01/1975	4th	COMP

***Figure 2.5** Correct rows from the student relation*

Your first reaction when you look at this sample of rows may be that it is invalid. However, the values for *student_id* for rows one and four are different and, therefore, each row is unique. This sample tells us there are two different people called Charlie Burton with the same birthday in the 4th year of the School of Computing and Mathematical Sciences. What a coincidence!

Each cell in a relation must contain only one piece of data (a cell is the point where a column and a row meet).

Column

student_id	title	firstname	surname
9701111	Mr	Charlie	Burton
9802600	Miss	Susan	Low
9802685	Mr	Alexander	Middleton
9807777	Mr	David	Wilson
9891000	Mr	John	Smith

Row

Cell

***Figure 2.6** Example of a cell in a relation*

The value of the cell in Figure 2.6 is 'Susan'. Every cell in the above relation contains only one value. Multi-valued cells are not allowed so the following relation would be invalid (Figure 2.7).

This example has multiple values in cells in the *potential_buyer_name* and *date_of_viewing* columns. These multi-valued cells are not permitted in a relational database. Only single-valued cells are allowed.

We say that relations that hold these multi-valued cells contain **repeating data items** and where there are one or more of these items they are referred to, collectively, as a **repeating group**.

property_id	client_name	potential_buyer_id	potential_buyer_name	date_of_viewing
P101	Smith	1282	Jones	17.04.2004
		1982	Perkins	19.04.2004
		2983	Patel	09.05.2004
		1282	Jones	29.05.2004
P106	Parker	1282	Jones	29.05.2004
		7225	Mitchell	23.04.2004

Figure 2.7 Property relation with invalid rows

Data items

Each piece of data in a relational database is a **data item**. Data items cannot be broken down into smaller elements of data. If we take the columns in the *department* relation – *dept_code*, *dept_name*, *location* and *ext_no* – each of these cannot be split into smaller items of data.

Addresses in database systems are typically stored as multiple data items (such as *house number*, *street*, *town* and *postcode*) rather than one data item (*address*). Data items are **atomic** because they cannot be decomposed into smaller items of data.

Using atomic data items increases the ease with which we can search and maintain the data in the database system.

Primary key

Each row in a relation must be unique. To ensure that this is the case each relation must have a **primary key**. A primary key is one or more columns of the relation whose values are used to uniquely identify each row of the relation.

department

dept_code	dept_name	location	ext_no
COMP	School of Computer and Mathematical Sciences	Building A	1234
ENG	School of Electronic and Electrical Engineering	West Annex	2136
MIS	School of Management and Information	Building C	4101
OENG	School of Mechanical and Offshore Engineering	Building B	2134

Figure 2.8 Department relation from the university example

The two tables (*department* and *student*) are part of a database used by a university. The university allocates a unique identifier to each department (*dept_code*) and each department has a different name. The university has many buildings on its campus and it is possible for departments to share accommodation. The university has an internal telephone system. All lecturers, departments and administration staff have their own extension number.

In the *department* table in Figure 2.8 there are a number of possible or **candidate keys** that we can consider before selecting the most appropriate key to be the primary key. These are:

- *dept_code*
- *dept_name*
- *location*
- *ext_no*.

Any of these four columns could be used to uniquely identify each row in the table. In order to select the most appropriate key it is important to understand a little more about the data (see box).

It becomes easier to select the most appropriate primary key from the candidate keys when you know a little more about the data. *Location* can be ruled out because departments can share accommodation (even though the sample data given does not show this!).

The *ext_no* could be used as a primary key because it is unique for each department, however the *ext_no* is also used by lecturers and administration staff and this would make it less attractive as a primary key.

The *dept_name* and the *dept_code* are both unique to each row. A primary key is used as a reference to each row in the table. The larger and more complex the key the more time it will take to use the key to find the required row of the table. With this in mind, the *dept_code* is a better primary key than the *dept_name* and would be the best choice as primary key.

Avoid meaningful primary keys

The *dept_code* in the university is an example of a meaningful primary key. The *dept_code* is related to the *dept_name*. But what do we do if a department changes its name? Do we change the *dept_code* in the *department* relation?

This would be acceptable if we were just concerned with the *department* relation but we also have to worry about all the data in the *student* relation. If the *dept_code* in the *department* relation is changed then every *dept_code* in the *student* relation with the previous value has to be changed to the new one.

If we do not update all the related *dept_code* values then it will look as though students are assigned to a department that does not exist!

Meaningful primary keys tend to change over time and this can introduce significant problems in a database system. Avoid using meaningful primary keys if you possibly can. Use arbitrary codes of numbers or letters instead.

It is not always possible to use completely meaningless primary keys. Sometimes you will have to include a time or a date in a primary key to distinguish between events. Be realistic when choosing primary keys and try to avoid meaningful primary keys when you can.

Compound primary keys

In some relations there is no one column that can act as a primary key. However, each row is unique because of the data values in the columns. For example:

viewings

property_id	client_name	potential_buyer_no	potential_buyer_name	date_of_viewing
P101	Smith	1282	Jones	17.04.2004
P101	Smith	1982	Perkins	19.04.2004
P101	Smith	2983	Patel	29.05.2004
P101	Smith	1282	Jones	29.05.2004
P106	Parker	1282	Jones	29.05.2004
P106	Parker	7225	Mitchell	23.04.2004

Figure 2.9 Example requiring compound key

In Figure 2.9 no single column contains a set of unique values.

- Because a property can be viewed more than once, *property_id* and *client_name* are repeated.

- Because one potential buyer can view one or more properties on several different occasions, *potential_buyer_no* and *potential_buyer_name* can appear more than once.

- Because any house can be visited more than once on the same day, the *date_of_viewing* is repeated. Note that the same person cannot view the same house twice on the same day.

This means that none of the columns can serve as a primary key on its own. However, a combination of *property_id*, *potential_buyer_no* and *date_of_viewing* is unique. This is because the combination of values in each of these three columns is never the same.

This combination of columns is our primary key. This is an example of a **compound key** (also known as a concatenated key) because it consists of more than one column.

To illustrate this further we will look at the rows that refer to potential buyer 1282:

property_id	client_name	potential_buyer_no	potential_buyer_name	date_of_viewing
P101	Smith	1282	Jones	17.04.2004
P101	Smith	1282	Jones	29.05.2004
P106	Parker	1282	Jones	29.05.2004

Figure 2.10 Rows for potential buyer 1282

Potential buyer 1282 is Mrs Jones. Her visits to view different properties are explained below from the data in Figure 2.10.

- In the first row she visits property P101 – key values are:

  property_id (P101)
  potential_buyer_no (1282)
  date_of_viewing (17.04.2004).

- The second row indicates that she visited property P101 again – key values are:

  property_id (P101)
  potential_buyer_no (1282)
  date_of_viewing (29.05.2004).

  Note that the date has changed and therefore our combination of three columns is still unique.

- In the final row Mrs Jones visits another property, P106. She does this on the same day that she viewed P101 for a second time – key values are:

  property_id (P106)
  potential_buyer_no (1282)
  date_of_viewing (29.05.2004).

  The only change from the previous row is the value for *property_id*. Our compound primary key of *property_id*, *potential_buyer_no* and *date_of_viewing* for the relation is unique.

A compound primary key should be made up of the smallest number of columns necessary to ensure the uniqueness of the primary key. As with all primary keys, the columns used in a compound key should be meaningless identifiers wherever possible.

Surrogate keys

A **surrogate key** is an arbitrary single column primary key which is created specifically for a relation. A surrogate key is created when the compound key for a relation is too complex to allow the key to be used efficiently or there is no unique collection of columns available in the relation.

When a surrogate key is required a new column is created to be the primary key of each row in the relation. If we take the property viewings example:

viewings

property_id	client_name	potential_buyer_no	potential_buyer_name	date_of_viewing
P101	Smith	1282	Jones	17.04.2004
P101	Smith	1982	Perkins	19.04.2004
P101	Smith	2983	Patel	29.05.2004
P101	Smith	1282	Jones	29.05.2004
P106	Parker	1282	Jones	29.05.2004
P106	Parker	7225	Mitchell	23.04.2004

Figure 2.11 A relation with a compound key

The columns that the primary key is constructed from are highlighted. This primary key is assembled from *property_id, potential_buyer_no* and *date_of_viewing*. We can remove this compound key and introduce a surrogate key in its place. This surrogate will be a single column primary key:

viewings

viewing_id	property_id	client_name	potential_buyer_no	potential_buyer_name	date_of_viewing
164	P101	Smith	1282	Jones	17.04.2004
165	P101	Smith	1982	Perkins	19.04.2004
166	P101	Smith	2983	Patel	29.05.2004
167	P101	Smith	1282	Jones	29.05.2004
168	P106	Parker	1282	Jones	29.05.2004
169	P106	Parker	7225	Mitchell	23.04.2004

Figure 2.12 A relation with a surrogate key

This single column primary key is much easier to work with than the previous three column compound primary key and is meaningless because it is an arbitrary number.

Foreign key

Foreign keys are vital in relational databases. Without foreign keys it is impossible to link data in separate relations. Relationships between relations in a database are created by linking a foreign key in one relation with its related primary key in a different relation.

student

student_id	title	firstname	surname	date_of_birth	year_of_study	dept_code
9701111	Mr	Charlie	Burton	05/01/1975	4th	COMP
9802600	Miss	Susan	Low	12/09/1986	2nd	OENG
9802685	Mr	Alexander	Middleton	28/05/1980	2nd	MIS
9806666	Mr	Sandy	Ogston	14/12/1982	2nd	ENG
9807777	Mr	David	Wilson	21/10/1984	2nd	ENG
9891000	Mr	John	Smith	19/02/1986	1st	COMP

department

dept_code	dept_name	location	ext_no
COMP	School of Computer and Mathematical Sciences	Building A	1234
ENG	School of Electronic and Electrical Engineering	West Annex	2136
MIS	School of Management and Information	Building C	4101
OENG	School of Mechanical and Offshore Engineering	Building B	2134

Figure 2.13 *Foreign key to primary key*

In Figure 2.13 above the foreign key *dept_code* in the *student* relation is linked to the primary key *dept_code* in the *department* relation. The value of one key can be used to look up the related value and hence the related data in the other relation.

For example, a secretary at the university that uses the above data would like to have a telephone message passed to a particular student. In order to do this she needs the *ext_no* for the department where the student can be found.

The secretary begins by searching the *student* relation for the required student. Once found this provides all the information about the student including the *dept_code* for the department that the student attends. The secretary takes this *dept_code* and looks for the matching *dept_code* in the *department* relation. Once the matching *dept_code* is found the secretary has the *ext_no* to contact the student. Figure 2.14 illustrates this.

Primary key–foreign key links can be used in both directions. In the example above the foreign key value was used to find the associated primary key value.

If a list of all the students attending a particular department was required, the value of *dept_code* for the department would be identified from the *department* relation. Then all the matching rows from the *student* relation (rows where the *dept_code* is equal to the value from the *department* relation) would be identified.

Foreign key from the primary key of the same relation

It is possible for a foreign key to reference a primary key within the same relation. For example, look at a sample relation used to record employees (Figure 2.15).

student

student_id	title	firstname	surname	date_of_birth	year_of_study	dept_code
9701111	Mr	Charlie	Burton	05/01/1975	4th	COMP
9802600	Miss	Susan	Low	12/09/1986	2nd	OENG
9802685	Mr	Alexander	Middleton	28/05/1980	2nd	MIS
9806666	Mr	Sandy	Ogston	14/12/1982	2nd	ENG
9807777	Mr	David	Wilson	21/10/1984	2nd	ENG
9891000	Mr	John	Smith	19/02/1986	1st	COMP

department

dept_code	dept_name	location	ext_no
COMP	School of Computer and Mathematical Sciences	Building A	1234
ENG	School of Electronic and Electrical Engineering	West Annex	2136
MIS	School of Management and Information	Building C	4101
OENG	School of Mechanical and Offshore Engineering	Building B	2134

Figure 2.14 Using keys

employee_id	firstname	lastname	department	manager_id
7384	Ingrid	West	Sales	8721
9827	Toby	Smith	Personnel	2341
9832	Amber	Rose	Sales	7384
6263	Megan	Jones	Sales	7384
2322	Simon	Cowell	Personnel	9827
3298	Andrew	Shaw	Warehouse	5172

Figure 2.15 Foreign key drawn from the primary key of the same relation

A manager is also an employee. Therefore the *manager_id*, although a different name from the primary key, is actually a foreign key that references the primary key, *employee_id*, of its own relation.

Relational databases depend on the use of primary and foreign keys to establish links, called relationships, between relations.

Data operators

There are four ways in which data are manipulated in a relational database system:

1 data is entered in to a relation

2 data is deleted from a relation

3 data is amended in a relation

4 data is retrieved from a relation.

These four operations use a variety of different data operators. In 1970, E F Codd, the creator of the relational database model, detailed operators which he called the **relational algebra**.

These relational database operators allow data to be inserted, amended, deleted and retrieved from a relational database. Most relational database management systems contain a set of operators which perform these functions. However, the detail of these operators is beyond the scope of the Higher Information Systems course.

Data integrity

Data integrity relates to the amount of trust we can place in the contents of a database. This means there must be a very close correlation between the facts stored in the database and the real world. In the example university database we believe that the fact '*student 9807777 attends the School of Electronic and Electrical Engineering*' is an accurate reflection of the operation of the university.

There are two types of integrity:

Entity integrity

Entity integrity relates to primary keys. This rule states that every relation must have a primary key and the column or columns selected for the primary key should be unique and not null (i.e. they must have a value).

Referential integrity

Referential integrity is concerned with foreign keys. The referential integrity rule states that foreign keys should have two states. Either the foreign key should be linked to the primary key of a related relation or, in very special circumstances, should have a null value.

In the first state, the value of the foreign key must exist in the linked relation as a primary key value. In the university example this means that the *dept_code* in the *student* relation cannot be a value that does not exist in the *dept_code* column of the *department* relation (Figure 2.16).

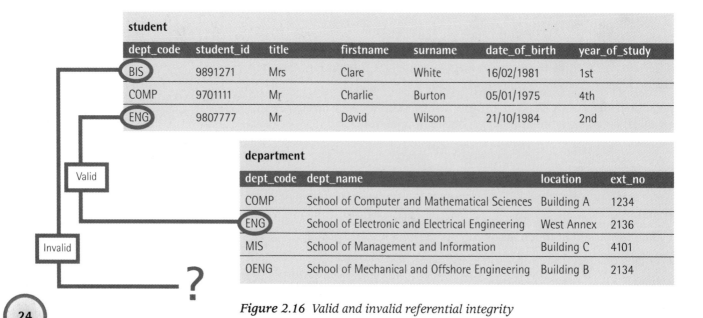

Figure 2.16 Valid and invalid referential integrity

In Figure 2.16 the value 'BIS' does not exist in the *dept_code* column of the *department* relation. This breaks the referential integrity rule. Only primary key values in departments (i.e. from the *dept_code* column of the *department* relation) can be foreign key values in the *dept_code* column of the *student* relation.

The second state for a foreign key is when it has a null (empty or unknown) value. A foreign key can only be a null value in special circumstances that depend on the rules of the organisation for which the database is being developed. Look at some more sample data from the employee relation from earlier in this chapter.

employee_id	firstname	lastname	department	manager_id
2322	Simon	Cowell	Personnel	9827
3298	Andrew	Shaw	Warehouse	5172
6262	Lindsey	Fleming	Sales	
7384	Ingrid	West	Sales	6262
9827	Toby	Smith	Personnel	2341
9832	Amber	Rose	Sales	6262

Figure 2.17 Example of a null value for a foreign key in a relation

Each manager is an employee and most, but not all, employees have a manager. The foreign key, *manager_id*, is drawn from the primary key, *employee_id*, of the same relation. But what happens when an employee is the most senior person in his or her department, i.e he or she has no manager?

Well, in this case, the value for *manager_id* is null because there is no available value to enter.

Questions

1. **a** Early information systems often had a number of drawbacks. Describe two of these problems.
   b How were these problems overcome?

2. Describe two features of a column in a relation database.

3. What is a repeating group?

4. What is an atomic data item?

5. Explain the difference between candidate keys and primary keys using a suitable example.

6. State the properties of a good primary key.

7. What is a compound primary key? Your answer should include an appropriate example.

8. What advantages do surrogate keys have over compound keys?

9. What is the purpose of a foreign key?

10. The term *null* is frequently used when working with relational database systems. What does it mean?

11. Four distinct manipulations can be applied to a database. What are they?

12. Entity and referential integrity are the types of data integrity that should be present in a relational database.
    Explain each of these terms using a suitable example.

13. Describe an instance when a foreign key might contain a null value.

Data Modelling
Building Blocks

Developing a model

The process of developing an information system can be divided into four main stages – analysis, design, implementation and evaluation. The development of a relational database system follows the same set of stages. At each stage of the first three stages a model of the relational database system is created (Figure 3.1).

These design stages can be summarised as follows:

- **Conceptual database design** – The process of constructing a model of the information used in a system, independent of *all* physical considerations. This means the model is an exact representation of the existing system and includes all the faults of that system.

- **Logical database design** – The process of constructing a model of the information presented in the conceptual model adapted to meet the rules of the relational data model. The logical database design is independent of a particular **relational database management system (RDBMS)** and all other physical considerations such as which computer the final system will run on.

- **Physical database design** – The process of producing a description for the implementation of the database. The physical database design is specific to the software and hardware that will be used to implement the logical design.

This process of designing a conceptual model then a logical data model then a physical model is know as database design methodology, i.e. a method of designing database systems.

Database design methodology (that is, the way databases are designed) is chiefly concerned with three things – entities, attributes and relationships.

Stage	Model developed
analysis	conceptual model
design	logical data model
implementation	physical model

Figure 3.1 *Stages of data modelling*

What is an entity?

An **entity** is something about which we want to record information. An entity is an object that exists and is distinguishable from other objects. An entity may be **concrete** (a person or a book, for example) or **abstract** (like a holiday or a concept). For instance:

- *Joanne Harris* with National Insurance number *NC 54 72 12 D* is an entity, as she can be uniquely identified as one particular person in the universe.

- The *Rental of Spiderman* with a rental date of *23/12/02* and DVD number of *6591* is an entity, as the transaction can be uniquely identified as one particular rental different from all other rentals.

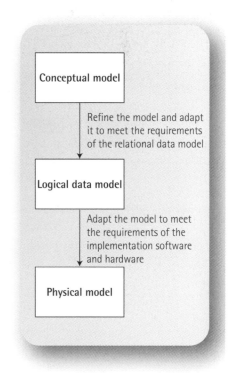

Figure 3.2 *Database design methodology*

Entity set

An **entity set** is a collection of entities of the same type (e.g. all the people who have an account at a bank). Entity sets can contain members from other entities, for example the entity set *employee* (all employees of the bank) and the entity set *customer* (all customers of the bank) may have members in common if someone who works at the bank also has an account at the bank.

Entity sets are very similar to relations (or tables) in a relational data model but may or may not meet all the rules for data structures that the relational database model specifies (see Chapter 2).

When giving a name to an entity set it is a common error to give it a name which is a plural, such as *customers*. This is wrong because an entity set should always be referred to as a singular collection of the entity it represents, e.g. *customer* **not** *customers*.

Attributes

An entity is represented by a set of **attributes**. Each attribute stores some data about the entity. For example *name*, *account_number*, *account_balance*, *street*, *city* are attributes of *customer* entity for the bank above.

Figure 3.3 *Entity and attributes (1)*

customer				
name	street	city	account_number	account_balance
James Innes	3 Crow Street	Glasgow	983271	£1902.98

Or, if the customer has more than one account:

Figure 3.4 *Entity and attributes (2)*

customer				
name	street	city	account_number	account_balance
James Innes	3 Crow Street	Glasgow	983271	£1902.98
			781721	£102.03
			197211	−£271.56

Notice that the second version of the entity has multiple values for some attributes. This is typical of entities identified as part of conceptual modelling. In a later chapter we will consider a method for removing these multi-valued cells in the entity. This method will produce a database design which conforms to the seven rules of the relational database model (see Chapter 2).

Domain constraints

The **domain** of an attribute is the set of permitted values (e.g. a name must only contain letters). Each domain has a set of **domain constraints**. These constraints apply to the type and value of the data that the attribute can hold. The domain constraints define the data that can be legally held by an attribute.

Null values

All attributes can be constrained by allowing or not allowing them to hold null values. A *null value* is an empty value rather than "" (empty quotes) or zero. This requires that an attribute defined as *NOT null* or *required* must be given a value.

To put it another way, all attributes can be constrained by presence (i.e. null or NOT null). If it is a requirement of the system that a value must be specified for the attribute then the attribute is defined as *NOT null* or *required*.

Data types

In Figure 3.5 each attribute (column) has a specific set of domain constraints that apply to it. Each attribute can store data of a particular type. These types are generally *text*, *integer*, *real*, *object*, *Boolean*, *date* and *time*.

Name	post_code	last_transaction	joint_account	account_type	account_opened	account_number	account_balance
Charlie Burton	G12 5TY	11:05	No	Current	12/05/2004	DX983	£1902.98

Figure 3.5 *Attributes with various domain constraints*

Text

Attributes which store data of the text data type store characters of text. These characters of text can, normally, be any of the symbols used in language such as a, b, F, G, !, &, 1, 2,), etc. Each of these symbols occupies one text character space in the attribute.

Size of text attributes

Attributes of text type can be constrained by length. If an attribute has a size of 30 then it can store null to 30 characters. All attributes of the text data type must be constrained by size because when the data is finally stored on paper or in a computer system they will occupy a specific amount of physical space or computer storage. If no size is specified then it is impossible to allocate the correct amount of storage space to the attribute.

Text attributes can also be constrained by one or more validation rules. These rules apply to the range of permitted values and format of the text.

Constrained by permitted values

In some circumstances the values of data that can be stored in a text attribute are very specific. Only certain values are allowed. For example, the current British cinema certificates which can be awarded to movies shown in the UK are U, PG, 12A, 15 and 18. Only these values are valid for an attribute which stores the classification of a film. Such an attribute would have a validation rule applied to it which would ensure that only those values could be stored by the attribute.

In Figure 3.5 the *account_type* is limited to either current, cheque, loan or cash. The value for the *account_type* is restricted to current, cheque, loan or cash and no other value may be stored by the attribute. Validation rules such as this would be enforced by the office clerk if the system is paper based or by the relational database management system if the system is computer based.

Constrained by range

In relatively rare cases, the valid values in a text attribute are from a range of letters. An example of this would be an attribute which stores the responses to a multiple-choice question. If the answers are A, B, C or D then the valid range of the text value stored is greater than or equal to A and less than or equal to D. This would be written as $> = $ *"A" AND* $< = $ *"D"*.

When such a range is used it refers not to the value of the letters but rather to the value of the ASCII (American Standard Code for Information Interchange) codes which are commonly used by computer systems to represent characters.

ASCII is a code for representing English characters as numbers, with each letter assigned a number from 0 to 127. For example, the ASCII code for upper-case M is 77 and the ASCII code for lower-case f is 102. 77 is less than 102 therefore 'M' is less than 'f' in terms of ASCII codes. See Figure 3.7 for a list of ASCII codes.

Constrained by format

Often the sequence of the text characters in an attribute is very important. The *account_number* shown in Figure 3.5 is of the format two letters followed by three numbers. The format of this is letter, letter, number, number, number. All values stored by this attribute must be of this format.

A common example of a format restricting the value of data in an attribute is a postcode. A postcode normally consists of a letter, another letter, a number, another number, a space, a number, a letter and another letter (LL99 9LL). There are exceptions to this which mean that there are actually six valid postcode formats.

Format	Example
L9▼9LL	M1▼1AA
L99▼9LL	M60▼1NW
LL9▼9LL	CR2▼6XH
LL99▼9LL	DN55▼1PT
L9L▼9LL	W1P▼1HQ
LL9L▼9LL	EC1A▼1BB

(▼ represents a space, 'L' indicates an alphabetic character and a '9' indicates a numeric character)

Figure 3.6 Valid postcode formats

Storage requirements

Text data is typically stored using ASCII or some similar method such as EBCDIC (Extended Binary Coded Decimal Interchange Code).

Most personal computers use ASCII codes to represent text, which makes it possible to transfer data from one computer to another. See Figure 3.7 for a list of commonly used characters and their ASCII equivalents.

Description	Char	ASCII
space		32
exclamation mark	!	33
(double) quotation marks	"	34
number sign	#	35
dollar sign	$	36
percent sign	%	37
ampersand	&	38
apostrophe	'	39
open parenthesis	(	40
close parenthesis	)	41
asterisk	*	42
plus sign	+	43
comma	,	44
minus sign/hyphen	-	45
division sign	÷	47
period, decimal point	.	46
slash, virgule, solidus	/	47
digit 0	0	48
digit 1	1	49
digit 2	2	50
digit 3	3	51
digit 4	4	52
digit 5	5	53
digit 6	6	54
digit 7	7	55
digit 8	8	56
digit 9	9	57
colon	:	58
semicolon	;	59
less-than sign	<	60
equal sign	=	61
greater-than sign	>	62
question mark	?	63

Description	Char	ASCII
commercial 'at' sign	@	64
capital A	A	65
capital B	B	66
capital C	C	67
capital D	D	68
capital E	E	69
capital F	F	70
capital G	G	71
capital H	H	72
capital I	I	73
capital J	J	74
capital K	K	75
capital L	L	76
capital M	M	77
capital N	N	78
capital O	O	79
capital P	P	80
capital Q	Q	81
capital R	R	82
capital S	S	83
capital T	T	84
capital U	U	85
capital V	V	86
capital W	W	87
capital X	X	88
capital Y	Y	89
capital Z	Z	90
left square bracket	[	91
backslash, reverse solidus	\	92
right square bracket	]	93
spacing circumflex accent	^	94
spacing underscore, low line	_	95

Description	Char	ASCII
spacing grave accent	`	96
small a	a	97
small b	b	98
small c	c	99
small d	d	100
small e	e	101
small f	f	102
small g	g	103
small h	h	104
small i	i	105
small j	j	106
small k	k	107
small l	l	108
small m	m	109
small n	n	110
small o	o	111
small p	p	112
small q	q	113
small r	r	114
small s	s	115
small t	t	116
small u	u	117
small v	v	118
small w	w	119
small x	x	120
small y	y	121
small z	z	122
left brace (curly bracket)	{	123
vertical bar	|	124
right brace (curly bracket)	}	125
tilde accent	~	126
delete	^?	127

Figure 3.7 ASCII codes

The standard ASCII character set uses just seven bits for each character. There are several larger character sets that use eight bits, which gives them 128 additional characters. This means that each text character occupies one byte of storage.

The extra characters are used to represent non-English characters, graphics symbols and mathematical symbols. Several companies and organisations have proposed extensions for these 128 characters. The DOS operating system uses a superset of ASCII called **extended ASCII** or **high ASCII**. A more universal standard is the ISO (International Standards Organisation) Latin 1 set of characters, which is used by many operating systems, as well as web browsers.

EBCDIC is another set of codes that is used on large IBM computers. Most EBCDIC character sets do not contain all of the characters defined in the ASCII code set but there is a special International Reference Version (IRV) code set that contains all of the characters in ISO Latin 1 set (and, therefore, ASCII). EBCDIC also uses eight bits (one byte) to store each character.

Integer

Attributes which store only whole numbers are integers. An attribute which is restricted to only integers can only store whole numbers such as 0, 1, –125 and 144457. As with all attributes it can also store a null value.

If a real number (a decimal such as 10.82) is stored by an attribute which is defined as an integer, then only the whole number part of the real number, i.e. 10, will normally be stored by the attribute. In this case the decimal part is chopped and lost even if the decimal number is nearer to the whole number above (i.e. 11) rather than the whole number below (i.e. 10).

Constrained by range

Attributes of integer type can be limited to specific ranges of numbers, a specific selection of numbers or to a specific format. Ranges of numbers and other data types are specified using the standard logical operators (Figure 3.8).

=	**Equal:** returns true if the term on the left equals the term on the right, otherwise returns false.
<>	**Not equal:** returns true if the term on the left does not equal the term on the right, otherwise returns false.
<	**Less than:** returns true if the term on the left is less than the term on the right, otherwise returns false.
>	**Greater than:** returns true if the term on the left is greater than the term on the right, otherwise returns false.
<=	**Less than or equal:** returns true if the term on the left is less than or equal to the term on the right, otherwise returns false.
>=	**Greater than or equal:** returns true if the term on the left is greater than or equal to the term on the right, otherwise returns false.
AND	Returns true if both the left-hand term and the right-hand term are true.
OR	Returns true if either the left-hand term or the right-hand term are true.
NOT	Returns true if the left-hand term is true and right-hand term is false, or if the right-hand term is true and the left-hand term is false.

Figure 3.8 Standard logical operators

The constraint *>5 AND <17* limits the acceptable values for an integer type attribute to 6, 7, 8, 9, 10, 11, 12, 13, 14, 15 or 16. The values 5 and 17 are not valid because they are outside the range. If the constraint was

$> = 5 \; AND \; < = 17$ then 5 and 17 would be valid because they are now within the specified range.

Style	Type	Size	Colour	Price
Chicago	jacket	12	blue	37.99
Chicago	trousers	8	red	24.75
London	dress	14	peach	29.80
L.A.	dress	16	black	24.99
Camden	jacket	10	red/black	18.99
L.A.	jacket	10	blue/white	42.80

Figure 3.9 Entities and attributes for clothes

Constrained by permitted values

Attributes of integer type can be limited to specific values. For example, the attribute *size* belongs to the entity *clothes* (Figure 3.9) and is used to hold the size of women's clothes in a shop. Women's clothes' sizes available in the shop are 6, 8, 10, 12, 14, 16 and 18. The attribute *size* is constrained to these seven values and no other values are permissible.

Constrained by format

An integer attribute may also be constrained to a specific number of digits. This is often used to ensure that the correct number of digits is entered. For example, 87 constrained by the format 9999 must be entered as 0087.

Storage requirements

Typically, an integer value can be stored in a number of different ways depending on the maximum and minimum sizes of the data to be stored. The storage terms used in Figure 3.10 are those common to most international standards.

Storage term	Range of numbers stored	Capacity of memory used
byte	stores numbers from 0 to 255 (no fractions)	1 byte
integer	stores numbers from –32,768 to 32,767 (no fractions)	2 bytes
long integer	(default) stores numbers from –2,147,483,648 to 2,147,483,647 (no fractions)	4 bytes

Figure 3.10 Common storage requirements of integer data types

Real numbers

Attributes of real number type can store any real number value. Real numbers are those numbers that are used to represent a continuous quantity (including zero and negatives). A real number can be thought of as a possible infinite decimal fraction, such as 324.823211247...

Storage is limited within computer systems, therefore real numbers are only stored to a specific number of decimal places – an infinite number of places would require infinite computer storage!

Constrained by range

Again, the standard logical operators (Figure 3.7) would be used to define the range of acceptable numbers. The constraint *> 5.15 AND < 17.22* limits the acceptable values for an integer type attribute to any number larger than 5.15 and less than 17.22. In this case the number 5.161 would be valid because it is greater than 5.15 and less than 17.22.

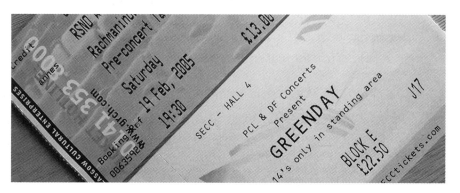

Figure 3.11 Sample concert ticket

Constrained by permitted values

As with integer attributes, attributes of the real number data type can be limited to specific values. An example of this would be an attribute *ticket_price* for which only the values 15.45, 17.50 and 18.35 are valid (i.e. these are the prices of the three available ticket types).

Constrained by format

Real numbers can be limited to a specific number of digits both before and after the decimal point. For example, the *account_balance* in Figure 3.5 is constrained to real numbers limited to two decimal places, as is the *ticket_price* shown in Figure 3.11.

Storage requirements

Typically a real value can be stored in a number of different ways depending on the maximum and minimum sizes of the data to be stored. The storage terms used in Figure 3.12 are those common to most international standards.

Storage term	Range of numbers stored	Capacity of memory used
single	decimal numbers –3.402823E38 to –1.401298E–45 for negative values and 1.401298E–45 to 3.402823E38 for positive values	4 bytes
double	–1.79769313486232E308 to –4.94065645841247E–324 for negative values and 4.94065645841247E–324 to 1.79769313486232E308 for positive values	8 bytes
currency	Numbers with up to 15 digits left of the decimal and 4 digits right of the decimal 922,337,203,685,477.5808 to 922,337,203,685,477.5807	8 bytes

Figure 3.12 Common storage requirements of real data types

Currency data types are used for financial data which is displayed with a currency symbol or symbols. Examples of this would be £14.99 where the £ is the currency symbol. Other currency symbols available include € (euro) and $ (dollar).

Object

An object is a file which is created with an application, such as a paint program or wordprocessor, which can be stored by an attribute. Modern computer systems enable users to create objects with one application and then link or embed them in a second application such as a relational database management system. An object, for example a picture or a spreadsheet, can be **linked** or **embedded** in an attribute.

Linked objects

A linked object displays the object's data, but the data remains stored in the source file. You can edit a linked object from the RDBMS and save changes to the source file, but it can still be opened and edited in the original application. When the information in the source file is changed, the change is reflected in the RDBMS.

For example, a database is used to store details of the wordprocessing documents produced by a company office. Every time a document is created its details are added to the database. In addition, each wordprocessing document is linked as an object within the database. When a specific document is required the database can be searched. The source document can then be found and edited, either via the database application or by loading the source file into the wordprocessing application.

Destination file

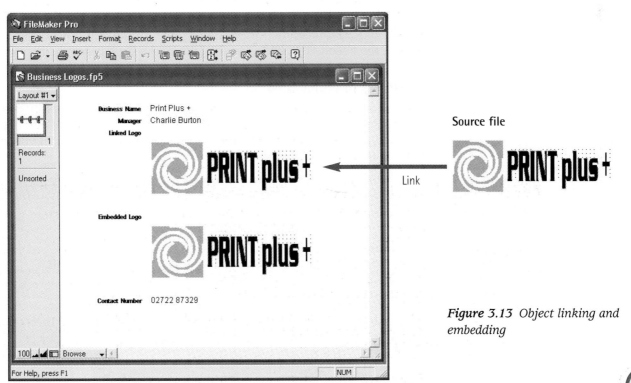

Figure 3.13 Object linking and embedding

Embedded objects

In contrast, an embedded object is a **copy** of the information created in the original application. Changes made to the source file are not reflected in the embedded object, and likewise changes made to the embedded object are not saved back to the source file.

There are advantages and disadvantages for both linking and embedding objects:

Advantages of linking an object

- The size of the destination file, the one which contains the link to the object, is kept at a minimum because the file does not include the linked object. The destination file only contains a reference to where the source file can be located within the computer's filing system.

- Updating the information in the source file automatically causes the destination file to update when opened. This ensures that the latest version of the object is always shown in the destination file.

- If you have to hold the same information in a number of documents, you only need to update the source file and all linked documents will be updated automatically.

Disadvantages of linking an object

- You have to have the destination and source files for the link to work, so you are storing two files not one.

- Updating the information in the source file automatically causes the destination file to update when opened. This may be a disadvantage in some situations when it is critical the linked object does not change, e.g. when the linked object is a snapshot of data for a particular period, such as a bill or an invoice.

- The source file and destination file have to remain in the same place within the computer system for the link to work. The path to the file (i.e. its location on the computer system) must not be changed. If the source file is moved or renamed then the destination file will not be able to locate the linked object because the path to the file has changed.

Advantages of embedding an object

- You can transfer the destination file to a different storage location or computer and the information will still be present because the contents of the embedded object have been copied and stored within the destination file.

- Changing the source file does not change the destination file because there is no connection between the embedded object and the source file.

Disadvantages of embedding an object

- Files created with embedded objects are much larger than those with linked objects. This is due to the size of the various embedded objects stored within the file.

- Changing the source file does not change the destination file. Therefore, over time, it is likely the source file and the embedded object will contain different data.

Link

An attribute of the link type holds a hyperlink or a location where external data can be found. This is different from an object in that it is the location of the external data that is stored and displayed rather than the external data itself.

A common example of the use of the link data type is the placement of uniform resource locators (URLs) within a database. A uniform resource locator is an address that specifies an Internet protocol (such as HTTP or FTP) and a location of an object, document, World Wide Web page, or other destination on the Internet or an intranet – for example: http://www.perfectpapers.net/.

Microsoft's desktop relational database package, Microsoft Access, has a link data type referred to as **hyperlink**. This data type can store either the path to a file or a URL. The path to a file uses the universal naming convention (UNC). This is a naming convention for files that provides a machine-independent means of locating a file. Rather than specifying a drive letter and path, a UNC name uses the syntax: \\server\share\path\file-name.

The 'server' is the computer system, the 'share' is the shared resource on the computer system (such as a hard disk or DVD-ROM drive), the 'path' holds details of the folder or folders within which the file is held and 'file-name' is the name of the file.

Boolean

An attribute of type Boolean has only two states or values (and null). It can be either true or false, yes or no, male or female, etc. The actual value stored depends on how the attribute is configured.

A common mistake when defining the attributes of entities is to use text or some other data type instead of Boolean. If only two states are required for the attribute then Boolean should be used as the data type because it reduces the amount of storage space required to store the data.

Boolean attributes typically occupy only a very small amount of computer memory (this can be as little as one bit) whereas text attributes require one byte (eight bits) per character!

What is a relationship?

A relationship describes how two entities are related. Relationships, together with entities and attributes, are the major building blocks of any relational database system.

Cardinality

A relationship can be thought of as a connection between two entities. There are three types of relationship, better known as the **cardinality** of the relationship:

- one-to-one
- one-to-many
- many-to-many.

One-to-one

A one-to-one relationship specifies that for one entity there is only one other corresponding entity. For example:

Example 1: mandatory/mandatory

Pupils in Anytown High School are each allocated a locker to use during their time at school. This locker is not shared and can be used only by the pupil to whom it has been allocated.

pupil_num	pupil_name	register_class		locker_num	locker_type
43781	Jennifer Brown	4A	——	232C	Vanguard
57842	Aveek Anderson	3E	——	234C	Guardian
23423	Scott Lowson	2F	——	728D	Athletic
23426	Wendy Alexander	2F	——	483B	Vanguard

Figure 3.14 *An example one-to-one relationship (mandatory/mandatory)*

For any **one** pupil there is only **one** locker.

The above is true as long as each pupil has a locker and every locker is allocated. This is called a **mandatory** relationship. That is a relationship that must exist in all cases.

Ordinality

Relationships can be one of two classes: **mandatory** (as in Example 1) or **optional**. This is referred to as the **ordinality** of the relationship.

While cardinality specifies the occurrences of a relationship, ordinality describes the relationship as either mandatory or optional. In other words, cardinality specifies the maximum number of relationships and ordinality specifies the absolute minimum number of relationships.

The relationship in Figure 3.14 is mandatory for *pupil* and mandatory for *locker*, therefore each pupil must have a locker and each locker must have a pupil.

But what happens if one pupil does not wish to have a locker or if one locker is not allocated to a pupil, or both?

Let us look at each of these cases in turn.

Example 2: optional/mandatory

Pupils in Anytown High School are allowed to choose whether or not to have a locker for use during their time at school. This locker is not shared and can only be used by the pupil to whom it has been allocated. Any lockers which are not allocated at the start of the year are removed to create more space in the pupil social areas.

This means that a pupil may or may not have a locker but each locker must have a pupil. Figure 3.15 illustrates this. The relationship is optional for *pupil* but is mandatory for *locker*. Pupil number 23426, Wendy Alexander, does not have a locker because the relationship with *locker* is optional but all the lockers do have pupils because the relationship with *pupil* is mandatory.

Warning!

You should not be asked about the ordinality of relationships as part of your Higher examination (it is part of Advanced Higher) but it is important to understand that the problems you will be solving at Higher level may involve optional and mandatory relationships. An understanding of this concept will be of use when carrying out the analysis, design and implementation of database systems.

---

pupil_num	pupil_name	register_class		locker_num	locker_type
43781	Jennifer Brown	4A	——	232C	Vanguard
57842	Aveek Anderson	3E	——	234C	Guardian
23423	Scott Lowson	2F	——	728D	Athletic
23426	Wendy Alexander	2F			

Figure 3.15 *Optional/mandatory*

Example 3: mandatory/optional

Pupils in Anytown High School are each allocated a locker to use during their time at school. This locker is not shared and can only be used by the pupil to whom it has been allocated. There are more lockers than pupils therefore a number of lockers will not be allocated. These will remain available for pupils who join during the school year.

This means that a pupil must have a locker but a locker need not have a pupil. The relationship is mandatory for *pupil* but optional for *locker* (see Figure 3.16).

pupil_num	pupil_name	register_class		locker_num	locker_type
43781	Jennifer Brown	4A	——	232C	Vanguard
57842	Aveek Anderson	3E	——	234C	Guardian
23423	Scott Lowson	2F	——	728D	Athletic
				483B	Vanguard

Figure 3.16 *Mandatory/optional*

Example 4: optional /optional

Pupils in Anytown High School are allowed to choose whether or not to have a locker for use during their time at school. This locker is not shared and can only be used by the pupil to whom it has been allocated. Any unallocated lockers will remain available for pupils who join during the school year.

This means that a pupil may or may not have a locker and a locker may or may not have a pupil. The relationship is optional for both.

pupil_num	pupil_name	register_class		locker_num	locker_type
43781	Jennifer Brown	4A	——	232C	Vanguard
57842	Aveek Anderson	3E	——	234C	Guardian
23423	Scott Lowson	2F	——	728D	Athletic
23426	Wendy Alexander	2F		483B	Vanguard

Figure 3.17 *Optional/optional*

One-to-many

A one-to-many relationship specifies that for one entity there can be many corresponding entities. Again, the relationship can be classed as mandatory or optional in different directions. For example:

Example 5: mandatory/mandatory

A local medical centre has several doctors that work for it. Each doctor has a list of patients and patients can see *only* the doctor on whose list they appear.

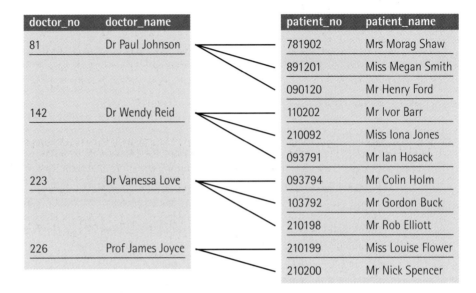

Figure 3.18 An example of a one-to-many relationship (mandatory/mandatory)

For any one doctor there are many patients, but for any one patient there is only one doctor. As it stands, this relationship is mandatory for *doctor* and mandatory for *patient*.

Example 6: optional/mandatory

A local medical centre has several doctors that work for it. The medical centre also employs a doctor to carry out research work. The research doctor does not have any patients. Apart from the research doctor, each doctor has a list of patients and patients can see only the doctor on whose list they appear.

Figure 3.19 An example of a one-to-many relationship (optional/mandatory)

The relationship is now optional for *doctor* but is still mandatory for *patient*. This is because the doctor carrying out research does not see any patients.

Example 7: mandatory/optional

A local medical centre has several doctors that work for it. Each doctor has a list of patients and patients can see *only* the doctor on whose list they appear. If a patient is unhappy with the doctor he or she is registered with then he or she can request to be removed from that doctor's list. When this happens the patient's details remain in the system until a vacancy is available with another doctor.

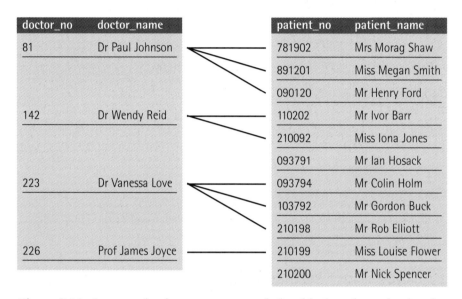

Figure 3.20 *An example of a one-to-many relationship (mandatory/optional)*

The relationship is mandatory for *doctor* but is optional for *patient* because a patient does not have to have a doctor.

Example 8: optional/optional

A local medical centre has several doctors that work for it. The medical centre also employs a doctor to carry out research work. The research doctor does not have any patients. Apart from the research doctor, each doctor has a list of patients and patients can see *only* the doctor on whose list they appear.

If a patient is unhappy with the doctor he or she is registered with then he or she can request to be removed from that doctor's list. When this happens the patient's details remain in the system until a vacancy is available with another doctor.

See Figure 3.21 on the next page.

It is now optional for a doctor to have patients and optional for a patient to have a doctor.

Many-to-many

A many-to-many relationship specifies that for one entity there can be many corresponding entities and vice versa.

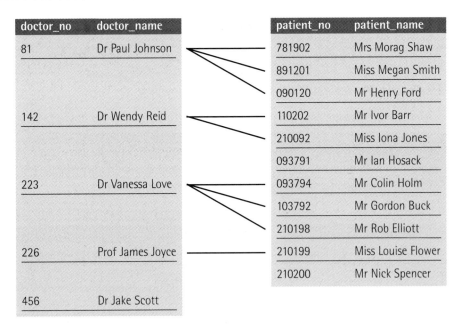

doctor_no	doctor_name
81	Dr Paul Johnson
142	Dr Wendy Reid
223	Dr Vanessa Love
226	Prof James Joyce
456	Dr Jake Scott

patient_no	patient_name
781902	Mrs Morag Shaw
891201	Miss Megan Smith
090120	Mr Henry Ford
110202	Mr Ivor Barr
210092	Miss Iona Jones
093791	Mr Ian Hosack
093794	Mr Colin Holm
103792	Mr Gordon Buck
210198	Mr Rob Elliott
210199	Miss Louise Flower
210200	Mr Nick Spencer

Figure 3.21 An example of a one-to-many relationship (optional/optional)

Example 9: mandatory/mandatory

A group of colleges has set up a netball league. The league is made up of teams and the teams have many players. One player can play for more than one team. Each team must have at least one player and each player must have at least one team.

team_id	team_name
KY91	St. Andrews
AB81	Ellon
ED12	Edinburgh
GL12	Glasgow
IV12	Inverness
DF12	Dunfermline
ST12	Stirling
BW19	North Berwick
AB12	Cults
PP12	Perth
DD61	Dundee

player_id	player_name
0021	Carol Keller
0145	Jo Andrews
0212	Kylie Scott
0895	Constance West
0992	Christina Hamilton
2616	Star West
4281	Adele Booker
5298	Iona McCrae
7291	Louise Ludd
8102	Kim White
9182	Madia Smith

Figure 3.22 An example of a many-to-many relationship (mandatory/mandatory)

For any one team there are *one or more* players and for any one player there are *one or more* teams. This is therefore a many-to-many relationship. In this example, the relationship is mandatory for *team* because each team must have at least one player, and mandatory for *player* because each player must have at least one team.

Client Nbr:	2711		Client Telephone:	0312 123198
Client Name:	West Homes Ltd		Client Fax:	0312 123199
Client Address:	14 Argos St Glasgow G23 9UJ		Contact Person:	John Michael Osbourne

Shipment Nbr	Insurance Ref	From	To	Date	Time	Van Reg
0012	NT9238	15 Andrews Cres. Dundee DD76 8TT	28 Westfield Pl. Dundee DD75 7YH	23/02/2004	09:30	P385 ASA
0010	RT8721	Arran House Inverness IV26 6TY	Harbour House Stonehaven AB22 8YU	24/02/2004	08:30	KY51 AFZ
0011	AD6701	267 Gill st. Stirling FK78 1MN	10a Lawson Rd Stirling FK78 2YT	24/02/2004	09:30	YT71 7YE

Figure 4.1b Sample from Client book, Case Study 1

ment is covered by an insurance policy. For insurance reasons each client can only have one removal in any one shipment. However, different clients can be allocated the same shipment number so that they are covered by the same insurance policy.

This allows Reed and Co. to pay for one policy to cover each shipment and bill this to all the clients who have removals as part of the shipment. The term shipment is used by Reed and Co to refer to all removals that are covered by the same insurance policy. Shipments don't travel in the same van and aren't linked in any other way to each other.

The Insurance Ref is the insurance policy number for the shipment. Look at the samples from the Client book (Figures 4.1a and 4.1b). From this you can see that each Shipment Nbr is only unique for each client and not for each removal.

The second book contains details of the removal vans that Reed and Co. owns. Each removal van has a unique registration number. To allocate a van to a removal the manager writes the van number against the removal in the *Client* book. Each van has only one removal allocated at a particular time and date and each removal only has one van allocated to it. This is a sample from the *Van* book (Figure 4.2):

Van Reg	Model	Make	Capacity	Fuel Type	Rental Cost
P385 ASA	Transit	Ford	11.89m³	Petrol	£90.00
KY51 AFZ	Convoy	LDV	16.85m³	Diesel	£100.00
YT71 7YE	LF	DAF	28.45m³	Diesel	£125.00
D842 YSA	Actros	Mercedes	36.10m³	Diesel	£150.00

Figure 4.2 Sample from Van book, Case Study 1

Entity–relationship occurrence modelling

The first step in constructing a conceptual model of any system is to examine the entities and relationships that currently exist within the system.

In a conceptual model it is relatively easy to identify the entities involved. Each document, each index card, each file in a system is an entity. Each collection of entities is an entity set.

Each of these entity sets deals with a specific collection of entities: bookings, customers, spare parts, etc. In Case Study 1 there are two entity sets – the *Client* book and the *Van* book. These entity sets are collections of the two entities – *Client* and *Van*.

All entities in an entity set must have the same attributes and each attribute must have a specific domain. Remember, a domain is the set of permitted values for an attribute and therefore defines what the attribute can and cannot store.

Entity–relationship (E/R) occurrence diagrams are achieved by looking at specific relationship occurrences and linking entity occurrences with lines, one line for each occurrence of the relationship.

Creating an E/R occurrence diagram

Entity–relationship occurrence modelling is a technique which helps to identify the relationship between two entities. In order to successfully use E/R occurrence modelling, a systems analyst must have a full understanding of the system being analysed, and sample data with which to work.

Identify the entities and their primary keys

The first process is to identify a primary key for each entity. In Case Study 1 there are two entities. The primary key for a *Van* entity is *Van Reg* because *Van Reg* is unique for each van. However, the primary key for a *Client* entity needs a bit more consideration.

Each client is uniquely identified by *Client Nbr* but a *Client* entity also stores details of the removals. Each removal has a *Shipment Nbr* but this is not unique because two different customers can have two different removals with the same number.

The problem is that all the attributes associated with a removal in a *Client* entity are multi-valued! This breaks Rule 7 of our seven relational database rules. Each cell in the table (the intersection of a column and a row) must contain only one value. We will learn how to fix this later in the book but for now we must accept that *Client Nbr* is the primary key of *Client* and that the attributes relating to a removal (*Shipment Nbr, Insurance Ref, From, To, Date, Time* and *Van Reg*) are multi-valued.

Create a list of primary key values

With the primary keys for each entity decided, the next step is to write down the primary key values so that the E/R occurrence diagram can be constructed. Figure 4.3 shows how this would be done for Case Study 1.

Figure 4.3 *Primary key values for Case Study 1*

Van Reg	Client Nbr
P385 ASA	2711
KY51 AFZ	0921
YT71 7YE	
D842 YSA	

In Figure 4.3 each primary value from the two sample pages from the *Client* book and the *Van* book have been listed.

Link primary keys

Once the list of the primary key values is completed, lines are drawn to illustrate how the values link together. Each line is one occurrence of the relationship between the two entities. Look at the first record for van P385 ASA in the *Client* data in the sample, and look at the value for *Client Nbr*. On the E/R occurrence diagram we draw a line between the *Van Reg* value and the *Client Nbr* value.

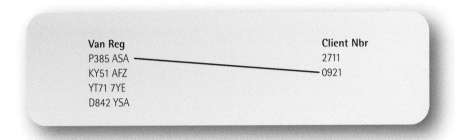

***Figure 4.4** Starting to create an E/R occurrence diagram*

This line indicates one 'link' between the *Van* entity set and the *Client* entity set. To complete the E/R occurrence diagram we add 'links' for all the remaining records from the sample data. To put it another way, we draw a line to represent each instance of the relationship between the two entity sets.

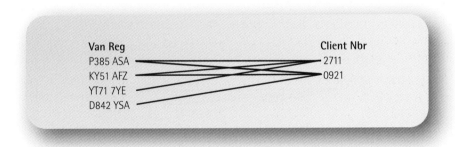

***Figure 4.5** Entity/occurrence diagram for Case Study 1*

What does this tell us about the relationship between *Client* and *Van*? Each van has one or more clients linked to it and each client has one or more vans linked to it.

One client has many vans and one van has many clients. The relationship between *Van* and *Client* is many-to-many. The pattern of the lines in the entity–relationship occurrence diagram can be used to identify the nature of the relationship between two entity sets.

When an E/R occurrence diagram is created, one of three patterns will appear in the lines. There is one pattern for each of the three relationship cardinalities: one-to-one, one-to-many and many-to-many. Each of the following examples demonstrates the pattern that appears for each of the relationships.

E/R occurrence diagram – one-to-one relationship

A company has a policy of allocating each employee a computer workstation connected to the company network. Each computer has a unique name and each employee has a unique payroll number. The following entity–relationship occurrence diagram was created (Figure 4.6):

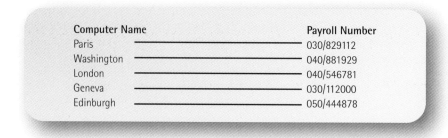

Figure 4.6 E/R occurrence diagram, one-to-one relationship

One *Computer Name* has one *Payroll Number* and one *Payroll Number* has one *Computer Name*. This is therefore an example of a one-to-one relationship.

E/R occurrence diagram – one-to-many relationship

Courses at Westhill University each have a unique course code. Students at the university each have a unique student ID. Students are only allowed to register for one course. At least 20 students enrol in each course at the university. The following entity–relationship occurrence diagram was created (Figure 4.7):

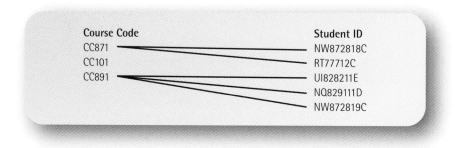

Figure 4.7 E/R occurrence diagram, one-to-many relationship

Each course has more than one student and each student has one course. This is, therefore, a one-to-many relationship.

E/R occurrence diagram – many-to-many relationship

Food suppliers have numerous outlets and outlets have numerous food suppliers. So, for example, Beefy Soup Co. sells soup to Big Store, ADSA Market and SafeCo shops. Big Store buys soup from Beefy Soup Co., Baters Ltd., Luxury Soup and McCampbells.

The entity–relationship occurrence diagram in Figure 4.8 was created.

Each food supplier has one or more outlets and each outlet has one or more food suppliers. This is therefore a many-to-many relationship.

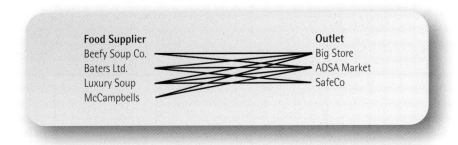

Figure 4.8 E/R occurrence diagram, many-to-many relationship

Entity relationship diagrams

Once the entities and relationships have been identified a tool is required to represent this structure. The **entity relationship diagram (ERD)** illustrates the logical structure of any database. It provides a pictorial method of illustrating entity sets, relationships, attributes and cardinality. A sample ERD for the Reed and Co. removals company is shown here.

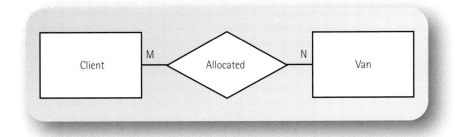

Figure 4.9 ERD for Reed and Co.

ERD connectors

The lines that connect the entity sets and relationships are annotated to show the cardinality of the relationship. An annotation is placed at either side of the relationship, next to the entity set, to show if the relationship is either one or many. This notation is based on mathematical set theory.

One-to-one relationships are shown by placing a 1 next to each of the entity sets (Figure 4.10).

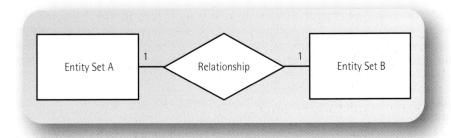

Figure 4.10 One-to-one ERD

One-to-many relationships are shown by placing a 1 on the one side of the relationship and an M on the many side (Figure 4.11).

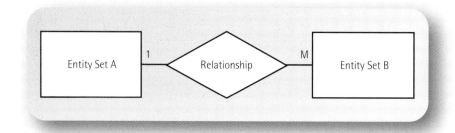

Figure 4.11 *One-to-many ERD*

Many-to-many relationships are shown by placing an M on one side of the relationship and an N on the other side. It is a very common mistake, when creating ERDs, to place an M on both sides of the relationship. **This is wrong!**

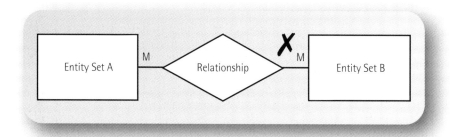

Figure 4.12 *Incorrect many-to-many ERD*

This is right (Figure 4.13):

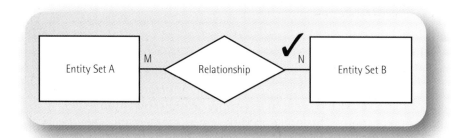

Figure 4.13 *Correct many-to-many ERD*

In mathematics, if the same variable is shown twice in the same equation it is assumed, correctly, that the two values are the same! If we used M twice for the same relationship in our ERD then we would be saying that for every record on one side of the relationship there is an equal number of matching records on the other side, and vice versa. This would not be the case.

The M in the ERD represents a value of more than one as does the N. This means that for each row in Entity Set A there may be more than one related row in Entity Set B, and for each row in Entity Set B there may be more than one related row in Entity Set A.

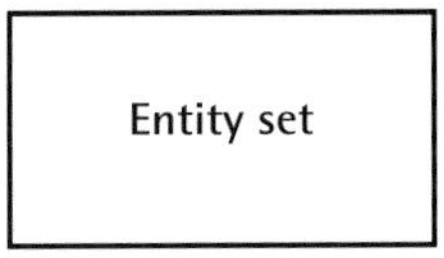 Entity set	A rectangle is used to represent each entity set. Remember, an entity set is a collection of entities. The name of the entity set is entered inside the rectangle to identify it. Remember the name must never be a plural, it must always be a singular, e.g. *person* rather than *people*.
 Relationship	The relationship between the two entity sets is shown as a diamond. Relationships illustrate how two entity sets share information. A short phrase is written inside the diamond to describe the relationship.
 Attribute	Attributes can be added to the ERD as ovals. The name of the attribute is entered inside the oval.
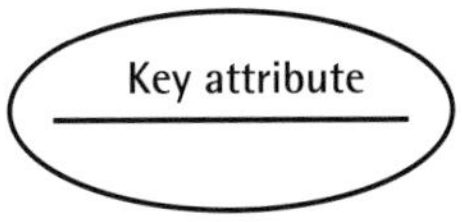 Key attribute	If an attribute is the primary key or part of the primary key for the entities in the entity set then its name is underlined inside the oval.
 Multi-valued attribute	Multi-valued attributes are shown with a double oval. The name of the attribute is written inside the ovals.
 Derived attribute	A derived attribute is one that is calculated from other attributes. For example, *pay* is an attribute that would be derived from *hours worked* and *hourly rate*.
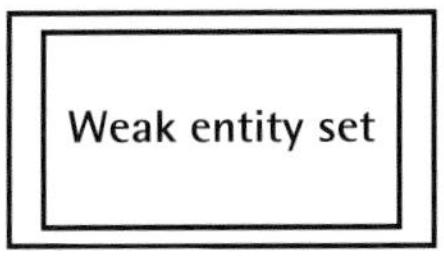 Weak entity set	A weak entity set is one that is created to remove a many-to-many relationship. We will learn more about this in the chapter on normalisation later in this book.
 Weak relationship	To connect a weak entity set with others, you should use a weak relationship notation. Again, more on this later.

Figure 4.14 ERD symbols

Here are some example ERDs based on the scenarios we looked at earlier for the entity–relationship occurrence diagrams.

One-to-one

A company has a policy of allocating each employee a computer workstation connected to the company network (Figure 4.15).

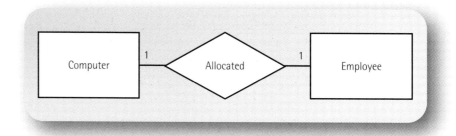

Figure 4.15 *One-to-one ERD,*
computer/employee

One-to-many

Courses at Westhill University each have a unique course code. Students at the university each have a unique student ID. Students are only allowed to register for one course. At least 20 students enrol in each course at the university.

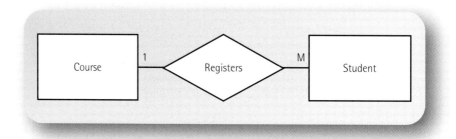

Figure 4.16 *One-to-many ERD,*
course/student

Many-to-many

Food suppliers have numerous outlets and outlets have numerous food suppliers.

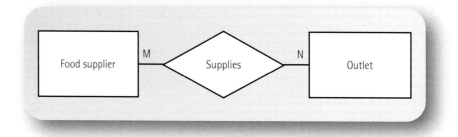

Figure 4.17 *Many-to-many ERD,*
supplier/outlet

Adding attributes

Attributes can be added to the entity relationship diagram to complete what we call the entity model, i.e. the recording (modelling) of the entities, relationships and attributes in the system. When an attribute is added to the ERD it is connected to the entity set to which it belongs by a line. The appropriate attribute symbol is used for the attribute. The completed ERD, including attributes, for Reed and Co. from Case Study 1 is shown in Figure 4.18.

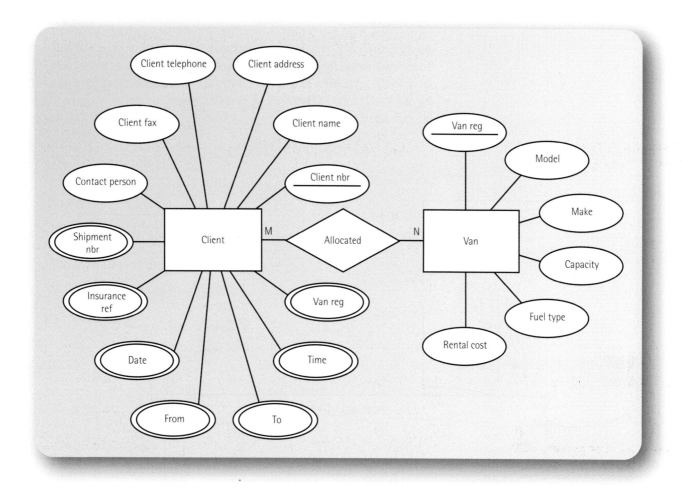

Figure 4.18 ERD for Reed and Co. with attributes

The alternative style

The alternative to using 1, M and N to identify relationships in an entity relationship diagram is to change the style of the connector line. A single straight line indicates that an entity set is at the one side of the relationship and a 'crow's foot' line indicates that an entity set is at the many side of a relationship (for example, see Figure 4.19).

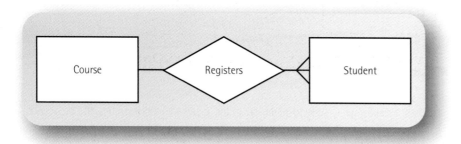

Figure 4.19 Sample of alternative notation for cardinality

Now that you have an understanding of entities, entity sets, relationships and attributes it is time to examine a second case study and produce entity–relationship occurrence diagrams and an entity relationship diagram.

Case Study 2

The Pine Furniture Company uses a system to record details of sales and products. All the information for the system is held on three separate sets of index cards. One set of index cards holds details of customers, another holds details of orders and the third holds details of products for sale. One sample of each index card is shown in Figure 4.20.

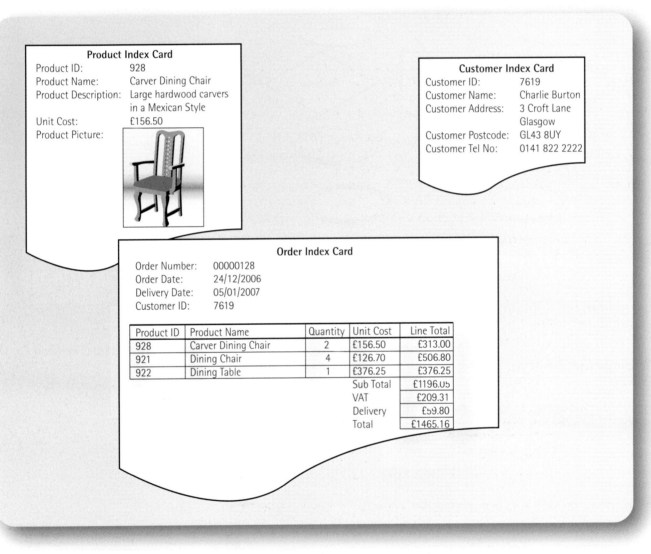

Product Index Card

Product ID:	928
Product Name:	Carver Dining Chair
Product Description:	Large hardwood carvers in a Mexican Style
Unit Cost:	£156.50
Product Picture:	

Customer Index Card

Customer ID:	7619
Customer Name:	Charlie Burton
Customer Address:	3 Croft Lane Glasgow
Customer Postcode:	GL43 8UY
Customer Tel No:	0141 822 2222

Order Index Card

Order Number:	00000128
Order Date:	24/12/2006
Delivery Date:	05/01/2007
Customer ID:	7619

Product ID	Product Name	Quantity	Unit Cost	Line Total
928	Carver Dining Chair	2	£156.50	£313.00
921	Dining Chair	4	£126.70	£506.80
922	Dining Table	1	£376.25	£376.25
			Sub Total	£1196.05
			VAT	£209.31
			Delivery	£59.80
			Total	£1465.16

Figure 4.20 Index cards for Case Study 2

When a customer wishes to place an order, a salesperson searches the customer index cards to see if a card already exists for the customer. If a card does not exist then a new card is made up and the customer is allocated a unique *Customer ID*.

The new *Customer ID* or the one from the existing customer index card is written on a blank order index card and the order is given a unique *Order Number*. The current date is entered as the *Order Date* on the card. The proposed *Delivery Date* is also entered on the card.

The customer informs the salesperson which items he or she wishes to order. The salesperson looks up each item in the product card index and enters the *Product ID*,

Product Name, Quantity and *Unit Cost.* A calculator is then used by the salesperson to work out the total for each line of the order and this value is entered under *Line Total.*

Once details of all the products have been entered on the order index card, the salesperson calculates the *Sub Total* by adding all the *Line Totals* together. The VAT is then calculated as 17.5% of the *Sub Total.* The delivery charge is always 5% of the *Sub Total.* This is also calculated and entered on the order index card. Finally, the *Total* is calculated by adding the *Sub Total, VAT* and *Delivery* together and entered on the card.

Now that we have some understanding of how the system works we can identify the entities, entity sets and relationships in the system.

E/R occurrence diagrams

There are three sets of index cards in the system. Each is an entity set: *Customer, Order* and *Product.* Each of these contains a collection of separate entities, for example *Customer* contains details of all the *Customer* entities.

We only need to create entity–relationship occurrence diagrams for entities which are related. Remember, a relationship is created by a primary and foreign key pair. The primary key of a *Product* is *Product ID* and the primary key of a *Customer* is *Customer ID. Product* and *Customer* are not related because there are no related attributes. There are no attributes of *Product* which appear in *Customer* and vice versa.

Therefore, we only need to create occurrence diagrams for *Customer/Order* and *Product/Order.*

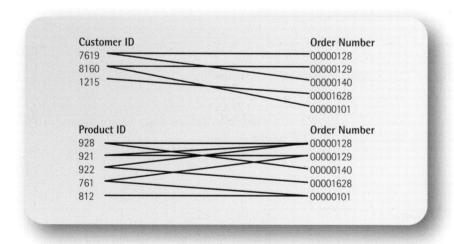

Figure 4.21 Entity–relationship occurrence diagrams for Case Study 2

From these diagrams we can see that the relationship between *Customer* and *Order* is one-to-many and the relationship between *Product* and *Order* is many-to-many. One customer can place one or more orders but one order can only be for one customer. One product can appear as part of one or more orders and one order can consist of one or more products.

The entity relationship diagram for this system is more complicated than the one constructed for Case Study 1. The easiest way to begin creating an ERD is to identify the entity set which links to the largest number of other entity sets. *Product* and *Customer* both link to one entity set but *Order* links to two entity sets. *Order* links to the largest number of entity sets so we place it at the centre of our ERD (Figure 4.22).

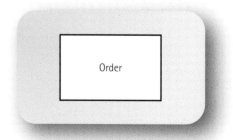

Figure 4.22 Starting to create the ERD for Case Study 2

This entity set links to two others so we now draw the diamond relationship symbols on either side of the entity (Figure 4.23).

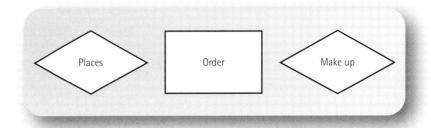

Figure 4.23 Adding relationships

Now add the connectors to the relationships and annotate the diagram on either side of the entity set to indicate the cardinality based on the E/R occurrence diagrams. We can use M on either side of the entity set because each M refers to a different relationship.

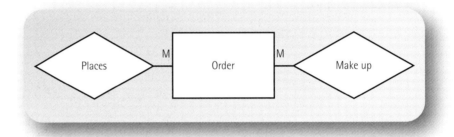

Figure 4.24 Adding connectors and cardinality

Now add the remaining entity sets, connectors and, again, annotate the diagram to indicate the cardinality.

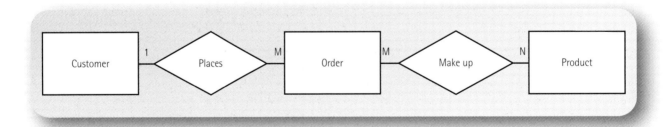

Figure 4.25 Completing the ERD

To complete the ERD we add the details of the attributes. There are atomic, multi-valued and derived attributes in this system. The attributes *Sub Total*, *VAT*, *Delivery* and *Total* are all calculated from values already held in the system. These attributes would not normally be stored by a computer-based database system because they would be calculated by the computer system as required. In the ERD these are the derived attributes identified using the dashed line around the attribute name.

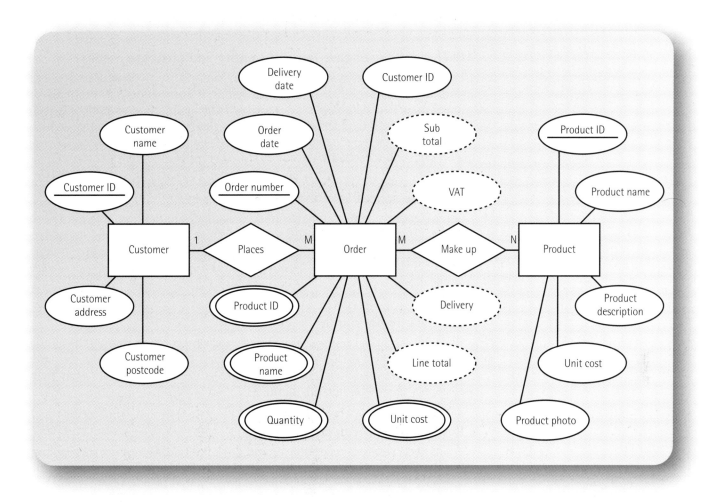

Figure 4.26 Completed ERD

An entity or entity set?

Entity sets and entities can be a little confusing. Remember, an *entity* is one thing, which is why, when we are trying to find the primary key, we try to find an attribute for each entity which makes it unique. If the correct attribute or attributes are chosen, their values will uniquely identify each entity in the entity set.

An *entity set* is a collection of entities. Each of the entities in an entity set must have the same attributes. When an entity relationship diagram is created it records how each entity set is related. When a database is created using software the entity sets become the tables, the attributes become the fields and each entity becomes a record in a table.

Notation and rules

Systems analysts have to develop systems which can be implemented on any appropriate database platform. This means that the notation they use, especially for fields (attributes in the database) and table names (entity sets in the database), needs to be one that most software packages can use as well!

In fact, it is a good idea to start with names for attributes and entity sets which can easily be implemented as field and table names in most RDBMS packages.

Some basic rules are:

Keep to all lower-case letters in entity and attribute names

Desktop database systems which run on just one computer are not normally case sensitive (it doesn't matter if something is in capitals or lower-case) but database systems which run online (i.e. as part of a web server) are often case sensitive and things can go wrong if you forget which fields or tables have capital letters. If you always keep to lower-case you won't have this problem.

Don't use spaces, use underscore (_) instead

Some database applications do not allow spaces in field or table names so it is good practice not to use spaces for these names. By using an underscore character rather than a space you can ensure that your chosen table and field names will be compatible with the greatest number of software applications.

Use meaningful names

Use table and field names that identify the object being named. In all the examples shown earlier the names given to the entities, entity sets and attributes identify their contents. If you store a customer's name then *customer_name* is a suitable identifier.

Keep it short (if you can)

Try to keep your entity, entity set and attribute names as short as possible. This can often be achieved by using a shortened form of the name, e.g. the attribute for a customer's telephone number could be *customer_tel_nbr* but remember to keep it meaningful!

Data dictionary

Another tool that a systems analyst can use to document a system is the data dictionary. A data dictionary is often called **metadata**. This is because a data dictionary is data about data. It is a description of the domain constraints that apply to each attribute of each entity. In other words, a data dictionary is a collection of data that describes the structure of a database.

A data dictionary is used to define the attributes and entities of which the system is composed. The data dictionary is very similar to a relational database table. Each column holds specific data relating to a particular domain while each row holds data specific to one attribute. Each row of the data dictionary defines the domain constraints for each attribute within the database system.

When a data dictionary is created, the systems analyst is essentially creating the design for the various database tables which will be created in the relational database management system. All relational database management systems have certain rules about how tables, fields and other properties of the database should be named and defined. These rules should be applied, where possible, to the data dictionary to make the transition from database design (i.e. the data dictionary) to implemented database (i.e. the database created using the RDBMS) easier.

A data dictionary contains the following columns:

Entity set

This is the name of the entity set. When the database is created using the RDBMS, the entity set name will be the name of the table.

Name

This column in the data dictionary is where the names given to the attributes of the entity are listed. Remember, when you are creating your attribute names, to follow the advice given earlier about meaningful names. The names given in this column will be the field names in the database table.

Type

The data held in the attribute will be constrained by type. The possible data types were defined in Chapter 3 in the section relating to domain constraints. These data types are text, integer, real, object, link, Boolean, date and time. As you complete this section of the data dictionary you should have some concept of the data types which are available in your RDBMS and how the standard data types (text, integer, real, object, link, Boolean, date and time) can be implemented using your RDBMS.

Size

Data items of text type are constrained by their maximum length. For attributes of the text type, the size column constrains the attribute to a specific maximum number of text characters. In a computer system the amount of available storage is limited therefore it is important to specify the maximum size required for any attribute to ensure this storage space can be reserved in computer memory.

Validation

Each attribute is constrained by the range of acceptable values. These domain constraints are one of four types:

- presence (are null values allowed or not)
- range (above/below certain values)
- permitted values (only one of a selection of values is allowed)
- format (the data entered must conform to a specific pattern and/or number of characters).

More detail about domain constraints is given in Chapter 3. One or more domain constraints can be entered in the validation column. Again, as you complete this column of the data dictionary, you should consider how you would implement each of the validation rules using your RDBMS.

Index/key

This column is used to identify primary and foreign keys and other items of data that might be commonly accessed in the database.

An index can be created for any attribute as a quick way to locate a record. Indices make it faster to find specific records and to sort records by the indexed attribute or attributes. The data entered against this column will be one of five possibilities.

Attribute property	Index entry
Attribute is primary key	Yes, primary key
Attribute is part of a compound primary key	Yes, compound key
Attribute is a foreign key	Yes, foreign key
Attribute is to be indexed	Yes
Attribute is not to be indexed	No

Figure 4.27 *Data dictionary index values*

Sometimes in a system it is useful to have the RDBMS index a field even if the field is not a key. An example of this would be an attribute which is commonly used in a search of a database, such as the *post_code* in a database used by a mail order company.

An index is a way of speeding up access to required data. A simple index is a table which contains two columns. The first column is the search key. The search key column contains a single occurrence of each of the values that appear in the indexed attribute. If the indexed attribute is a primary key then the index will contain the same number of records as the entity from which the attribute is drawn.

The second column of the index is a pointer and points to the first record in the table which has an attribute equal to the search key.

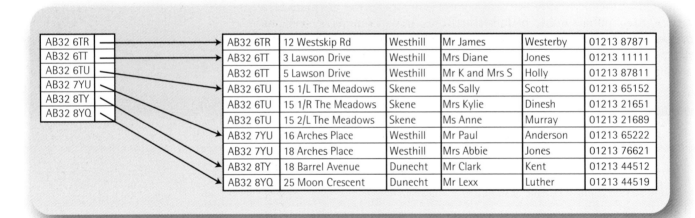

Figure 4.28 *A simple index and related table of data*

When a search is carried out for a *post_code* in the example in Figure 4.28, rather than initially searching the main table the RDBMS searches the index for the value required. When the required *post_code* is found the RDBMS reads the value for the pointer and jumps to that location in the main table. All the records with the matching *post_code* can then be read from the main table.

As you might imagine, every time a change is made to the main table the index must also be updated because the position of the records in the table changes as records are created and deleted. These updates take some time for the processor to complete. If too many indices are created then these, rather than speeding up the system, will slow it down. This is because the time gained from using the indices in searches will be lost, since the system will spend too much time maintaining the indices as the data in the table change!

The example in Figure 4.28 is a very simple index. There are far more complex and more efficient ways of indexing tables, however these are beyond the requirements of this course.

Creating the data dictionary

The data dictionary is laid out as a table. The columns contain the items listed above while each row holds data specific to one attribute. Each row of the data dictionary defines the domain constraints for each attribute within the database system.

Entity Set	Name	Type	Size	Validation	Index/Key
customer	customer_nbr	Integer	> 0	required	Yes, primary key
customer	customer_name	Text	50	required	No
customer	customer_address	Text	255	required	No
customer	customer_postcode	Text	8	any valid postcode format	No
customer	customer_tel_nbr	Text	22		No
order	customer_nbr	Integer		required	Yes, foreign key
order	order_number	Integer		required	Yes, primary key
order	order_date	Date/Time		dd/mm/yyyy, required	No
order	delivery_date	Date/Time		dd/mm/yyyy, required	No
...	...	...	...	...	...

Figure 4.29 Partial sample of a data dictionary

At this stage, all attributes, including multi-valued and derived attributes, are entered into the data dictionary. For multi-valued attributes, the data dictionary details how only one occurrence of each attribute is stored (for example, see Figure 4.30):

...	...	...	...	...	...
order	sub_total	Real		the sum of line_totals for order, required	No
order	vat	Real		17.5% of sub_total, required	No
order	delivery	Real		5% of sub_total, required	No / No
order	line_total	Real		unit_cost x quantity, required	No
order	unit_cost	Real		> 0, required	No
order	quantity	Integer		> 0, required	No
order	product_name	Text	35	required	No
order	product_id	Integer		required	Yes, foreign key
...	...	...	...	...	...

Figure 4.30 Continuation of partial sample of a data dictionary

Notice that the names given to the entities are different from those that appear on the forms in Figure 4.20 and the ERD (Figure 4.26). This is because the naming rules have been applied. Spaces have been replaced with the underscore character and lower-case characters have been used throughout.

Questions

1. The primary keys of each of the following entities are underlined.
   Produce entity–relationship occurrence models for a, b and c below.

   a Student and Tutor

   Student

<u>Student No</u>	18728	Firstname:	Joseph
DOB:	06/02/1989	Surname:	Millar

Course ID	Course Name	Credits	Tutor ID
D561	Computing	1	1989
D766	Hardware Sys	1	7817
C991	DB Design	2	7817

   Tutor

Tutor ID	Tutor Name	Tutor Extension
1989	Mr Boyd	761
7817	Mrs Hammond	991
6516	Mr George	123

   b Employee and Department

   Employee

Employee ID	Department ID	Employee Name
AD191	002	Harry Ward
ER123	001	George Clooney
GH818	003	Dawn Smith
AD154	002	Stephanie Swift
TY176	001	Lorreta Went

   Department

Department ID	Department
001	Sales
002	HR
003	Manufacturing

   c Driver and Taxi

   Driver

Driver ID	Driver Name	Taxi
03	Jo Fleming	TY52 8UQ
15	Ian Smith	AS51 2ER
18	Pat Page	VJ53 7KL

Taxi

Reg Number	Carries	Disabled Access
TY52 8UQ	5	Yes
AS51 2ER	4	No
VJ53 7KL	8	Yes

2. For each of a, b and c above draw an entity relationship diagram. Include the entity sets, attributes and relationships.

3. The BusyBee Cleaning Company specialises in providing cleaning services for domestic clients. Each client has a set of requirements. For example, Mrs R Jones requires cleaning services from Monday to Friday, 7 am until 9 am, but Mr P Nuttall only requires cleaning services on a Wednesday from 10 am until 1 pm.

Whenever a new client is taken on, a BusyBee administrator assesses how many cleaning staff are required for the premises, then assigns staff to the job by adding them to the bottom of the client's card. Two sample index cards from the system are shown below:

Client

Client Ref: 7800   *Client Name*:   Mrs R Jones

Tel Nbr: 0938 827381

Requirements:

Monday to Friday, 7 am to 9 am

Cleaner ID	Cleaner Name
A78	Jordon Wong
D12	Sheila Wood

Cleaner

Cleaner ID	Cleaner Name	Cleaner Tel No
A78	Jordon Wong	01452 58456
D12	Sheila Wood	01452 98987
CY67	Gordon Freeman	01452 57745
B15	Fran Rose	01345 89765

From the above information, create

a an entity–relationship occurrence model to discover the relationship between the two entities

b an ERD to illustrate the relationship and entity sets of the system

c a data dictionary for the system.

4. Describe three factors which should be considered when selecting names for database columns.

5. What is the purpose of the validation column in a data dictionary?

6. Explain the purpose of an index in a relational database system.

Normalisation

Normalisation is a set of steps which, when properly carried out, removes many of the common problems of relational database design.

The normalisation process contains four steps which take us from the conceptual model of the database system to the logical data model. Remember, the logical data model is a design for the database system which meets the requirements of the relational database model which we looked at in Chapter 2.

The relational data model has seven rules. Each rule must be adhered to if a database system is to be implemented using relational database tools. We can test a conceptual database model against these rules to see if the model meets these requirements.

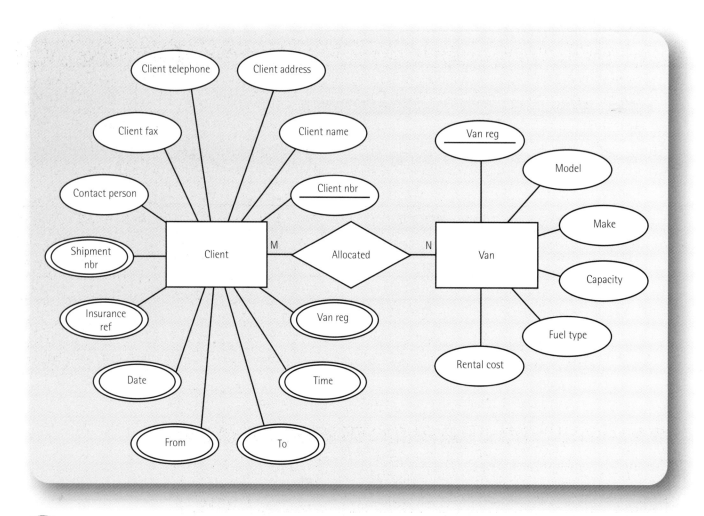

Figure 5.1 *ERD for Case Study 1*

If we change the seven relational database rules into questions we can use these to test if the conceptual model is valid, that is, meets all the rules!

		Answer
1.	Does every relation in the database have a unique name?	Yes
2.	Does every column in a relation have a unique name within that relation?	Yes
3.	Are all entries in a column of the same kind?	Yes
4.	Is the ordering of columns in each relation not significant?	Yes
5.	Is each row in each relation unique?	Yes
6.	Is the order of the rows not important in the relation?	Yes
7.	Does each cell in the table (the intersection of a column and a row) contain only one value?	No

This conceptual model, like most conceptual models, does not meet the requirements of the relational database model. Many of the requirements have been met because of the work carried out to create the conceptual model. If we consider the sample data for Case Study 1 and view the data as relations (i.e. tables), it is possible to see some of the problems.

Figure 5.2 Sample data table for Case Study 1

client

client_nbr	client_name	client_address	client_telephone	client_fax	contact_person	shipment_nbr	insurance_ref	from	to	date	time	van_req
2711	West Homes Ltd	14 Argos St Glasgow G23 9UJ	0312 123198	0312 123199	John Michael Osbourne	0012	NT9238	15 Andrews Cres Dundee DD76 8TT	28 Westfield Pl. Dundee DD75 7YH	23/02/2004	09:30	P385 ASA
						0010	RT8721	Arran House Inverness IV26 6TY	Harbour House Stonehaven AB22 8YU	24/02/2004	08:30	KY51 AFZ
						0014	QW1211	267 Gill St Stirling FK78 1MN	10a Lawson Rd Stirling FK78 2YT	24/02/2004	09:30	YT71 7YE
0921	Great Arwoods Plc.	18 New Parlie St Edinburgh EH87 9QQ	0327 989127	0327 981111	Vicky Kenn	0012	NT9238	3 Abercrombie St Aberdeen AB15 7YU	18 Drummond Pl Aberdeen AB11 8TR	23/02/2004	09:30	KY51 AFZ
						0010	RT8721	5 West Beach Finchley NW9 8YU	12 Dorset St Leeds L87 8HU	24/02/2004	08:30	P385 ASA
						0011	AD6701	The Lodge Heathsville West Moore WM8 3HJ	15 Smith Heights Bothwill G56 7ER	24/02/2004	11:30	D842 YSA

van

van_reg	model	make	capacity	fuel_type	rental_cost
P385 ASA	Transit	Ford	11.89 m³	Petrol	£90.00
KY51 AFZ	Convoy	LDV	16.85 m³	Diesel	£100.00
YT71 7YE	LF	DAF	28.45 m³	Diesel	£125.00
D842 YSA	Actros	Mercedes	36.10 m³	Diesel	£150.00

Each relation has a unique name, therefore satisfying Rule 1 of the relational database model. Each column within each relation has been allocated a unique name, therefore satisfying Rule 2. The data dictionary has defined the domain constraints for each column, therefore satisfying Rule 3. Rules 4 and 6 are satisfied because there is no dependence on the sequence of data stored. We've selected a primary key for each relation to uniquely identify each row, therefore satisfying Rule 5.

The problem is with Rule 7 because there are multi-valued cells in the *Client* relation. We need to find a way of removing these multi-valued cells. The multi-valued cells create a many-to-many relationship between *Client* and *Van*.

Problems with database designs

There are a number of common problems which we need to correct in this database design before it can be implemented using relational database management software.

Problems with many-to-many relationships

We can see why the many-to-many relationship is a problem if we look at the data in the relation *Client* in Figure 5.2 above. Notice that there are multiple values for *shipment_nbr*, *insurance_ref*, *from*, *to*, *date*, *time* and *van_reg*. The two major problems they present are:

- There is no way to know exactly how any of the values in the multi-valued cells relate to one another. Currently, we might try to assume that, because the data for removals is shown in rows, this indicates some sort of order. But each item of data is not actually held in a row. It is held in a multi-valued cell within a row. For example, the value of the *shipment_nbr* attribute for the *client_nbr* 2771 is: 0012, 0010, 0014 (Figure 5.3).

  There is no way to know which of these values should be associated with the values for *van_reg*: P385 ASA, KY51 AFZ, YT71 7YE (Figure 5.4).

shipment_nbr
0012
0010
0014

Figure 5.3 shipment_nbr, a multi-valued cell

van_reg
P385 ASA
KY51 AFZ
YT71 7YE

Figure 5.4 van_reg, another multi-valued cell

From
15 Andrews Cres
Dundee
DD76 8TT
Arran House
Inverness
IV26 6TY
267 Gill St
Stirling
FK78 1MN

Figure 5.5 To complete a search the values need to be separated

- Searching the table is very difficult. If, for example, we want to know which removals are from Dundee, the RDBMS will need to perform some kind of processing to separate each of the multiple values in the *from* attribute and then match these to the text 'Dundee' (Figure 5.5).

It would be much easier if each of the multi-valued cells could be broken down so that each value was in its own cell. Normalisation is a process which removes multi-valued cells and improves the overall design of the database (Figure 5.6).

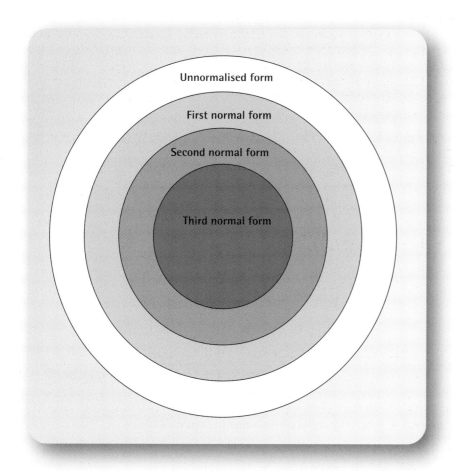

Figure 5.6 *Stages of normalisation*

There are four steps which we carry out as part of the normalisation process. These are described below.

Creation of UNF from source documents

The first step of normalisation is to produce an unnormalised form (UNF) based on the conceptual data dictionary and ERD.

When we create the UNF we start to reduce the amount of redundant data in the system. To begin the UNF we first write down all attributes of the system in a vertical list.

Notice that the columns of both the relations are listed in Figure 5.7. Now we remove any column which appears more than once. This means that one occurrence of *van_reg* will be removed.

We now have a list of columns which belong to the system. In fact, we have created one relation which consists of all the columns in the system. For this relation we have to identify all the potential primary keys. These potential primary keys are called **candidate keys**.

The best primary keys are those that are single columns but there are other possible combinations which are just as valid.

The potential keys for this relation are: *client_nbr*, *van_reg* and *shipment_nbr*. Any of these would be a potential starter primary key for this relation. If we apply the rules of normalisation then it doesn't matter

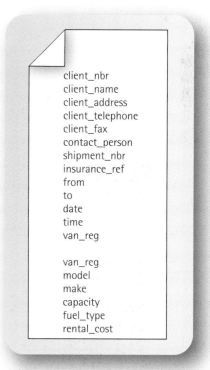

Figure 5.7 *Beginning to create a UNF*

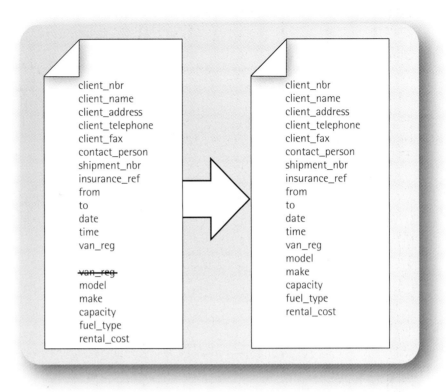

Figure 5.8 Removing duplicate columns to create a UNF

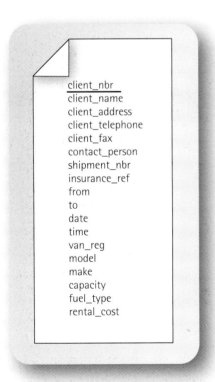

Figure 5.9 UNF in progress with primary key underlined

which of these keys is chosen. We'll choose *client_nbr* now, but later we'll see what happens if either of the other two are chosen.

Now we underline the chosen primary key (Figure 5.9).

For each record of this primary key there are multi-valued cells. These multi-valued cells are called a **repeating group**. Figure 5.10 shows the primary key values and the repeating cells for each primary key.

In the unnormalised form we show these repeating data items, the repeating group, indented to show the attributes containing multi-valued cells (Figure 5.11).

Finally, we give the relation a name and enclose the attributes in round brackets to show that they belong to the relation (Figure 5.12).

This is the completed UNF from which we produce the first normal form. The first step in moving from a conceptual model to a logical data model is now complete.

There are several problems with this normal form. The problems which we identified earlier about accessing and searching the data held in the multi-valued cells are still present in the UNF and need to be removed by applying the rule for first normal form.

Figure 5.10 Primary key values, and repeating cells for each primary key

client_nbr	client_name	client_address	client_telephone	client_fax	contact_person	shipment_nbr	insurance_ref	from	to	date	time	van_req	model	make	capacity	fuel_type	rental_cost
2711	West Homes Ltd	14 Argos St Glasgow G23 9UJ	0312 123198	0312 123199	John Michael Osbourne	0012	NT9238	15 Andrews Cres Dundee DD76 8TT	28 Westfield Pl. Dundee DD75 7YH	23/02/2004	09:30	P385 ASA	Transit	Ford	11.89 m³	Petrol	£90.00
						0010	RT8721	Arran House Inverness IV26 6TY	Harbour House Stonehaven AB22 8YU	24/02/2004	08:30	KY51 AFZ	Convoy	LDV	16.85 m³	Diesel	£100.00
						0014	QW1211	267 Gill St Stirling FK78 1MN	10a Lawson Rd Stirling FK78 2YT	24/02/2004	09:30	YT71 7YE	LF	DAF	28.45 m³	Diesel	£125.00
0921	Great Arwoods Plc.	18 New Parlie St Edinburgh EH87 9QQ	0327 989127	0327 981111	Vicky Kenn	0012	NT9238	3 Abercrombie St Aberdeen AB15 7YU	18 Drummond Pl Aberdeen AB11 8TR	23/02/2004	09:30	KY51 AFZ	Convoy	LDV	16.85 m³	Diesel	£100.00
						0010	RT8721	5 West Beach Finchley NW9 8YU	12 Dorset St Leeds L87 8HU	24/02/2004	08:30	P385 ASA	Transit	Ford	11.89 m³	Petrol	£90.00
						0011	AD6701	The Lodge Heathsville West Moore WM8 3HJ	15 Smith Heights Bothwill G56 7ER	24/02/2004	11:30	D842 YSA	Actros	Mercedes	36.10 m³	Diesel	£150.00

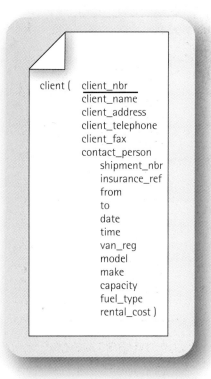

```
client_nbr
client_name
client_address
client_telephone
client_fax
contact_person
    shipment_nbr
    insurance_ref
    from
    to
    date
    time
    van_reg
    model
    make
    capacity
    fuel_type
    rental_cost
```

Figure 5.11 *UNF in progress with repeated group indented*

```
client (   client_nbr
           client_name
           client_address
           client_telephone
           client_fax
           contact_person
               shipment_nbr
               insurance_ref
               from
               to
               date
               time
               van_reg
               model
               make
               capacity
               fuel_type
               rental_cost )
```

Figure 5.12 *Completed UNF*

First normal form

First normal form eliminates the repeating group by putting the group into a new relation and connecting it to the original relation with a one-to-many relationship. We say a relation is in first normal form if there are no multi-valued cells within it. Each cell must contain one atomic value.

Look again at Figure 5.10. To change this into first normal form we create a new relation to represent the repeating group. All the columns that belong to the repeating group will be removed to this new relation.

In Case Study 1, Reed and Co., the columns that were indented in the UNF are the repeating group. These are separated to create a new relation called *removal*.

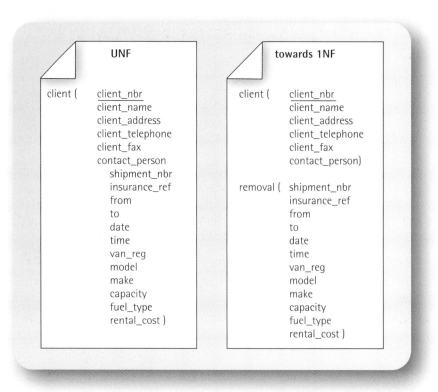

Figure 5.13 Moving from UNF to 1NF

The problem with the 1NF created in Figure 5.13 above is there is no relationship between *client* and *removal* because there are no columns which appear in both to link them. There is no primary/foreign key pairing to create the relationship.

In order to complete the 1NF, the primary key of the UNF relation is copied across to the new relation, which contains the UNF repeating group, to create a foreign key. The primary key of the new relation is then selected and underlined.

For Case Study 1, the UNF primary key (*client_nbr*) is copied into the *removal* relation to create a foreign key. This links the *client* relation to the *removal* relation using a primary/foreign key pair. This creates the one-to-many relationship linking *client* to *removal*.

The primary key of *removal* is identified from the information given about the system in the Case Study 1 notes in Chapter 4. Each *shipment_nbr* is unique for each client but not for the system overall, therefore both *shipment_nbr* and *client_nbr* are required to identify a unique removal (remember, a client can only have one removal in a shipment for insurance purposes). This means that the primary key of *removal* is a compound key of *shipment_nbr* and *client_nbr*.

The relationship between *client* and *removal* is a one-to-many relationship, as shown in the ERD in Figure 5.15.

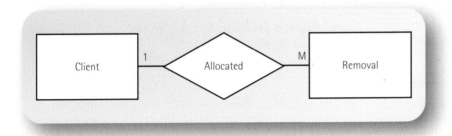

Figure 5.15 ERD of 1NF for Case Study 1

The database design in 1NF satisfies all the rules of the relational database model but contains a significant amount of **data redundancy**.

Data redundancy

Data redundancy refers to the amount of data in a database that is not required. The aim of good relational database design is to reduce data redundancy by:

- ensuring that each item of data is stored only once within the database
- ensuring that only data that cannot be calculated from other data held in the database are stored.

Redundant data is data that appears more than once in the database or data that can be calculated from values already held in the database, i.e. derived attributes identified in the ERD.

The relations in Figure 5.15 illustrate the data in the Case Study 1, 1NF shown in Figure 5.14.

As you can see from Figure 5.16, all the data for each van appears every time the van is used for a removal. Also, the insurance reference is typed in every time a removal is allocated to a shipment. This is very inefficient in terms of operating the database and a waste of storage space. Imagine the time spent typing in all the van details every time a removal is booked for a client, or the possibility of a mistake when entering an insurance reference!

There are three common problems with relations that contain redundant data:

Insertion problem

If Reed and Co. were to buy a new removal van, where would the data about it be entered in the database? There is nowhere in any of the relations to add the details of a van unless the van has been booked for a removal.

This is known as an **insertion problem** and is a common problem with flat-file and poorly constructed relational databases.

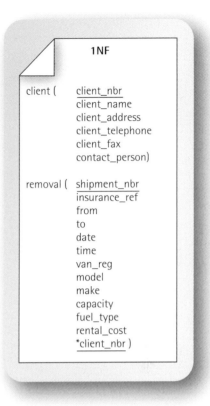

Figure 5.14 The complete 1NF for Case Study 1

Modification problem

If Reed and Co. decided to change the *rental_cost* of the van with registration number KY51 AFZ there is no way, in the current relations, that this change can be made without updating more than one record.

It may take a considerable amount of time to update every required record with the new *rental_cost*. More importantly, updating all these records might lead to inconsistencies in the data if a mistake is made entering the new value or if some records are missed out.

This is known as a **modification problem** and is common with flat-file and poorly constructed relational databases.

Deletion problem

What happens if the removal for *client_nbr* 2711 with *shipment_number* 0014 is deleted? Deleting this record will delete all the data about the van with *van_reg* YT71 7YE! This van is not used in any other removal therefore its details will be lost when the record is deleted.

This is known as a **deletion problem** and is also common with flat-file and poorly constructed relational databases.

To remove these problems we need to modify the relations by applying the second and third normal form rules.

shipment_ nbr	insurance_ ref	from	to	date	time	van_req	model	make	capacity	fuel_ type	rental_ cost	client_ nbr
0012	NT9238	15 Andrews Cres Dundee DD76 8TT	28 Westfield Pl. Dundee DD75 7YH	23/02/2004	09:30	P385 ASA	Transit	Ford	11.89 m³	Petrol	£90.00	2711
0010	RT8721	Arran House Inverness IV26 6TY	Harbour House Stonehaven AB22 8YU	24/02/2004	08:30	KY51 AFZ	Convoy	LDV	16.85 m³	Diesel	£100.00	2711
0014	QW1211	267 Gill St Stirling FK78 1MN	10a Lawson Rd Stirling FK78 2YT	24/02/2004	09:30	YT71 7YE	LF	DAF	28.45 m³	Diesel	£125.00	2711
0012	NT9238	3 Abercrombie St Aberdeen AB15 7YU	18 Drummond Pl Aberdeen AB11 8TR	23/02/2004	09:30	KY51 AFZ	Convoy	LDV	16.85 m³	Diesel	£100.00	0921
0010	RT8721	5 West Beach Finchley NW9 8YU	12 Dorset St Leeds L87 8HU	24/02/2004	08:30	P385 ASA	Transit	Ford	11.89 m³	Petrol	£90.00	0921
0011	AD6701	The Lodge Heathsville West Moore WM8 3HJ	15 Smith Heights Bothwill G56 7ER	24/02/2004	11:30	D842 YSA	Actros	Mercedes	36.10 m³	Diesel	£150.00	0921

Figure 5.16 1NF with sample data for Case Study 1

client_ nbr	client_ name	client_ address	client_ telephone	client_ fax	contact_ person
2711	West Homes Ltd	14 Argos St Glasgow G23 9UJ	0312 123198	0312 123199	John Michael Osbourne
0921	Great Arwoods Plc.	18 New Parlie St Edinburgh EH87 9QQ	0327 989127	0327 981111	Vicky Kenn

Second normal form

A relation is in second normal form (2NF) if every column within it is entirely dependent on the whole of the key and not just part of the key. Second normal form *only* applies to relations that have a compound key.

If a relation has a single column primary key then it is automatically in second normal form. In the 1NF identified in Figure 5.16, *client* has a single column primary key therefore *client* is in second normal form.

Removal has a primary key of *shipment_nbr* and *client_nbr*. This means we must test it to ensure that it is in second normal form. If it is not, we need to make some changes to the relation to place it in second normal form.

Partial dependency

To test if something is in second normal form we use the following question:

> Is the key needed to find all the values in the relation or will just part of the key do?

The key of *removal* is *shipment_nbr* and *client_nbr*. Each client can only have one removal as part of a shipment but a client can have any number of removals as long as they are allocated to different shipments. Each shipment has an *insurance_ref* allocated which is a reference to the insurance details for the shipment.

The same *shipment_nbr* appears against a number of different client removals. This means that to uniquely identify anything that is part of a removal requires both the *shipment_nbr* and the *client_nbr*.

But are both *shipment_nbr* and *client_nbr* required to uniquely identify each column in the relation *removal*? Each shipment contains a number of removals, each one for a different client, and each one with its own values for *from*, *to*, *date*, *time*, *van_reg*, etc. However, all the removals which are part of the same shipment have the same *insurance_ref* and *shipment_nbr*.

This means that if the value for *shipment_nbr* is known then the value for *insurance_ref* can be found without requiring the *client_nbr*. To put it in database terminology, *insurance_ref* is **partially depended** on the primary key *shipment_nbr* and *client_nbr* because it depends only on part of the key, i.e. *shipment_nbr*.

To remove this partial dependency, a new relation is created called *shipment* into which *shipment_nbr* and *insurance_ref* are placed. *Shipment_nbr* remains in *removal* as part of the primary key but it is now a foreign key as well.

By creating the *shipment* relation the amount of data redundancy in the system is reduced because *insurance_ref* is now stored only once for each shipment. *Shipment_nbr* is still required as part of the primary key of *removal* and is also required in *removal* to create the relationship with *shipment*.

The relationship between *shipment* and *removal* is a one-to-many relationship, as shown in the ERD for the second normal form (Figure 5.20).

Even though the amount of redundant data has been reduced there is still redundant data in the system. Every time a van is used for a removal all the details about the van (*van_reg*, *model*, *make*, *capacity*, *fuel_type*, *rental_cost*) are included in the record.

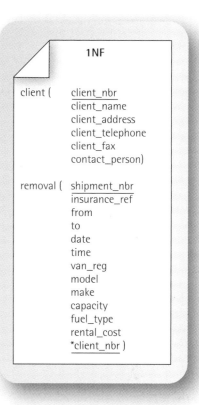

Figure 5.17 *The complete 1NF for Case Study 1*

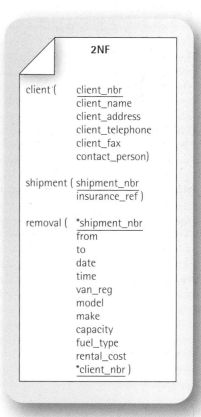

Figure 5.18 *The complete 2NF for Case Study 1*

shipment_ nbr	from	to	date	time	van_req	model	make	capacity	fuel_ type	rental_ cost	client_ nbr
0012	15 Andrews Cres Dundee DD76 8TT	28 Westfield Pl. Dundee DD75 7YH	23/02/2004	09:30	P385 ASA	Transit	Ford	11.89 m³	Petrol	£90.00	2711
0010	Arran House Inverness IV26 6TY	Harbour House Stonehaven AB22 8YU	24/02/2004	08:30	KY51 AFZ	Convoy	LDV	16.85 m³	Diesel	£100.00	2711
0014	267 Gill St Stirling FK78 1MN	10a Lawson Rd Stirling FK78 2YT	24/02/2004	09:30	YT71 7YE	LF	DAF	28.45 m³	Diesel	£125.00	2711
0012	3 Abercrombie St Aberdeen AB15 7YU	18 Drummond Pl Aberdeen AB11 8TR	23/02/2004	09:30	KY51 AFZ	Convoy	LDV	16.85 m³	Diesel	£100.00	0921
0010	5 West Beach Finchley NW9 8YU	12 Dorset St Leeds L87 8HU	24/02/2004	08:30	P385 ASA	Transit	Ford	11.89 m³	Petrol	£90.00	0921
0011	The Lodge Heathsville West Moore WM8 3HJ	15 Smith Heights Bothwill G56 7ER	24/02/2004	11:30	D842 YSA	Actros	Mercedes	36.10 m³	Diesel	£150.00	0921

Figure 5.19 *2NF with sample data for Case Study 1*

client_ nbr	client_ name	client_ address	client_ telephone	client_ fax	contact_ person
2711	West Homes Ltd	14 Argos St Glasgow G23 9UJ	0312 123198	0312 123199	John Michael Osbourne
0921	Great Arwoods Plc.	18 New Parlie St Edinburgh EH87 9QQ	0327 989127	0327 981111	Vicky Kenn

shipment_ nbr	insurance_ ref
0012	NT9238
0010	RT8721
0014	QW1211
0011	AD6701

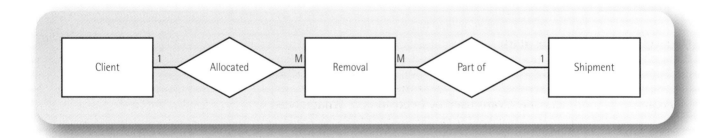

Figure 5.20 *ERD of 2NF for Case Study 1*

Third normal form

A relation is in third normal form if all the columns depend on the primary key and not on any other column.

In the second normal form for Case Study 1, (Figure 5.18) there are currently three relations. Each relation has a primary key and each relation is correctly in second normal form.

All the columns in the *client* relation depend on the primary key of *client_nbr*. There is no other column within *client* that could be used as a primary key for some or all of the columns.

The *shipment* relation contains the primary key of *shipment_nbr* and the column *insurance_ref*. Shipment must be in third normal form because there are only two columns in the relation and there is no other column for some or all of the relation to be dependent on.

The *removal* relation still contains a large amount of redundant data because the details of a van are repeated every time the van is used for a removal. The purpose of normalisation is to remove redundant data to create relations which efficiently store data. The *removal* relation contains the primary key of *shipment_nbr* and *client_nbr* and the columns *from*, *to*, *date*, *time*, *van_reg*, *model*, *make*, *capacity*, *fuel_type* and *rental_cost*.

Transitive dependency

If a van's *van_reg* is known, can the values for *model*, *make*, *capacity*, *fuel_type* and *rental_cost* be found? Does *van_reg* uniquely identify each van? Yes, it can and yes it does.

This means details for each van depend on the *van_reg* rather than the primary key of *shipment_nbr* and *client_nbr*. It also means that *model*, *make*, *capacity*, *fuel_type* and *rental_cost* are **transitively dependent** on the primary key *shipment_nbr* and *client_nbr*.

They are actually dependent on *van_reg* but because *van_reg* in *removal* depends on *shipment_nbr* and *client_nbr*, then *model*, *make*, *capacity*, *fuel_type* and *rental_cost* are also dependent on *shipment_nbr* and *client_nbr*. The dependence on *van_reg* is **through** the primary key of *shipment_nbr* and *client_nbr* which makes it transitive, i.e. moving through.

To place the *removal* relation in third normal form, the transitively dependent columns are removed to a new relation, *van*, with the primary key of *van_reg*. *Van_reg* remains in *removal* to create the relationship between *van* and *removal*.

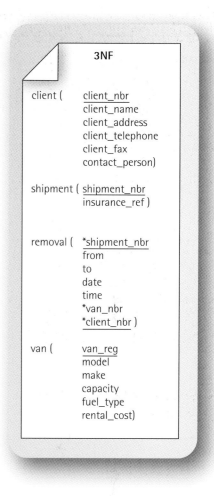

Figure 5.21 The complete 3NF for Case Study 1

Adding a surrogate key

This system is now correctly in third normal form but there is a small problem. The column *van_reg* is a meaningful primary key. It contains the actual registration numbers of the vans used by Reed and Co. What if Reed and Co. sells one of the vans and buys a new one to replace it?

Look at Figure 5.22. Now, if a van is replaced, only the details in *van* need to be amended. The values for *van_nbr* in *removal* don't need to change because the new van has simply replaced the old van for the removal.

Data redundancy removed

By examining the sample data organised in the four relations it is possible to see that the data redundancy has been removed from the UNF that was created earlier (Figure 5.23).

Each relation is linked to other relations by a one-to-many relationship created using primary/foreign key pairs, each relation is in third normal form and each relation satisfies the seven relational database rules (Figure 5.24).

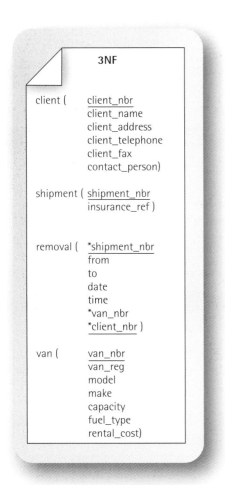

3NF

client (client_nbr
             client_name
             client_address
             client_telephone
             client_fax
             contact_person)

shipment (shipment_nbr
                insurance_ref)

removal (*shipment_nbr
              from
              to
              date
              time
              *van_nbr
              *client_nbr)

van (van_nbr
             van_reg
             model
             make
             capacity
             fuel_type
             rental_cost)

Figure 5.22 The complete 3NF for Case Study 1 with surrogate key

Figure 5.23 3NF with sample data for Case Study 1

shipment_nbr	from	to	date	time	van_nbr	client_nbr
0012	15 Andrews Cres Dundee DD76 8TT	28 Westfield Pl. Dundee DD75 7YH	23/02/2004	09:30	001	2711
0010	Arran House Inverness IV26 6TY	Harbour House Stonehaven AB22 8YU	24/02/2004	08:30	002	2711
0014	267 Gill St Stirling FK78 1MN	10a Lawson Rd Stirling FK78 2YT	24/02/2004	09:30	003	2711
0012	3 Abercrombie St Aberdeen AB15 7YU	18 Drummond Pl Aberdeen AB11 8TR	23/02/2004	09:30	002	0921
0010	5 West Beach Finchley NW9 8YU	12 Dorset St Leeds L87 8HU	24/02/2004	08:30	001	0921
0011	The Lodge Heathsville West Moore WM8 3HJ	15 Smith Heights Bothwill G56 7ER	24/02/2004	11:30	004	0921

client_nbr	client_name	client_address	client_telephone	client_fax	contact_person
2711	West Homes Ltd	14 Argos St Glasgow G23 9UJ	0312 123198	0312 123199	John Michael Osbourne
0921	Great Arwoods Plc.	18 New Parlie St Edinburgh EH87 9QQ	0327 989127	0327 981111	Vicky Kenn

shipment_nbr	insurance_ref
0012	NT9238
0010	RT8721
0014	QW1211
0011	AD6701

van_nbr	van_reg	model	make	capacity	fuel_type	rental_cost
001	P385 ASA	Transit	Ford	11.89 m³	Petrol	£90.00
002	KY51 AFZ	Convoy	LDV	16.85 m³	Diesel	£100.00
003	YT71 7YE	LF	DAF	28.45 m³	Diesel	£125.00
004	D842 YSA	Actros	Mercedes	36.10 m³	Diesel	£150.00

Insertion, modification and deletion problems resolved

This third normal form has removed the insertion, modification and deletion problems which we discussed after the first normal form was created. Each item of non-key data in the system is recorded only once.

Insertion

If Reed and Co. buys an additional van it can be added to the *van* relation before it is allocated to any removals. Likewise, an *insurance_ref* can be recorded for *shipment* before any removals are allocated to the shipment, or a new client can be added to the *client* relation before a removal is inserted.

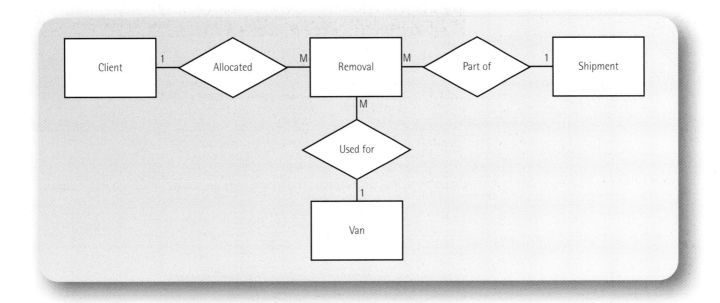

Figure 5.24 ERD of 3NF for Case Study 1

Modification

If a client changes address then only the details in the *client* relation need to be modified. Likewise, if a shipment is allocated a different insurance policy, only the *insurance_ref* in *shipment* needs to be modified. If a van is sold and replaced then only the van details in *van* need to be modified.

Deletion

If any of the rows of the relations are deleted only the data relevant to that relation is lost. If a removal is deleted then this does not delete any van, client or shipment details. A client can be deleted from the *client* relation without having any direct impact on any of the other relations.

What about referential integrity?

Referential integrity can be applied to relations by the RDBMS. Referential integrity means that no foreign key value can exist without a related primary key value in the related relation.

For example, if referential integrity is enforced between *client* and *removal* then a removal cannot be inserted without a matching *client_nbr* being present in *client*. The *client_nbr* 2281 in *removal* in Figure 5.25 does not exist in *client* which means that this removal has been booked for a client that does not exist!

Cascade modifications

If a primary key value is modified then the related foreign key values should also be modified if referential integrity is being enforced (Figure 5.26).

If the primary key value for a client is modified then this modification should be cascaded to the related foreign keys. This means that if the primary key value changes then the changes should be copied to all the related rows.

shipment_nbr	from	to	date	time	van_nbr	client_nbr
0012	15 Andrews Cres Dundee DD76 8TT	28 Westfield Pl. Dundee DD75 7YH	23/02/2004	09:30	001	2711
0010	Arran House Inverness IV26 6TY	Harbour House Stonehaven AB22 8YU	24/02/2004	08:30	002	2711
0014	3 Abercrombie St Aberdeen AB15 7YU	18 Drummond Pl Aberdeen AB11 8TR	23/02/2004	09:30	002	0921
0014	3 Croft Court Westhill AB56 7YU	The Manor Blairgowrie FK89 7YU	25/02/2004	08:30	003	2281

client_nbr	client_name	client_address	client_telephone	client_fax	contact_person
2711	West Homes Ltd	14 Argos St Glasgow G23 9UJ	0312 123198	0312 123199	John Michael Osbourne
0921	Great Arwoods Plc.	18 New Parlie St Edinburgh EH87 9QQ	0327 989127	0327 981111	Vicky Kenn

?

Figure 5.25 *Referential integrity failure – no matching primary key for foreign key*

Cascade deletions

This is also true for when a client is deleted. If a primary key value has been deleted all related foreign key values should also be deleted in order to maintain referential integrity. This means that if *client_nbr* 2771 were deleted from *client*, the related rows in *removal* would also have to be deleted because the foreign key *client_nbr* in *removal* no longer has a matching primary key value of 2771 in *client* (Figure 5.27).

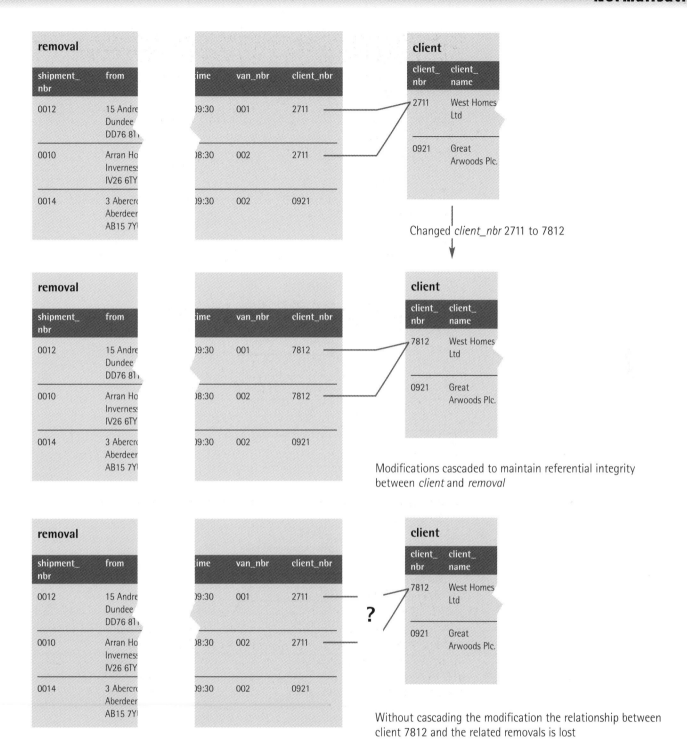

Figure 5.26 *Referential integrity – cascade modifications*

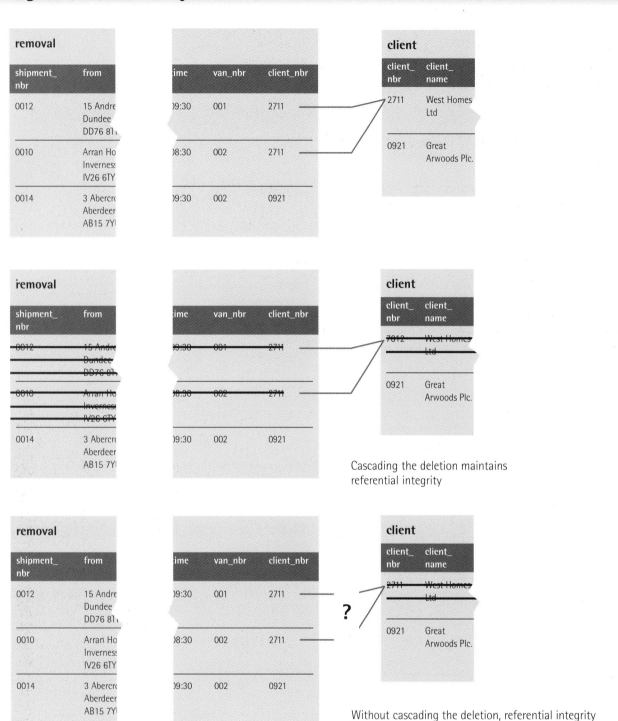

Cascading the deletion maintains referential integrity

Without cascading the deletion, referential integrity is broken because there is no matching primary key value for the foreign key *client_nbr* in *removal*

Figure 5.27 *Referential integrity – cascade delete*

Summary of normalisation

The process of normalisation can be quite difficult to grasp but the steps involved are relatively straightforward:

- **Step 1** – Create a UNF (select a primary key and indent the repeating group for this primary key).
- **Step 2** – Remove the repeating group to a new relation and include the primary key of the UNF as a foreign key.

- **Step 3** – Remove partial dependencies, columns which depend on part of a compound key and not the whole of the key, to a new relation.

- **Step 4** – Remove transitive dependencies, columns which depend on a non-key column within the relation, to a new relation.

Normalisation – does it always work out the same way?

It does not matter which of the potential primary key columns is chosen as the primary key for the unnormalised form. The final third normal form will always be the same provided the normalisation process is completed correctly.

For example, there were three possible correct unnormalised forms from which it is possible to begin the normalisation process, as shown in Figure 5.28.

To prove that the normalisation will always give the same result in third normal form we will now work through each of the other two unnormalised forms.

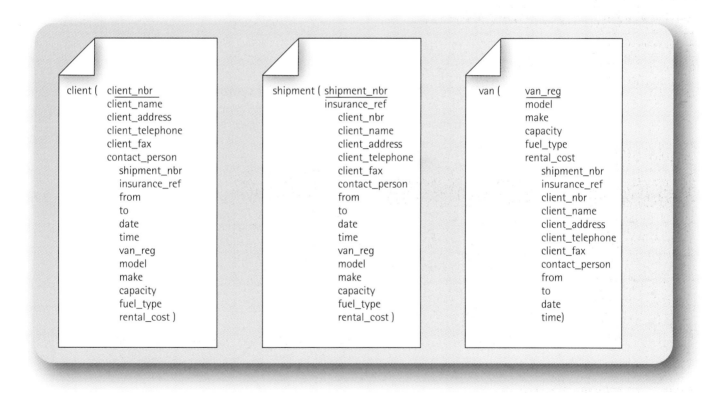

Figure 5.28 *Possible UNFs for Case Study 1*

Case Study 1 – Variation 1

1NF

The repeating group is removed to a new relation and the primary key of the UNF is carried across as a foreign key in the new relation to create the one-to-many relationship. The details of removals, vans and clients are moved to a new relation called removal.

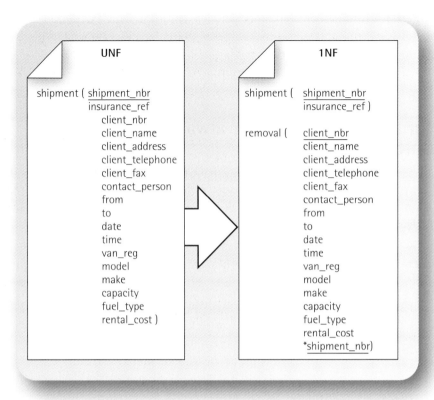

Figure 5.29 *Possible UNF to 1NF for Case Study 1*

2NF

The partial key dependencies are removed to new relations. The client columns only depend on part of the primary key, *client_nbr*. These can be removed to a new relation – *client*. (See Figure 5.30.)

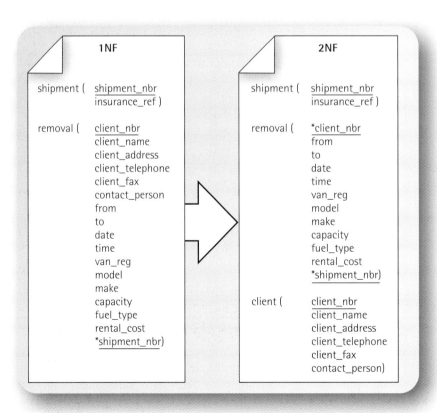

Figure 5.30 *Possible 1NF to 2NF for Case Study 1*

3NF

Remove transitive dependencies to new relations. The details for each van depend on *van_reg* rather than the primary key of *client_nbr* and *shipment_number*. The van details are removed to a new relation called *van* (Figure 5.31).

Case Study 1 – Variation 2

1NF

The repeating group is removed to a new relation and the primary key of the UNF is carried across as a foreign key in the new relation to create the one-to-many relationship. For one van there are repeating values for *removals*, *shipments* and *clients* (Figure 5.32).

2NF

The partial key dependencies are removed to new relations. There are two sets of partial key dependencies here, one for shipments and one for clients. *Insurance_ref* depends on *shipment_nbr*, and *client_name*, *client_address*, *client_telephone*, *client_fax*, *contact_person* all depend on *client_nbr* (Figure 5.33).

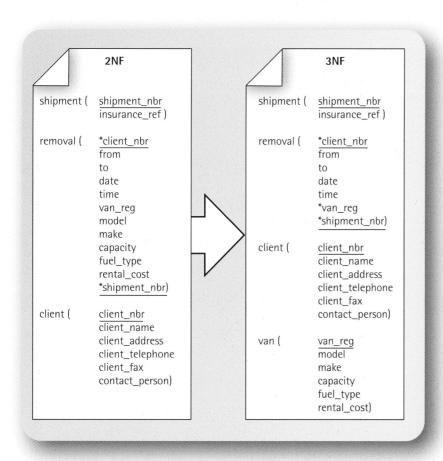

Figure 5.31 Possible 2NF to 3NF for Case Study 1

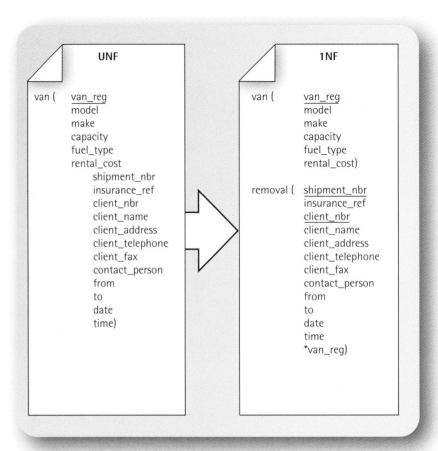

Figure 5.32 Possible UNF to 1NF for Case Study 1

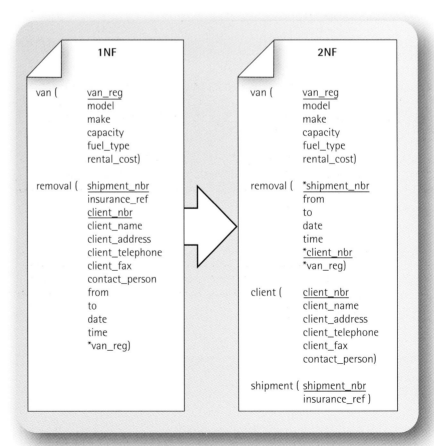

Figure 5.33 Possible 1NF to 2NF for Case Study 1

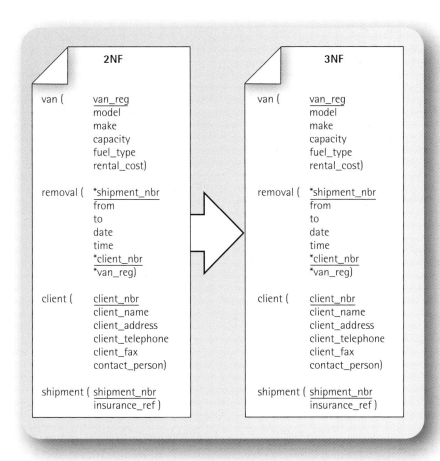

Figure 5.34 *Possible 2NF to 3NF for Case Study 1*

3NF

Remove transitive dependencies to new relations. There are no transitive dependencies in this second normal form so it is now automatically in third normal form. All the columns depend on the primary key and not on any other column (Figure 5.34).

As you can see from the working above, it does not matter which primary key is chosen provided all the normalisation steps are carried out correctly. The final 3NF will always be the same irrespective of which route is taken to reach it.

Case Study 2

Case Study 2 concerns a card index system used by the Pine Furniture Company to record details of customers, orders and products. The ERD for the system is shown in Figure 5.35.

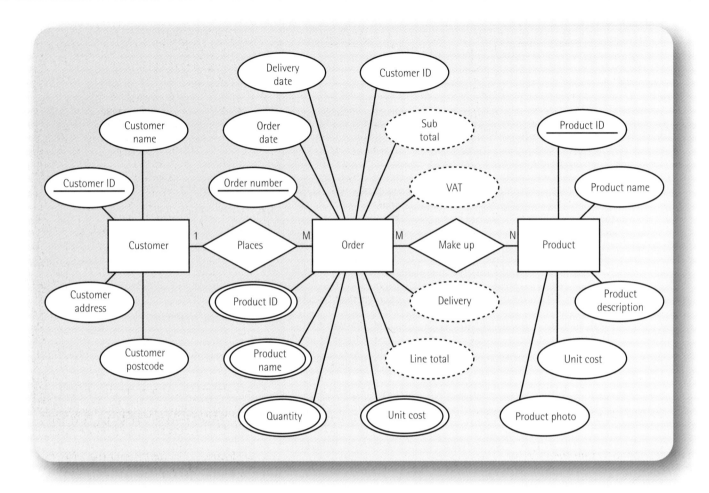

Figure 5.35 *Completed ERD for Case Study 2*

Unnormalised form

The first stage of normalisation is to create a UNF (unnormalised form). Again, start by listing all of the attributes of the entities. These will be the columns in the relations which are created as part of normalisation (Figure 5.36).

Next, remove any attributes which are derived or duplicated. Remember, good databases don't store data that can be calculated from other data items within the database and we only need to store each item of data once (Figure 5.37).

Sub_total, *vat*, *delivery* and *line_total* are all derived from other stored values in the database. *Customer_id*, *unit_cost*, *product_id* and *product_name* appear more than once so one instance of each is removed from the UNF.

Now we select a primary key from the possible keys available. The possible keys are *customer_id*, *order_number* and *product_id*. We shall select *customer_id* as the primary key. (Figure 5.38).

Finally, for the primary key of *customer_id* we show the repeating group by indenting the repeating data items. The UNF is also given a name to identify it as a relation and enclosed in curved brackets (Figure 5.39).

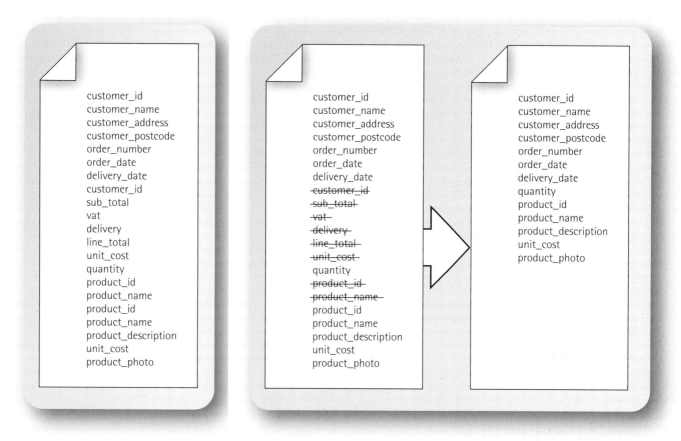

customer_id
customer_name
customer_address
customer_postcode
order_number
order_date
delivery_date
customer_id
sub_total
vat
delivery
line_total
unit_cost
quantity
product_id
product_name
product_id
product_name
product_description
unit_cost
product_photo

Figure 5.36 *Starting the UNF for Case Study 2*

customer_id
customer_name
customer_address
customer_postcode
order_number
order_date
delivery_date
~~customer_id~~
~~sub_total~~
~~vat~~
~~delivery~~
~~line_total~~
~~unit_cost~~
quantity
~~product_id~~
~~product_name~~
product_id
product_name
product_description
unit_cost
product_photo

customer_id
customer_name
customer_address
customer_postcode
order_number
order_date
delivery_date
quantity
product_id
product_name
product_description
unit_cost
product_photo

Figure 5.37 *Continuing the UNF for Case Study 2*

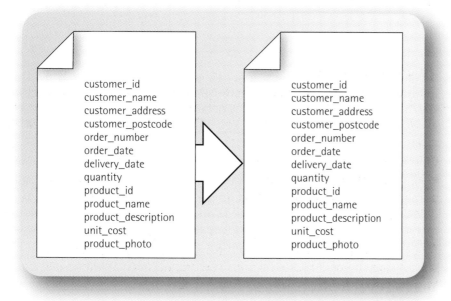

customer_id
customer_name
customer_address
customer_postcode
order_number
order_date
delivery_date
quantity
product_id
product_name
product_description
unit_cost
product_photo

customer_id
customer_name
customer_address
customer_postcode
order_number
order_date
delivery_date
quantity
product_id
product_name
product_description
unit_cost
product_photo

Figure 5.38 *Continuing the UNF for Case Study 2*

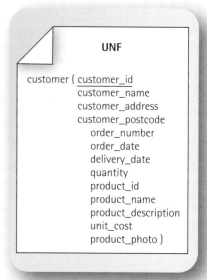

UNF

customer (<u>customer_id</u>
    customer_name
    customer_address
    customer_postcode
    order_number
    order_date
    delivery_date
    quantity
    product_id
    product_name
    product_description
    unit_cost
    product_photo)

Figure 5.39 *Continuing the UNF for Case Study 2*

First normal form

To create the first normal form the repeating group is removed to a new relation and the primary key of the UNF is copied across to create a foreign key (Figure 5.40).

The primary key of the new relation is now identified to complete the first normal form. Each order has a unique *order_number*, however there are multiple products on each order which means both *order_number* and *product_id* are required to uniquely identify each row in the relation (Figure 5.41).

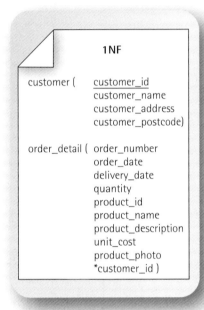

Figure 5.40 (left) Starting the 1NF for Case Study 2

Figure 5.41 (right) Complete 1NF for Case Study 2

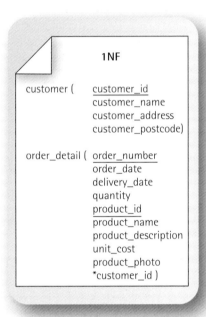

Second normal form

Second normal form states that all partial dependencies should be removed. These are dependencies on part of but not the entire primary key. In the 1NF above, the product details depend on the *product_id* and not on the whole of the primary key of *order_number* and *product_id*. To create the 2NF these details are removed to a new relation and *product_id* remains in *order_detail* as a foreign key (and also part of the primary key).

Also, the details of an order are dependent on *order_number* and not on the primary key of *order_number* and *product_id*. The columns specific to an order are removed to create a new relation called *order*. The only column that depends on the entire primary key is *quantity* which is the amount of a product to be supplied (Figure 5.42).

Third normal form

Third normal form states that all transitive dependencies must be removed. The second normal form does not contain any columns which depend on non-key columns in the relations. This means that the second normal form is also the correct third normal form. (See Figure 5.43.)

The ERD for Case Study 2 is now much easier to create because there are no derived or repeating attributes (Figure 5.44).

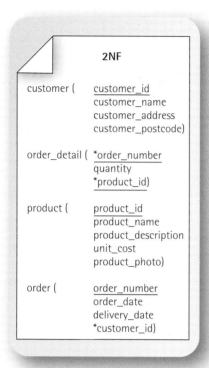

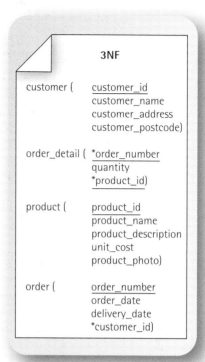

Figure 5.42 *Complete 2NF for Case Study 2*

Figure 5.43 *Complete 3NF for Case Study 2*

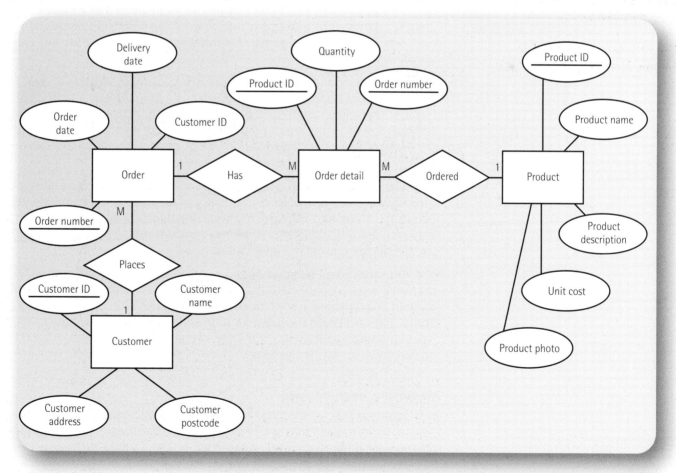

Figure 5.44 *ERD for Case Study 2 in 3NF*

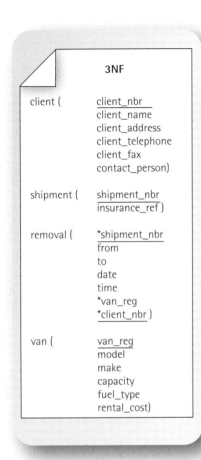

3NF

client (<u>client_nbr</u>
          client_name
          client_address
          client_telephone
          client_fax
          contact_person)

shipment (<u>shipment_nbr</u>
          <u>insurance_ref</u>)

removal (*<u>shipment_nbr</u>
          from
          to
          date
          time
          *van_reg
          *<u>client_nbr</u>)

van (<u>van_reg</u>
          model
          make
          capacity
          fuel_type
          rental_cost)

Figure 5.45 *Case Study 1 in 3NF*

Moving to implementation

Once the normalisation is complete the next stage is to prepare for the implementation of the system using relational database management software. To produce an implementation the following items are required:

- a final entity relationship diagram representing the third normal form
- a data dictionary based on the third normal form.

The systems analyst is often not part of the team that produces the final database system. The database programming team will work from the analyst's documents to produce the working system. The entity relationship diagram and the data dictionary are the core documents for specifying the relations and the relationships to be implemented.

Weak entity sets and weak relationships

The ERD symbols which we looked at earlier included symbols for a **weak entity set** and a **weak relationship**. These symbols can be introduced into the entity relationship diagram to provide additional information about the entity sets and relationships represented. A weak entity set contains a collection of **weak entities**.

Weak entity

A weak entity is an entity which uses the primary key of a related entity set as part of its primary key. Weak entities are often created when a repeating group is removed to produce a first normal form with a compound key. Any entity which has a single attribute primary key is a strong entity (Figure 5.45).

In Case Study 1, the entity *removal* is a weak entity because it uses the primary keys of both *shipment* and *client* as its primary key. A strong entity has a primary key which does not include any attribute of another entity whereas a weak entity contains at least one part of its primary key which is the primary key of another relation. Weak entities are shown in the ERD using a double rectangle rather than a single one.

The relationship between a weak entity and the entity which supplies part of its primary key is a weak relationship. In Case Study 1, the relationship between *removal* and *shipment* is a weak relationship, as is the relationship between *removal* and *client*. Weak relationships are shown in the ERD by using a double diamond (Figure 5.46).

The ERD above has been amended to show the weak entity *removal* and the weak relationships *allocated* and *part of*. Weak entities can be implemented in a database system but they cannot exist without a related strong entity. This is because the related strong entity provides part of the primary key of the weak entity, therefore if the strong entity does not exist then the related weak entity cannot exist.

Removing weak entities

It is common practice to remove weak entities by adding a surrogate key. That is, to introduce a new arbitrary identifier such as, for Case Study 1, *removal_nbr* in *removal*. If this was introduced as a single attribute primary key for *removal* then the entity changes into a strong entity because it no longer relies on any other entity for part of its key.

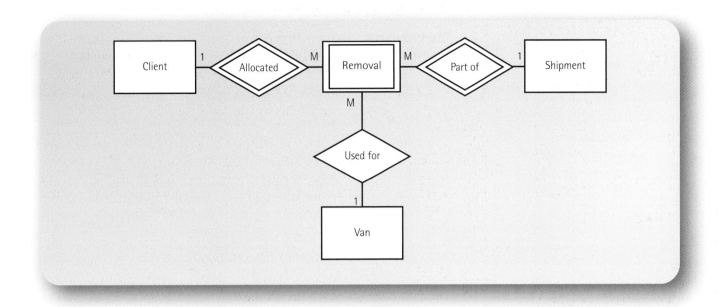

Figure 5.46 *ERD for Case Study 1 in 3NF*

Producing a system – the short method

Often the initial ERD and data dictionary will be omitted from the analysis stage. The minimum you will be required to produce as part of the analysis and design of a database system prior to implementation will be:

- a set of entities in third normal form (having shown the correct UNF, 1NF and 2NF)
- an entity relationship diagram based on this third normal form
- a data dictionary based on the third normal form.

Questions

1. Lovell and Watson Publishing currently makes use of a paper-based system to keep track of books and their customers. A card index is used to record details of the books. Each book has a unique identifier called an ISBN and each author has a unique Author ID. Each author can write one or more books. Each book has only one author.

A Customer Order Report is kept for each customer and is updated when a new order is received. A customer can order the same book on more than one occasion. Customers only place one order per day.

One example of a Book Card and two examples of a Customer Order Report are shown below.

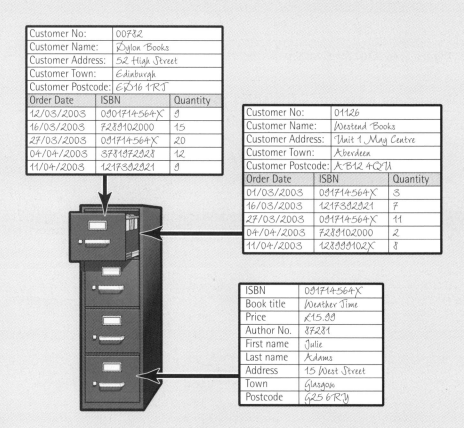

Customer No:	00782	
Customer Name:	Dylon Books	
Customer Address:	52 High Street	
Customer Town:	Edinburgh	
Customer Postcode:	ED16 1RJ	
Order Date	ISBN	Quantity
12/03/2003	0901714564X	9
16/03/2003	7289102000	15
27/03/2003	091714564X	20
04/04/2003	3781972928	12
11/04/2003	1217392921	9

Customer No:	01126	
Customer Name:	Westend Books	
Customer Address:	Unit 1 May Centre	
Customer Town:	Aberdeen	
Customer Postcode:	AB12 4QU	
Order Date	ISBN	Quantity
01/03/2003	091714564X	3
16/03/2003	1217392921	7
27/03/2003	091714564X	11
04/04/2003	7289102000	2
11/04/2003	128999102X	8

ISBN	091714564X
Book title	Weather Time
Price	£15.99
Author No.	87281
First name	Julie
Last name	Adams
Address	15 West Street
Town	Glasgow
Postcode	G25 6RY

a Produce an unnormalised form for this system.

b Convert this UNF into 3NF. Show all your working (i.e. 1NF and 2NF) as part of the process.

c Create an entity relationship diagram to illustrate the relationships that exist between the entities in third normal form.

2. ScotGas is a company that inspects gas central heating systems for its customers. The inspection manager is responsible for ensuring that inspections are carried out by the company's inspectors. The inspection manager has a record of each customer held in a card index and has an Inspection Visits Book which contains details of the inspectors and the inspections each has been assigned to.

One example of a Customer Index Card and two examples of the Inspection Visits details are shown below.

Inspector No:	20780
Inspector Name:	Charlie D Burton
Inspector Mobile No:	07
Inspection Area:	Ed
Inspector Qualification:	Ga

Inspection Date	Inspection
17/05/2004	09.30
17/05/2004	10.30
17/05/2004	12.30
17/05/2004	15.00
18/05/2004	09.00

Inspector No:	00782
Inspector Name:	Kyle Molt
Inspector Mobile No:	07181 989881
Inspection Area:	Edinburgh
Inspector Qualification:	Gas Fitter II, Electrical I

Inspection Date	Inspection Time	Customer No	Inspection Type
16/05/2004	11.30	1782	Domestic
16/05/2004	12.30	4144	Domestic
16/05/2004	14.30	5162	Commercial
17/05/2004	15.30	2291	Domestic
18/05/2004	09.00	2291	Domestic

Customer No	1782
Customer Name	Margo Wash
Customer Address	Bedrock of Ginn IV, Ervin Kip EK89 9UI
Customer Tel No	01829 98292

Each inspector has a unique reference number as does each customer. Customers are only allowed one inspection per day.

a Produce an unnormalised form for this system.

b Convert this UNF into 3NF. Show all your working (i.e. 1NF and 2NF) as part of the process.

c Create an entity relationship diagram to illustrate the relationships that exist between the entities in third normal form.

d Consider each of the entities you have created. Are there any alternatives to the *Inspector No* and *Customer No* as primary keys? Identify these alternatives and discuss their suitability.

e Create a data dictionary for the entity with a primary key of *Customer No*.

Queries

A relational database system is of little use unless there are methods for managing the data structures (the metadata from the data dictionary and the relationships from the ERD), manipulating the data in the tables and controlling how the data is viewed and who has access to the database.

Queries are one method of completing all or some of these tasks depending on the RDBMS being used. Some relational database management systems have query systems which allow complete control of every part of the database management. Others, such as Microsoft's Access, have query systems which are focused on manipulating the database (i.e. creating, modifying, deleting and reading data) and have other, separate, tools for database definition and control.

There are a wide number of different methods to query relational databases. This chapter is concerned with the theory of extracting data from a database and the various types of query which it is possible to create.

Structured query language

Structured query language (SQL) is a standardised query language for requesting information from a database. It consists of a number of text commands that can be used to create query statements which instruct a relational database to carry out a range of operations. The operations can be related to the structure of the database, the data held within the tables and the access and control of the database users.

SQL was originally created by IBM, but many software companies developed versions of it. It was adopted as a standard by the American National Standards Institute (ANSI) in 1986 and by the International Standards Organisation (ISO) in 1987.

In their SQL standard, the ANSI declared that the official pronunciation for SQL is 'es queue el'. However, many database professionals have adopted the pronunciation 'sequel'. This reflects the language's original name, Sequel, before trademark conflicts caused IBM to change the name to SQL.

SQL is a 'common language' which is well known to database users. SQL consists of a number of commands and a defined syntax. The syntax is the collection of rules used to govern how SQL statements are constructed.

E F Codd, who created the relational database concept, stated that:

'a relational database may support several languages and various modes of terminal use (for example, fill-in-the-blanks mode). However, there must be at least one language whose statements are expressible, per some well-defined syntax, as character strings and that is comprehensive in supporting *all* of the following items:

- data definition

- view definition

- data manipulation

- integrity constraints

- transaction boundaries (begin, commit and rollback)'

Codd is saying that all relational database systems must have some method of:

- defining the structure of tables
- creating different views of the data by extracting it from the database in particular ways
- manipulating that data in the tables
- enforcing the relational database rules (such as entity integrity and referential integrity)
- controlling the processing of the database using text-based commands.

Keep in mind that Codd was writing this when the Apple Macintosh, which defined the graphical user interface, was barely one year old. Most people at that time considered computers with GUIs to be little more than toys. There are many relational database systems which do not support SQL but use their own graphical query language. Technically, these would not conform to Codd's statement because they do not have a command-line, text-based syntax. These RDBMSs still contain all the functionality defined by Codd and therefore there is no specific disadvantage to using any of these to manage your relational database.

There are three parts to SQL:

- a data definition language (DDL)
- a data manipulation language (DML)
- a data control language (DCL).

Data definition language

The DDL is used to define and modify the database structure. It consists of commands to create, modify and delete tables and fields. For Case Study 1, there are a total of four tables to create for the final system in 3NF. The structure for each of the tables in the database can be set up using the CREATE TABLE statement. The SQL statement to create the *client* table is shown in Figure 6.1.

INT defines the *client_nbr* as an integer value and CHAR defines the remaining fields as character strings of the length given in brackets. The primary key is defined as *client_nbr*. This information is written as system tables which the RDBMS creates to record the structure of the database it is maintaining (Figure 6.2).

To remove a table from the database the DROP TABLE statement is used. This removes all data present in the table and removes the table definition from the system tables (Figure 6.3).

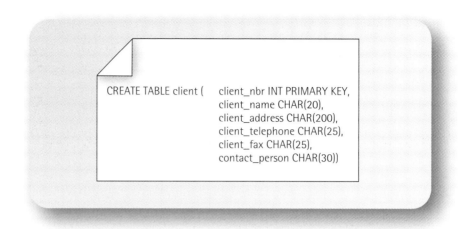

Figure 6.1 Sample CREATE TABLE SQL statement

Field	Type	Attributes	Null	Default
client_nbr	int(11)		No	0
client_name	char(20)		Yes	NULL
client_address	char(200)		Yes	NULL
client_telephone	char(25)		Yes	NULL
client_fax	char(25)		Yes	NULL
contact_person	char(30)		Yes	NULL

Figure 6.2 Sample table structure in an SQL database

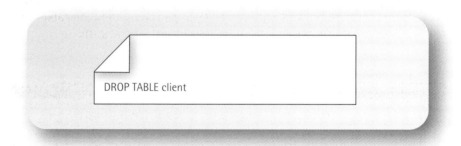

Figure 6.3 Sample DROP TABLE SQL statement

Certain modifications to the tables are also allowed. It is possible to change the properties of the fields and add fields to and remove fields from tables.

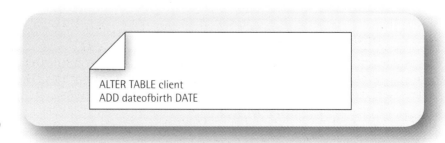

Figure 6.4 Sample ALTER TABLE – ADD SQL statement

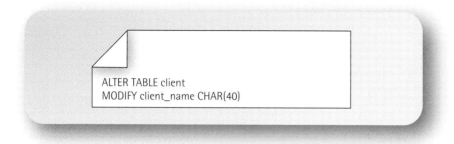

Figure 6.5 Sample ALTER TABLE – MODIFY SQL statement

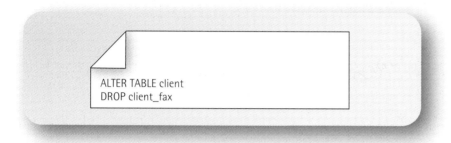

Figure 6.6 Sample ALTER TABLE – DROP SQL statement

In the examples in Figures 6.4 to 6.6, the ADD statement adds *dateofbirth* as a column with the data type DATE to the table *client*, the MODIFY statement changes the size of the *client_name* field from 20 to 40 characters and the DROP statement removes the *client_fax* field from the table. The resulting table structure in an SQL database might look like this:

Field	Type	Attributes	Null	Default
client_nbr	int(11)		No	0
client_name	char(40)		Yes	NULL
client_address	char(200)		Yes	NULL
client_telephone	char(25)		Yes	NULL
contact_person	char(30)		Yes	NULL
dateofbirth	date		Yes	NULL

Figure 6.7 Sample modified table structure in an SQL database

Data manipulation language

The data manipulation language part of SQL allows data to be entered, modified, deleted and read from the database. This is the key part of SQL for most users.

Data is entered using the INSERT statement (Figure 6.8).

If the list of values is the same sequence as the sequence of fields when defined, then the field names can be omitted (Figure 6.9).

One record has been inserted into the SQL database, as shown in Figure 6.10.

INSERT INTO client (client_nbr, client_name, client_address, client_telephone, contact_person, dateofbirth)
VALUES (0921, "Great Arwoods Plc.", "18 New Parlie St, Edinburgh, EH87 9QQ", "0327 989127", "Vicky Kenn", 1986-02-13);

Figure 6.8 Sample INSERT SQL statement

INSERT INTO client
VALUES (0921, "Great Arwoods Plc.", "18 New Parlie St, Edinburgh, EH87 9QQ", "0327 989127", "Vicky Kenn", 1986-02-13);

Figure 6.9 Sample INSERT SQL statement without field names

client_nbr	client_name	client_address	client_telephone	contact_person	date of birth
921	Great Arwoods Plc.	18 New Parlie St, Edinburgh, EH87 9QQ	0327 989127	Vicky Kenn	1986-02-13

Figure 6.10 Sample record in an SQL database

The ongoing data in the database can be maintained using the UPDATE and DELETE SQL statements. These statements modify field values or delete records from the table or tables.

UPDATE client
SET contact_person = "Jane McPherson"
WHERE client_name = "Great Arwoods Plc."

Figure 6.11 Sample UPDATE SQL statement

This update would be shown in the SQL database as:

client_nbr	client_name	client_address	client_telephone	client_fax	contact_person
921	Great Arwoods Plc.	18 New Parlie St, Edinburgh, EH87 9QQ	0327 989127	0327 981111	Jane McPherson

Figure 6.12 Sample updated record in an SQL database

To remove this record from the SQL database the DELETE statement would be used. The primary key value for this record is 0921 because *client_nbr* is the primary key. The DELETE statement is used to remove the record with this primary key value.

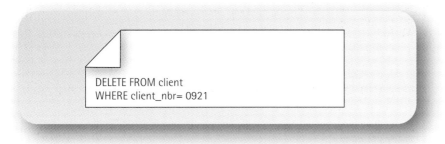

```
DELETE FROM client
WHERE client_nbr= 0921
```

Figure 6.13 Sample DELETE SQL statement

Although SQL does allow data definition and data control (see later) it was principally designed for extracting data from a database. This is accomplished by the SELECT statement.

SELECT query

The SELECT query is the most common and easiest to understand. Selecting data from a database is by far the most common use of SQL. The SELECT query allows data to be selected from tables in the database according to specific criteria. At its very simplest a query extracts data from one table in the database.

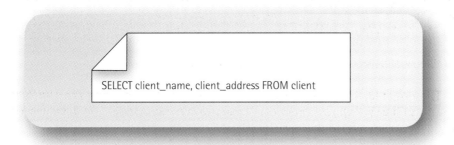

```
SELECT client_name, client_address FROM client
```

Figure 6.14 Sample SELECT SQL statement

This selects all of the values for the fields *client_name* and *client_address* from the table *client*. The values that are the result of a query are called an **answer table** because the output is the answer to the query.

client_name	client_address
Great Arwoods Plc.	18 New Parlie St, Edinburgh, EH87 9QQ
West Homes Ltd	14 Argos St, Glasgow, G23 9UJ
Smith National Ltd.	Unit 16, Cults Industrial Estate, Aberdeen, AB15 9SA
Anderson PLC	17 Manor House, Dollar, FK87 8YJ

Figure 6.15 SELECT query answer table from an SQL database

WHERE clause

A SELECT query can make use of criteria to narrow down the answer table results. We can look for a single value or a range of values and so on, by adding a WHERE clause to the SELECT statement.

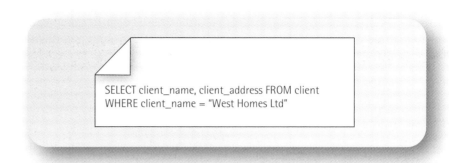

Figure 6.16 *SELECT query with simple WHERE clause*

This will produce an answer table where the value for *client_name* is equal to 'West Homes Ltd'.

Figure 6.17 *SELECT query with simple WHERE clause answer table*

client_name	client_address
West Homes Ltd	14 Argos St, Glasgow, G23 9UJ

There is no limit to the number of conditions which can be given in the WHERE clause. These conditions are used to select specific records based on the field values and to enforce the relationships between tables.

Joining tables

Selecting data from individual tables does have its uses but the true power of relational databases is only apparent when data is selected from multiple tables at the same time. This is very easy to do using SQL because all that is required are the table names and the details of the primary and foreign keys. Consider the following sample tables:

client

client_nbr	client_name	client_address	client_telephone	client_fax	contact_person
921	Great Arwoods Plc.	18 New Parlie St, Edinburgh, EH87 9QQ	0327 989127	0327 981111	Jane McPherson
2711	West Homes Ltd	14 Argos St, Glasgow, G23 9UJ	0312 123198	0312 123199	John Michael Osbourne
3761	Smith National Ltd.	Unit 16, Cults Industrial Estate, Aberdeen, AB15 9SA	0617 812781	0617 812782	Peter Southward
6151	Anderson PLC	17 Manor House, Dollar, FK87 8YJ	08771 827128	08771 827611	Jim Mulligan

van

van_reg	model	make	capacity	fuel_type	rental_cost
D842 YSA	Actros	Mercedes	36.10	Diesel	150.00
KY51 AFZ	Convoy	LDV	16.85	Diesel	100.00
P385 ASA	Transit	Ford	11.89	Petrol	90.00
YT71 7YE	LF	DAF	28.45	Diesel	125.00

shipment

shipment_nbr	insurance_ref
0010	RT8721
0011	AD6701
0012	NT9238
0014	QW1211

Cont'd ...

removal

removal_nbr	shipment_nbr	removal_from	removal_to	removal_date	removal_time	van_reg	client_nbr
1	0012	3 Abercrombie St Aberdeen AB15 7YU	18 Drummond Pl Aberdeen AB11 8TR	2004-02-23	09:30:00	KY51 AFZ	921
2	0010	5 West Beach Finchley NW9 8YU	12 Dorset St Leeds L87 8HU	2004-02-24	08:30:00	P385 ASA	921
3	0014	The Lodge Heathsville West Moore WM8 3HJ	15 Smith Heights Bothwill G56 7ER	2004-02-24	11:30:00	D842 YSA	921
4	0012	15 Andrews Cres Dundee DD76 8TT	28 Westfield Pl Dundee DD75 7YH	2004-02-23	09:30:00	P385 ASA	2711
5	0010	Arran House, Inverness IV26 6TY	15 Smith Heights Bothwill G56 7ER	2004-02-24	08:30:00	KY51 AFZ	2711
6	0011	267 Gill St Stirling FK78 1MN	10a Lawson Rd Stirling FK78 2YT	2004-02-24	09:30:00	YT71 7YE	2711

Figure 6.18 Sample relational database tables – Case Study 1

The three tables *shipment*, *van* and *client* are all related through the *removal* table because *removal* contains three foreign keys: *shipment_number*, *van_reg* and *client_nbr*. These foreign keys relate back to the primary keys of the tables.

A simple query to select some of the removal and client details for the removal with a *removal_nbr* equal to 1 is shown in Figure 6.19:

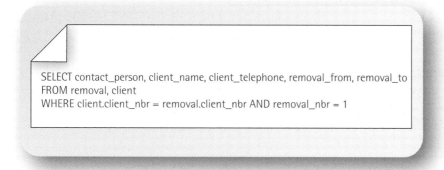

```
SELECT contact_person, client_name, client_telephone, removal_from, removal_to
FROM removal, client
WHERE client.client_nbr = removal.client_nbr AND removal_nbr = 1
```

Figure 6.19 SELECT query with simple WHERE condition across two tables

The first line of this query indicates the fields to be selected from the tables, and the second line specifies the source of the fields, i.e. the *removal* and the *client* tables. The third line states how the tables are linked together (client.client_nbr = removal.client_nbr) and which *removal_nbr* is required (removal_nbr = 1).

Figure 6.20 shows how the query selects the required data from the tables. The shaded columns indicate fields which are not required by the query as part of the answer table, the columns outlined in black are the columns

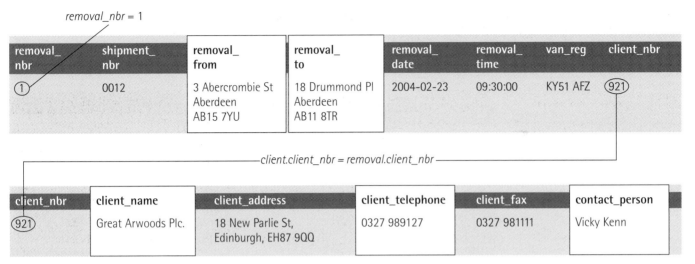

removal_nbr = 1

removal_nbr	shipment_nbr	removal_from	removal_to	removal_date	removal_time	van_reg	client_nbr
1	0012	3 Abercrombie St Aberdeen AB15 7YU	18 Drummond Pl Aberdeen AB11 8TR	2004-02-23	09:30:00	KY51 AFZ	921

client.client_nbr = removal.client_nbr

client_nbr	client_name	client_address	client_telephone	client_fax	contact_person
921	Great Arwoods Plc.	18 New Parlie St, Edinburgh, EH87 9QQ	0327 989127	0327 981111	Vicky Kenn

Figure 6.20 *Diagram of SELECT query with simple WHERE condition across two tables*

selected by the query and the circled values are the values specified by the WHERE clause of the query. The query would, therefore, produce the answer table shown in Figure 6.21.

contact_person	client_name	client_telephone	removal_from	removal_to
Vicky Kenn	Great Arwoods Plc.	0327 989127	3 Abercrombie St Aberdeen AB15 7YU	18 Drummond Pl Aberdeen, AB11 8TR

Figure 6.21 *Answer table for SELECT query with simple WHERE condition joining two tables*

In the query, the WHERE clause contains the *client_nbr* field from both tables. To remove any possible ambiguity each *client_nbr* is identified with the table to which it belongs: *client.client_nbr* and *removal.client_nbr*.

The condition WHERE client.client_nbr = removal.client_nbr joins the two tables together using the equal values for *client_nbr*. This uses the primary and foreign key values of *client_nbr*.

Multiple joins

Using the same syntax it is possible to create more complex queries which extract data from a number of related tables (Figure 6.22).

Figure 6.22 *SELECT query with WHERE condition joining multiple tables*

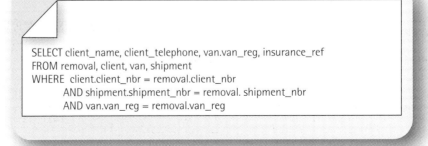

```
SELECT client_name, client_telephone, van.van_reg, insurance_ref
FROM removal, client, van, shipment
WHERE  client.client_nbr = removal.client_nbr
       AND shipment.shipment_nbr = removal. shipment_nbr
       AND van.van_reg = removal.van_reg
```

Each of the matching records from the database is extracted according to the query conditions. Figure 6.23 illustrates how the data for the first record in the answer table is selected.

client_nbr	client_name	client_address	client_telephone	client_fax	contact_person
921	Great Arwoods Plc.	18 New Parlie St, Edinburgh, EH87 9QQ	0327 989127	0327 981111	Vicky Kenn
2711	West Homes Ltd	14 Argos St, Glasgow, G23 9UJ	0312 123198	0312 123199	John Michael Osbourne
3761	Smith National Ltd.	Unit 16, Cults Industrial Estate, Aberdeen, AB15 9SA	0617 812781	0617 812782	Peter Southward
6151	Anderson PLC	17 Manor House, Dollar, FK87 8YJ	08771 827128	08771 827611	Jim Mulligan

client.client_nbr = removal.client_nbr

removal_nbr	shipment_nbr	removal_from	removal_to	removal_date	removal_time	van_reg	client_nbr
1	0012	3 Abercrombie St Aberdeen AB15 7YU	18 Drummond Pl Aberdeen AB11 8TR	2004-02-23	09:30:00	KY51 AFZ	921
2	0010	5 West Beach Finchley NW9 8YU	12 Dorset St Leeds L87 8HU	2004-02-24	08:30:00	P385 ASA	921
3	0014	The Lodge Heathsville West Moore WM8 3HJ	15 Smith Heights Bothwill G56 7ER	2004-02-24	11:30:00	D842 YSA	921
4	0012	15 Andrews Cres Dundee DD76 8TT	28 Westfield Pl Dundee DD75 7YH	2004-02-23	09:30:00	P385 ASA	2711
5	0010	Arran House, Inverness IV26 6TY	15 Smith Heights Bothwill G56 7ER	2004-02-24	08:30:00	KY51 AFZ	2711
6	0011	267 Gill St Stirling FK78 1MN	10a Lawson Rd Stirling FK78 2YT	2004-02-24	09:30:00	YT71 7YE	2711

shipment.shipment_nbr = removal.shipment_nbr

van.van_reg = removal.van_reg

shipment_nbr	insurance_ref
0010	RT8721
0011	AD6701
0012	NT9238
0014	QW1211

van_reg	model	make	capacity	fuel_type	rental_cost
D842 YSA	Actros	Mercedes	36.10	Diesel	150.00
KY51 AFZ	Convoy	LDV	16.85	Diesel	100.00
P385 ASA	Transit	Ford	11.89	Petrol	90.00
YT71 7YE	LF	DAF	28.45	Diesel	125.00

Figure 6.23 Linking the foreign and primary keys in a query

The answer table that this query produces contains six rows. The way that the SELECT query locates the data for the first row of this answer table is shown in Figure 6.23.

client_name	client_telephone	van_reg	insurance_ref
Great Arwoods Plc.	0327 989127	KY51 AFZ	NT9238
Great Arwoods Plc.	0327 989127	P385 ASA	RT8721
Great Arwoods Plc.	0327 989127	D842 YSA	QW1211
West Homes Ltd	0312 123198	P385 ASA	NT9238
West Homes Ltd	0312 123198	KY51 AFZ	RT8721
West Homes Ltd	0312 123198	YT71 7YE	AD6701

Figure 6.24 Answer table for multiple table query

Even though no fields are shown in the answer table from the *removal* table, the query is still based on links which use the foreign keys within the *removal* table, and their related primary keys, to join the tables together.

Wildcards in SELECT

If you require all of the fields from a table to be included in your answer table then the query can make use of the * (asterisk) wildcard.

Figure 6.25 SELECT query using wildcard

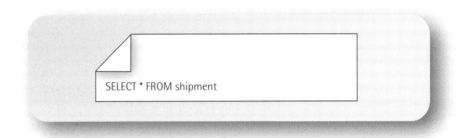

```
SELECT * FROM shipment
```

shipment_nbr	insurance_ref
0010	RT8721
0011	AD6701
0012	NT9238
0014	QW1211

Figure 6.26 Answer table generated using wildcard

This query would produce the answer table shown in Figure 6.26, with all the fields of the table *shipment*.

The * wildcard can be used to select data from multiple tables, however the relationship between the tables should always be specified otherwise the results will be incorrect. If no relationship is specified in the WHERE condition of the query then the answer table will contain records for every possible combination of rows from the two tables – that's normally a lot of records!

Figure 6.27 SELECT query using wildcard

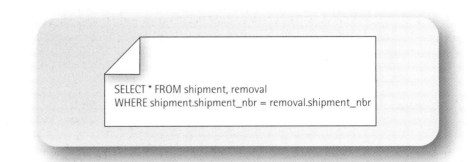

```
SELECT * FROM shipment, removal
WHERE shipment.shipment_nbr = removal.shipment_nbr
```

shipment_nbr	insurance_ref	removal_nbr	shipment_nbr	removal_from	removal_to	removal_date	removal_time	van_reg	client_nbr
0010	RT8721	2	0010	5 West Beach Finchley NW9 8YU	12 Dorset St Leeds L87 8HU	2004-02-24	08:30:00	P385 ASA	921
0010	RT8721	5	0010	Arran House Inverness IV26 6TY	15 Smith Heights Bothwill G56 7ER	2004-02-24	08:30:00	KY51 AFZ	2711
0011	AD6701	6	0011	267 Gill St Stirling FK78 1MN	10a Lawson Rd Stirling FK78 2YT	2004-02-24	09:30:00	YT71 7YE	2711
0012	NT9238	1	0012	3 Abercrombie St Aberdeen AB15 7YU	18 Drummond Pl Aberdeen AB11 8TR	2004-02-23	09:30:00	KY51 AFZ	921
0012	NT9238	4	0012	15 Andrews Cres Dundee DD76 8TT	28 Westfield Pl Dundee DD75 7YH	2004-02-23	09:30:00	P385 ASA	2711
0014	QW1211	3	0014	The Lodge Heathsville West Moore WM8 3HJ	15 Smith Heights Bothwill G56 7ER	2004-02-24	11:30:00	D842 YSA	921

The answer table in Figure 6.28 displays all the fields from both the *shipment* and *removal* tables in the database. There are two *shipment_nbr* columns because *shipment_nbr* is a field in both tables.

Figure 6.28 SELECT query using wildcard across two joined tables

Sorting using a query

The ORDER BY clause can be added to the SELECT statement to sort the answer table on one or more fields. For example, to sort the *van* table into descending order of *rental_cost* the SQL statement would be:

```
SELECT * FROM van ORDER BY rental_cost DESC
```

Figure 6.29 Sorting using ORDER BY

This will produce the answer table shown in Figure 6.30.

van_reg	model	make	capacity	fuel_type	rental_cost
D842 YSA	Actros	Mercedes	36.10	Diesel	150.00
YT71 7YE	LF	DAF	28.45	Diesel	125.00
KY51 AFZ	Convoy	LDV	16.85	Diesel	100.00
P385 ASA	Transit	Ford	11.89	Petrol	90.00

Figure 6.30 Sorted answer table

It is possible to use the ORDER BY clause to sort the answer table by multiple fields. An example of this would be to sort the *removal* table into ascending order of *shipment_nbr* and then, when the *shipment_nbr* values are equal, to sort the table by descending *client_nbr*.

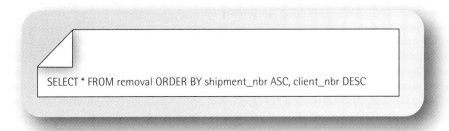

SELECT * FROM removal ORDER BY shipment_nbr ASC, client_nbr DESC

Figure 6.31 Sorting using ORDER BY

removal_ nbr	shipment_ nbr	removal_ from	removal_ to	removal_ date	removal_ time	van_reg	client_nbr
5	0010	Arran House Inverness V26 6TY	15 Smith Heights Bothwill G56 7ER	2004-02-24	08:30:00	KY51 AFZ	2711
2	0010	5 West Beach Finchley NW9 8YU	12 Dorset St Leeds L87 8HU	2004-02-24	08:30:00	P385 ASA	921
6	0011	267 Gill St Stirling FK78 1MN	10a Lawson Rd Stirling FK78 2YT	2004-02-24	09:30:00	YT71 7YE	2711
4	0012	15 Andrews Cres Dundee DD76 8TT	28 Westfield Pl Dundee DD75 7YH	2004-02-23	09:30:00	P385 ASA	2711
1	0012	3 Abercrombie St Aberdeen AB15 7YU	18 Drummond Pl Aberdeen AB11 8TR	2004-02-23	09:30:00	KY51 AFZ	921
3	0014	The Lodge Heathsville West Moore WM8 3HJ	15 Smith Heights Bothwill G56 7ER	2004-02-24	11:30:00	D842 YSA	921

Figure 6.32 Answer table sorted using ORDER BY

Aggregating values using a query

It is possible to group the results of a query to produce summary information. This is called **aggregation**. A simple example of this would be if we wanted to display only the clients who have records in the *removal* table, i.e. those for whom you had arranged removals.

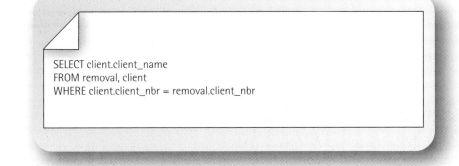

SELECT client.client_name
FROM removal, client
WHERE client.client_nbr = removal.client_nbr

Figure 6.33 Sorting using ORDER BY

This query will produce an answer table which displays all of the values for *client_name*, one for each record in *removal*.

If there were many thousands of removals this would be a very difficult answer table to understand. It would be better to show only one occurrence of each *client_name*. This would be an aggregation of the data displayed in the table in Figure 6.34.

client_name
Great Arwoods Plc.
Great Arwoods Plc.
Great Arwoods Plc.
West Homes Ltd
West Homes Ltd
West Homes Ltd

Figure 6.34 Sorting using ORDER BY

```
SELECT client.client_name
FROM removal, client
WHERE client.client_nbr = removal.client_nbr
GROUP BY client.client_nbr
```

Figure 6.35 Aggregating using GROUP BY

By adding the GROUP BY clause, only one occurrence of each *client_name* is shown for each unique *client_nbr* (Figure 6.36).

When an aggregated value is required, such as a total, average, maximum, minimum, etc., the GROUP BY clause is used to group the results of the query together so that the aggregated value can be calculated.

client_name
Great Arwoods Plc.
West Homes Ltd

Figure 6.36 Answer table produced using GROUP BY in a query

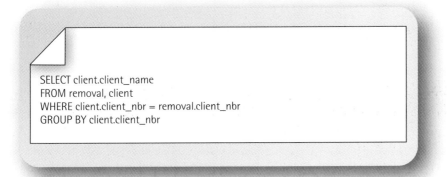

```
SELECT client.client_name, AVG(van.rental_cost)
FROM removal, client, van
WHERE client.client_nbr = removal.client_nbr  AND removal.van_reg = van.van_reg
GROUP BY client.client_nbr
```

Figure 6.37 Aggregating using GROUP BY

This query shows the average of *rental_cost* for all the removals for each client. AVG(van.rental_cost) calculates the average rental cost for the group of records based on the GROUP BY clause. The WHERE clause gives the relationships which are used to link the tables specified in the FROM clause, i.e. *removal*, *client* and *van*. This produces the answer table shown in Figure 6.38.

client_name	AVG(van.rental_cost)
Great Arwoods Plc.	113.333333
West Homes Ltd	105.000000

Figure 6.38 Aggregating using GROUP BY

Using an alias

The AVG(van.rental_cost) is not very user friendly. The name for this column can be changed using the AS keyword. This allows the query to give a different name, an **alias**, to the column in the answer table.

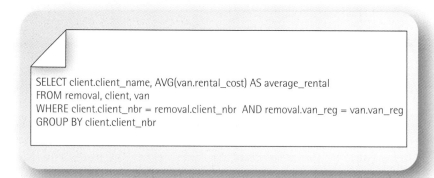

```
SELECT client.client_name, AVG(van.rental_cost) AS average_rental
FROM removal, client, van
WHERE client.client_nbr = removal.client_nbr  AND removal.van_reg = van.van_reg
GROUP BY client.client_nbr
```

Figure 6.39 Using AS to give an alias to a column

client_name	average_rental
Great Arwoods Plc.	113.333333
West Homes Ltd	105.000000

Figure 6.40 Answer with alias column

Performing calculations

Queries are used to perform calculations using the data held in the database tables. Both numerical and non-numerical fields can be used as part of a calculation. If the management of Reed and Co., which runs the removals system, wants to find out how much clients would pay for removals if a 20 per cent discount were given, the query shown in Figure 6.41 would be used.

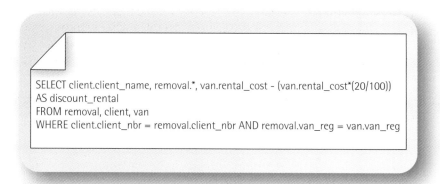

```
SELECT client.client_name, removal.*, van.rental_cost - (van.rental_cost*(20/100))
AS discount_rental
FROM removal, client, van
WHERE client.client_nbr = removal.client_nbr AND removal.van_reg = van.van_reg
```

Figure 6.41 Calculation in a query

This query calculates 20 per cent of *van.rental_cost* and then deducts this from the *van.rental_cost*. The values produced are displayed in a column with the alias *discount_rental*. All the details from removal are shown in the answer table because of the use of the wildcard – *removal** (Figure 6.42)

Queries can be constructed to perform almost any calculation required. SQL provides all the standard computing arithmetical operators: plus (+), minus (–), multiply (*), divide (/) as well as a large range of mathematical functions such as maximum (MAX), minimum (MIN), average (AVG), total (SUM) and count (COUNT).

client_ name	removal_ nbr	shipment_ nbr	removal_ from	removal_ to	removal_ date	removal_ time	van_reg	client_ nbr	discount_ rental
Great Arwoods Plc.	1	0012	3 Abercrombie St Aberdeen AB15 7YU	18 Drummond Pl Aberdeen AB11 8TR	2004-02-23	09:30:00	KY51 AFZ	921	80.00
Great Arwoods Plc.	2	0010	5 West Beach Finchley NW9 8YU	12 Dorset St Leeds L87 8HU	2004-02-24	08:30:00	P385 ASA	921	72.00
Great Arwoods Plc.	3	0014	The Lodge Heathsville West Moore WM8 3HJ	15 Smith Heights Bothwill G56 7ER	2004-02-24	11:30:00	D842 YSA	921	120.00
West Homes Ltd	4	0012	15 Andrews Cres Dundee DD76 8TT	28 Westfield Pl Dundee DD75 7YH	2004-02-23	09:30:00	P385 ASA	2711	72.00
West Homes Ltd	5	0010	Arran House Inverness IV26 6TY	15 Smith Heights Bothwill G56 7ER	2004-02-24	08:30:00	KY51 AFZ	2711	80.00
West Homes Ltd	6	0011	267 Gill St Stirling FK78 1MN	10a Lawson Rd Stirling FK78 2YT	2004-02-24	09:30:00	YT71 7YE	2711	100.00

Figure 6.42 Answer table with calculation

Data control language

The third group of SQL keywords is the data control language. DCL allows alternate views of the data in the tables to be created. These views are stored ways of viewing the data in the tables which can be accessed by users of the system as if the views were actual tables. The definition of the views is stored by the RDBMS and this creates a 'virtual' table. When a user requests a view (using a SELECT query) the definition is used to extract the required data from database tables.

A view of a database system could be created using the SQL statement in Figure 6.43:

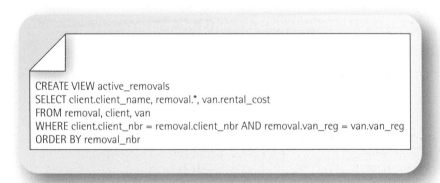

```
CREATE VIEW active_removals
SELECT client.client_name, removal.*, van.rental_cost
FROM removal, client, van
WHERE client.client_nbr = removal.client_nbr AND removal.van_reg = van.van_reg
ORDER BY removal_nbr
```

Figure 6.43 Creating a view using DCL

Each view is held as a table definition by the RDBMS so that users can access them. To the user the request to display the view is just like that for a table (Figure 6.44).

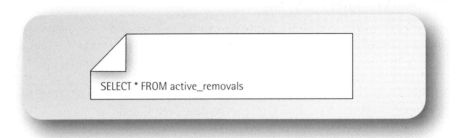

Figure 6.44 *Selecting a view*

DCL also handles the authorisation aspects of data and permits the user to control who has access to see or manipulate data within the database. It uses two main keywords to do this:

- GRANT – authorises a user to perform an operation
- REVOKE – removes or restricts the capability of a user to perform an operation.

The example in Figure 6.45 gives a user, cburton, permission to insert data and update data for the view, called *active_removals*, created above. The second example (Figure 6.46) removes the permission to select data or insert data for this view.

Figure 6.45 *Granting permissions using DCL*

Figure 6.46 *Revoking permissions using DCL*

Graphical query tools

A graphical tool allows the user to construct queries without requiring a working knowledge of SQL. There are many of these graphical tools available; some are stand-alone products which interface with existing SQL databases. Others, such as the query languages for Microsoft Access and FileMaker Pro, are embedded within a complete relational database management system.

Queries in Microsoft Access

Microsoft Access is the database part of Microsoft's very successful office suite of applications. Microsoft Access does have a version of SQL built into the database engine which it uses, and it is possible to use this to completely control the database using the DDL, DML and DCL components. However, this is rarely done because Access includes graphical and user-friendly tools to replace SQL. These graphical tools include a table designer, form editor, report editor and a query tool.

The query tool allows the user to select the tables to be queried, define relationships between them, select fields to be included and set criteria to find specific values for fields.

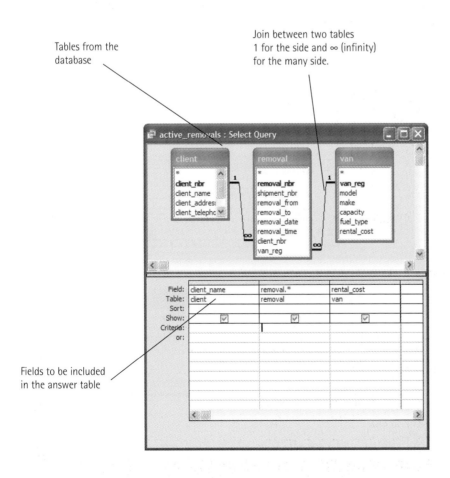

Figure 6.47 Query design, from Microsoft Access

Graphical query tools allow complex queries to be created using a visual method. This is easier for the less experienced user, because he or she does not need to learn the relatively complex SQL, but it is not as flexible as SQL for more experienced users.

The Microsoft Access query shown in Figure 6.47 will show the *client_name* from the *client* table, all the fields from the *removal* table because the * wildcard has been used, and the *rental_cost* from *van*. Only the records which are linked by the matching primary/foreign key values will be shown. The primary keys for each table are shown in **bold** in each table object in the query. The related foreign keys are shown against the table **join**. The join represents the relationship between the tables in the query.

Normally the relationships which were defined when the database was created will be shown in the query, however, just as with SQL, it is possible to remove these relationships from the query and specify new relationships.

Graphical SELECT query – Microsoft Access

The very simplest graphical query is a SELECT query. The simple SELECT query in Figure 6.48 will extract the *client_name* and *client_address* from the *client* table.

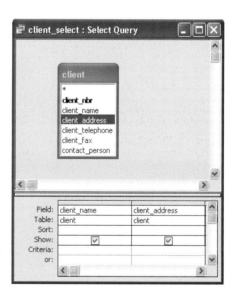

Figure 6.48 Simple SELECT query, from Microsoft Access

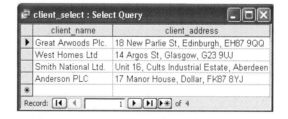

Figure 6.49 Simple SELECT query answer table, from Microsoft Access

Joining tables – Microsoft Access

With Microsoft Access, joining tables is simply a matter of adding the required tables to the query design. The defined relationships, which are established elsewhere in the package, are shown by default between the related tables (Figure 6.50).

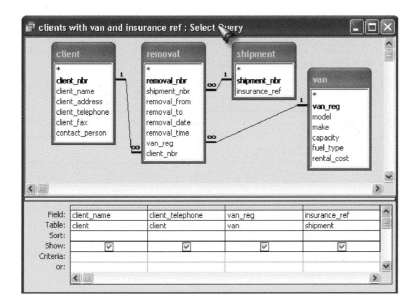

Figure 6.50 SELECT query across joined tables, from Microsoft Access

This query will produce the same answer table as shown in Figure 6.24. The data is taken from each of the related tables but uses fields in *removal* to create the relational joins between the tables.

client_name	client_telephone	van_reg	insurance_ref
Great Arwoods Plc.	0327 989127	KY51 AFZ	NT9238
Great Arwoods Plc.	0327 989127	P385 ASA	RT8721
Great Arwoods Plc.	0327 989127	D842 YSA	QW1211
West Homes Ltd	0312 123198	P385 ASA	NT9238
West Homes Ltd	0312 123198	KY51 AFZ	RT8721
West Homes Ltd	0312 123198	YT71 7YE	AD6701

Figure 6.51 Answer table for SELECT query across joined tables, from Microsoft Access

Adding criteria to a query – Microsoft Access

Criteria can be added to any query to select records with particular field values. The above query can be very easily amended to show details for 'Great Arwoods Plc.' The value 'Great Arwoods Plc.' is added to the criteria row in the query design to select only matching field values.

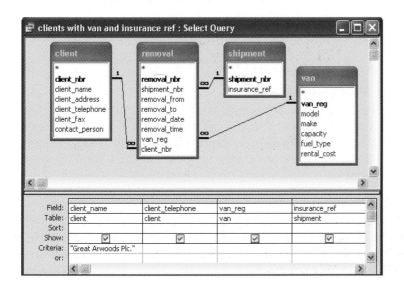

Figure 6.52 Query across joined tables with criteria, from Microsoft Access

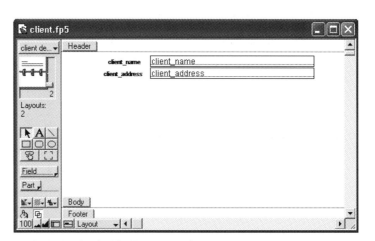

Figure 6.53 Answer table for query across joined tables with criteria, from Microsoft Access

Queries in FileMaker Pro

FileMaker, Inc's FileMaker Pro database product uses individual files to store its tables. There is no query tool as there is with Microsoft Access. To extract data from the database various user views are created, similar to the user views which can be created in SQL database products.

Graphical SELECT query – FileMaker Pro

Each view, called a **layout**, can contain specific fields from a variety of tables. The very simplest view is just of the fields within the current database file (table).

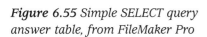

Figure 6.54 Simple SELECT query, from FileMaker Pro

Figure 6.55 Simple SELECT query answer table, from FileMaker Pro

Joining tables – FileMaker Pro

Within FileMaker Pro, relationships are defined between the tables and enforced by validation. There is no direct way of enforcing referential integrity but it can be enforced by using validation rules to ensure that foreign key values are only selected from related primary key values (Figure 6.56).

To create a query a new view is produced. The view may contain fields from the current database table and/or fields from related tables.

The layout shown in Figure 6.57 extracts data from each of the tables which are related to *removal*. This is the same query as shown in Figures 6.22, 6.23 and 6.24 and produces the answer table shown in Figure 6.58.

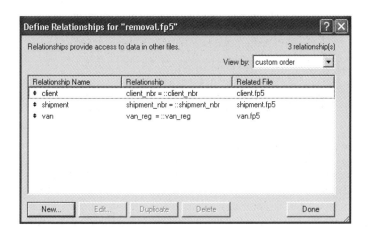

Figure 6.56 Relationships defined, from FileMaker Pro

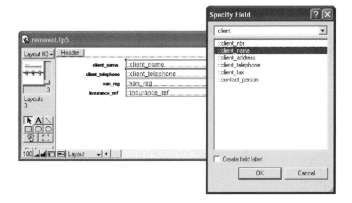

Figure 6.57 Creating a layout using related tables, from FileMaker Pro

Figure 6.58 Answer table using related tables, from FileMaker Pro

Notice that the name given to *client_name* is *client::client_name*. This means that the client name shown is from the *client* table rather than the *removal* table, within which this layout is created.

Adding criteria to a query – FileMaker Pro

FileMaker layouts do not store search criteria such as we might state in an SQL WHERE clause. Whenever criteria are required in a query a separate **find** operation must be carried out using the required layout. The layout in Figure 6.58 can be used to find details of records for Great Arwoods Plc. only by selecting the find view and then entering the required criteria.

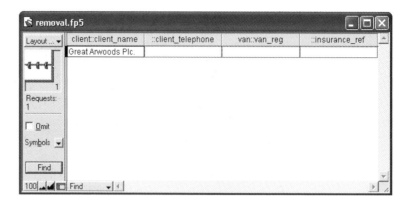

Figure 6.59 Creating a layout, from FileMaker Pro

Figure 6.60 Answer table produced by find, from FileMaker Pro

Queries in PremiumSoft's Navicat

Navicat by PremiumSoft is a powerful MySQL database administration tool. Navicat provides a powerful set of tools that are sophisticated enough for professional developers, yet easy to learn for new users. It provides a range of tools for the free MySQL database system which are very similar to those offered by Microsoft Access and FileMaker Pro.

MySQL is a web-based database system which is used for a wide variety of applications, from web-based content management systems (which control the content of websites) to large payroll systems for international companies.

Navicat provides a range of tools which make it easier to use SQL by replacing the text-based command language with graphical tools (Figure 6.61).

The query shown in Figure 6.61 will produce an answer table containing the *client_name* from the *client* table, all of the fields from *removal*, and *rental_cost* from the *van* table. In a method very similar to Microsoft Access, Navicat allows users to join tables using drag and drop links between fields. These links are shown as lines connecting the tables.

Navicat can interrogate the database and show the answer table produced by the query (Figure 6.62).

Navicat's query tools are very similar to the query tools which we examined for Microsoft Access and FileMaker Pro.

List of available tables

Relationship between tables

Area shows tables in the query

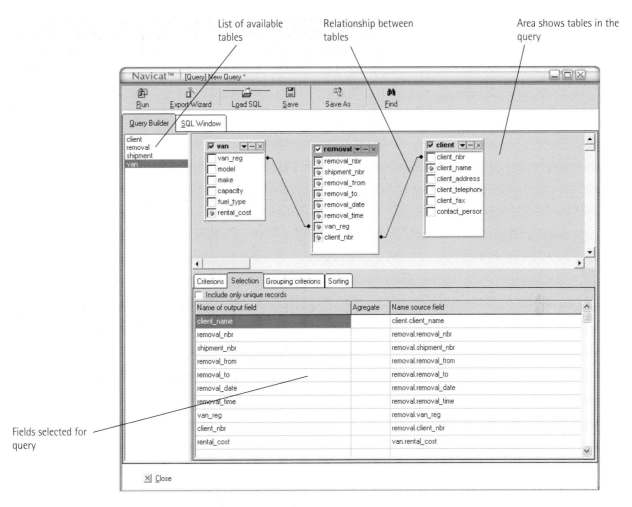

Fields selected for query

Figure 6.61 Sample query, from Navicat

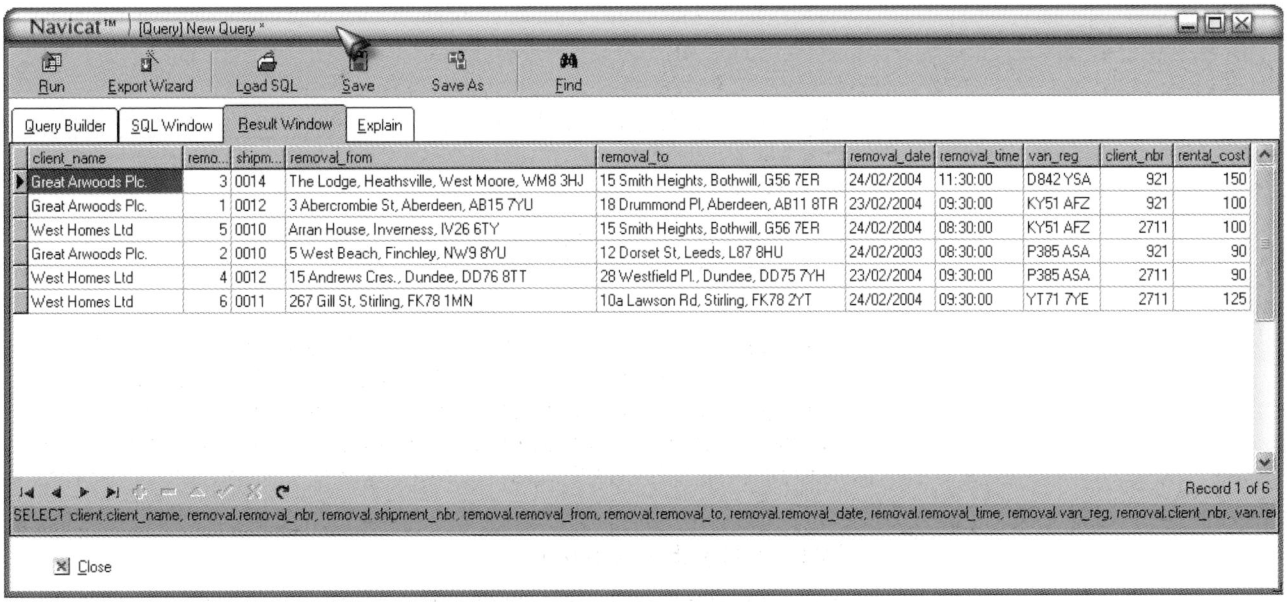

Figure 6.62 Sample answer table, from Navicat

Questions

1. What is the main purpose of queries in a database system?

2. What is SQL?

3. Describe the purpose of each of the following:
   a Data definition language
   b Data manipulation language
   c Data control language.

4. What does the FROM clause in an SQL statement specify?

5. Use the following tables to answer the questions below.
   a Construct the answer table for the SQL statement:
   SELECT cars.regno, fname, sname
   WHERE customer.licence = rental.licence
   AND rental.regno = car.regno
   AND sname = 'Johnstone'
   b Explain how the relational database uses the primary/foreign keys to produce this answer table. Refer to the matching of the keys in your answer.
   c What will the following SQL statement calculate?
   SELECT sum(hire_cost*no_of_days) FROM car, rental WHERE car.regno = rental.regno
   GROUP BY licence

   Note: You do not have to produce the answer table. Explain what will be produced.

customer

licence	fname	sname	address1	address2	address3	postcode	phone
BELLZ17	Bobby	Bell	45 Aberdeen Avenue	Tarves	Aberdeenshire	AB26 1ZZ	(0965)24789
COOPE22	Alice	Cooper	15 Fare Park Drive	Westhill	Aberdeenshire	AB32 2ED	(0234)57829
FRENC99	Tommy	French	28 Buckie Road	Dyce	Aberdeen	AB12 4GB	(0224)24333
GREEN23	Sara	Barnes	Flat 2/L	16 Perth Road	Dundee	DD21 8UI	(0382)22466
JOHNS12	Brian	Johnstone	1 Main Road	Alloa	Clackmannanshire	FK10 1EB	(0259)43343
JOHNS17	Brian	Johnstone	10 Main Road	Alloa	Clackmannanshire	FK10 1EB	(0259)44444
MCLEA56	Elizabeth	McLean	15 Weensland Road	Hawick	Borders	TD9 8LB	(0333)33333
ROBER44	Gary	Roberts	1 Buckie Lane	Banff	Aberdeenshire	AB45 3ED	(0261)12745

Cont'd ...

car

regno	make	model	colour	type	insurance	hire_cost
P334SXC	Ford	Fiesta	Blue	Small Hatch	6	£25.00
P335SXC	Ford	Fiesta	Blue	Small Hatch	6	£25.00
T202FHF	Ford	Transit	White	Van	10	£35.00
T34 BXC	Rover	45	Green	Family Hatch	9	£40.00
V111BBB	Audi	A5	Yellow	Executive Saloon	14	£50.00
V919RFV	Ford	Mondeo	Green	Executive Saloon	11	£45.00

rental

regno	date	licence	no_of _days
T202FHF	02-May-05	BELLZ17	1
V111BBB	19-May-05	COOPE22	1
P335SXC	01-Mar-05	FRENC99	1
T202FHF	09-Mar-05	FRENC99	7
T202FHF	16-Mar-05	FRENC99	7
T34 BXC	23-Apr-05	GREEN23	4
T34 BXC	20-May-05	GREEN23	1
T34 BXC	29-Apr-05	JOHNS12	2
P334SXC	24-Apr-05	JOHNS12	4
P334SXC	18-Mar-05	JOHNS17	2
V919RFV	21-Apr-05	MCLEA56	5
T34 BXC	06-May-05	ROBER44	7
P335SXC	19-Mar-05	ROBER44	7

6. Compare graphical query tools with SQL. What are the advantages and disadvantages for inexperienced and experienced users?

Reports

A report is a formal way of presenting output from a database system. Essentially, reports are SELECT queries which use additional text formatting functions to present a document which is appropriate for a variety of users.

Reports are created by a **report writer,** also called a **report generator**, which is usually part of a database management system. The report writer extracts information from one or more tables and presents the information in a specified format. Most report writers allow you to select records that meet certain conditions, by using a query, and to display selected fields in rows and columns.

You can also format data into pie charts, bar charts and other diagrams. Once you have created a format for a report, you can save the format specifications in a file and continue re-using it for new data.

Architecture of database reports

Database reports as documents normally have a defined layout. A typical database report may make use of all, some or one of these layout areas within its design.

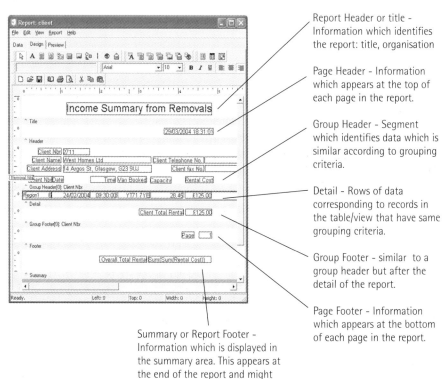

Report Header or title - Information which identifies the report: title, organisation

Page Header - Information which appears at the top of each page in the report.

Group Header - Segment which identifies data which is similar according to grouping criteria.

Detail - Rows of data corresponding to records in the table/view that have same grouping criteria.

Group Footer - similar to a group header but after the detail of the report.

Page Footer - Information which appears at the bottom of each page in the report.

Summary or Report Footer - Information which is displayed in the summary area. This appears at the end of the report and might include overall totals, averages, etc.

Figure 7.1 Sample report layout, from Navicat

The report writer looks like any other software application which a user might encounter. The major difference is that the report writer does not contain a document, it contains a layout. The layout can be used to generate many different styles of document, all based on the data held in the database tables.

Report bands

The areas within the report are called **bands**. All report layouts (also called templates) consist of bands and **controls** (fields and other RDBMS objects such as field names and calculations) that define how the report will look. The only required band in the report is the Detail band.

Detail band

The Detail band usually contains fields from the answer table to display the data for the report. The rule is that the Detail band is shown (in any report) once for every record in the answer table. So you need to create only one layout in the Detail band to define how all records in the Detail band will be shown. A report which has only a Detail band is the simplest type of report.

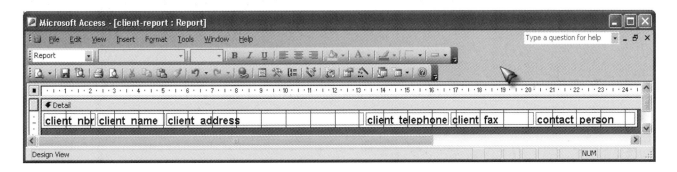

Figure 7.2 Detail-only report layout, from Microsoft Access

The above report layout, from Microsoft Access, contains only the Detail band. The report produced by this will contain only data. There will be no data headings, field names or summary information.

Figure 7.3 Detail-only report document, from Microsoft Access

The report (in Figure 7.3) is produced by the report layout in Figure 7.2. As you can see, only one report layout is required to display each row in the answer table of the source query.

Group header/footer bands

A Group band in a report groups together equal values from a number of records. For example, the answer table in Figure 7.4 has a number of columns which contain the same values for some of the records.

client_ nbr	client_ name	client_ address	client_ telephone	client_ fax	removal_ nbr	removal_ date	removal_ time	van_ reg	capacity	rental_ cost
921	Great Arwoods Plc.	18 New Parlie St Edinburgh EH87 9QQ	0327 989127	0327 981111	1	23/02/2004	09:30	KY51 AFZ	16	100
921	Great Arwoods Plc.	18 New Parlie St Edinburgh EH87 9QQ	0327 989127	0327 981111	2	24/02/2004	08:30	P385 ASA	11	90
921	Great Arwoods Plc.	18 New Parlie St Edinburgh EH87 9QQ	0327 989127	0327 981111	3	24/02/2004	11:30	D842 YSA	36	150
2711	West Homes Ltd	14 Argos St Glasgow G23 9UJ	0312 123198	0312 123199	4	23/02/2004	09:30	P385 ASA	11	90
2711	West Homes Ltd	14 Argos St Glasgow G23 9UJ	0312 123198	0312 123199	5	24/02/2004	08:30	KY51 AFZ	16	100
2711	West Homes Ltd	14 Argos St Glasgow G23 9UJ	0312 123198	0312 123199	6	24/02/2004	09:30	YT71 7YE	28	125

Figure 7.4 Answer table with equal column values

The values for *client_nbr*, *client_name*, *client_address*, *client_telephone* and *client_fax* are all the same for the first three records and the last three records. These values can be grouped together in a report layout by placing the *client_nbr*, *client_name*, *client_address*, *client_telephone* and *client_fax* fields in a Group band in the report.

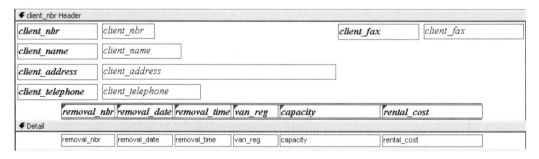

Figure 7.5 Report layout with grouping header

Figure 7.5 shows the field labels (in bold) and the fields themselves. Notice that the client details are in the Group band *client_nbr* Header and that the headings for the fields in the Detail band are also shown in the group header. This is because the headings for *removal_nbr*, *removal_date*, *removal_time*, *van_reg*, *capacity* and *rental cost* need only be shown once for each client.

You can see from Figure 7.6 that each client's details are only shown once for the matching removal information. The client's details have been grouped together for equal values of *client_nbr*.

client_nbr	921		client_fax	0327 981111
client_name	Great Arwoods Plc.			
client_address	18 New Parlie St, Edinburgh, EH87 9QQ			
client_telephone	0327 989127			

removal_nbr	removal_date	removal_time	van_reg	capacity	rental_cost
2	24/02/2004	08:30	P385 ASA	11	90
1	23/02/2004	09:30	KY51 AFZ	16	100
3	24/02/2004	11:30	D842 YSA	36	150

client_nbr	2711		client_fax	0312 123199
client_name	West Homes Ltd			
client_address	14 Argos St, Glasgow, G23 9UJ			
client_telephone	0312 123198			

removal_nbr	removal_date	removal_time	van_reg	capacity	rental_cost
6	24/02/2004	09:30	YT71 7YE	28	125
4	23/02/2004	09:30	P385 ASA	11	90
5	24/02/2004	08:30	KY51 AFZ	16	100

Figure 7.6 Report with group header and detail

As well as using a group header we can also use a group footer. For example, depending on the requirements of the report, some details, for each client, might be better placed below the Detail band, such as summary totals for clients or other information.

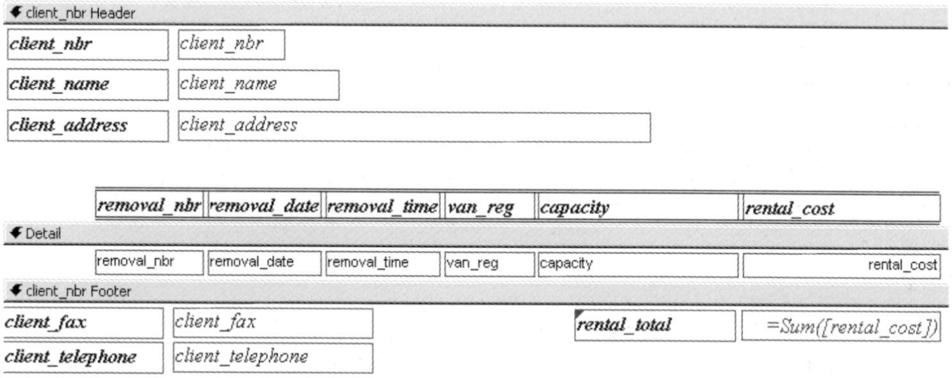

Figure 7.7 Report layout with group header and footer

In the layout above, the *client_fax* and *client_telephone* details are shown in the Footer band underneath the Detail band. Also shown is a calculated database object which uses the SUM function to calculate the total of *rental_cost* for each unique *client_nbr*. This total is for each unique *client_nbr* because the group footer groups together equal values of *client_nbr*.

client_nbr	921
client_name	Great Arwoods Plc.
client_address	18 New Parlie St, Edinburgh, EH87 9QQ

removal_nbr	removal_date	removal_time	van_reg	capacity	rental_cost
2	24/02/2004	08:30	P385 ASA	11	£90.00
1	23/02/2004	09:30	KY51 AFZ	16	£100.00
3	24/02/2004	11:30	D842 YSA	36	£150.00

client_fax	0327 981111		rental_total	£340.00
client_telephone	0327 989127			

client_nbr	2711
client_name	West Homes Ltd
client_address	14 Argos St, Glasgow, G23 9UJ

removal_nbr	removal_date	removal_time	van_reg	capacity	rental_cost
6	24/02/2004	09:30	YT71 7YE	28	£125.00
4	23/02/2004	09:30	P385 ASA	11	£90.00
5	24/02/2004	08:30	KY51 AFZ	16	£100.00

client_fax	0312 123199		rental_total	£315.00
client_telephone	0312 123198			

Figure 7.8 Report with group header and footer

Using multiple group header/footer bands

It is possible to build up complex reports using several Group bands. There are often several ways to group information in a report and these can be layered to help the user understand the information stored in the database.

For example, in the Reed and Co. case study, clients are allocated vans for removals. A report might be required to show, for each client, an overview of the vans and the removal to which the vans are allocated. This report should have two Group bands, one for *client* and one for *van*. The removals for each van and client would then be shown in the Detail band.

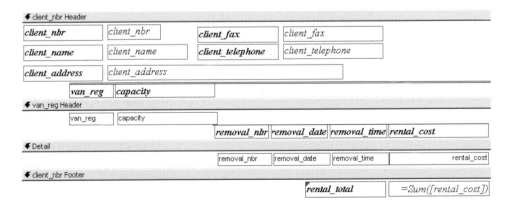

Figure 7.9 Report layout with group header and footer

A sample of the resulting report is shown in Figure 7.10.

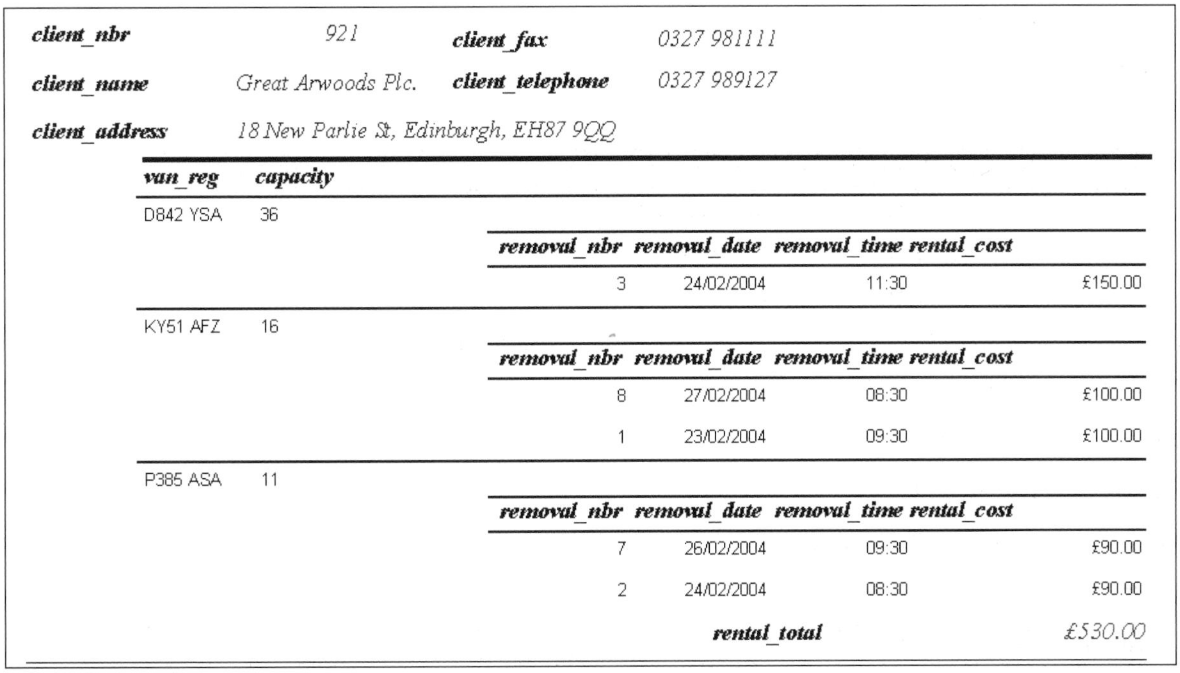

client_nbr	921	client_fax	0327 981111
client_name	Great Arwoods Plc.	client_telephone	0327 989127
client_address	18 New Parlie St, Edinburgh, EH87 9QQ		

van_reg	capacity				
D842 YSA	36				

		removal_nbr	removal_date	removal_time	rental_cost
		3	24/02/2004	11:30	£150.00

van_reg	capacity
KY51 AFZ	16

		removal_nbr	removal_date	removal_time	rental_cost
		8	27/02/2004	08:30	£100.00
		1	23/02/2004	09:30	£100.00

van_reg	capacity
P385 ASA	11

		removal_nbr	removal_date	removal_time	rental_cost
		7	26/02/2004	09:30	£90.00
		2	24/02/2004	08:30	£90.00
				rental_total	£530.00

Figure 7.10 Report with group header and footer

You can see from this sample that all the records for the client are shown, but are broken down using the Report bands to make the information presented easier to understand.

Page header/footer

A Page Header band can contain one or more lines of text that appear at the top of each page of the report. Once you specify the text that should appear in the header, the report writer automatically inserts it in the report. Similarly, the page footer can contain similar objects to the report header but appears at the bottom of each page.

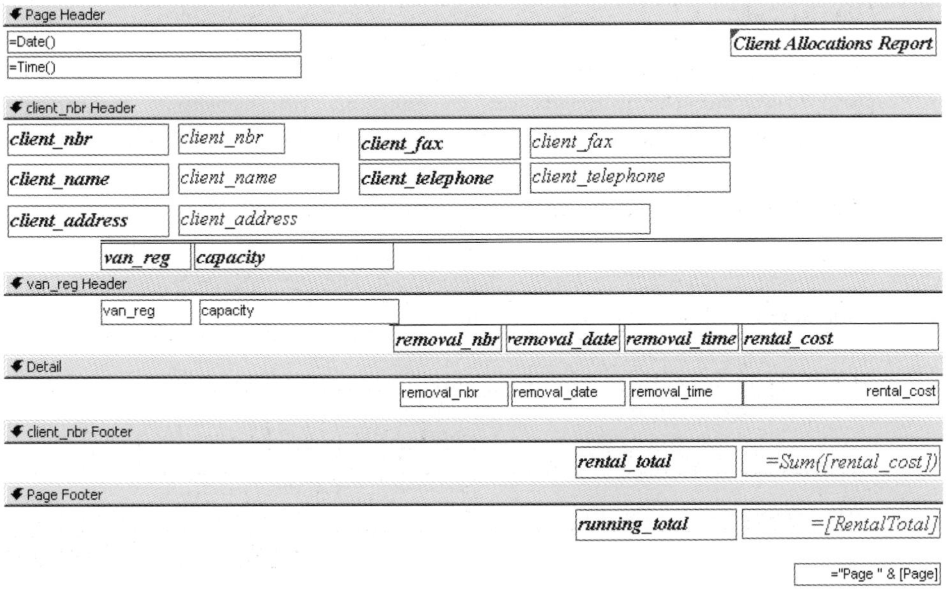

Figure 7.11 Report layout with group header and footer

Most report writers will allow you to use special symbols in the header or footer that represent changing values. For example, you can enter a symbol for the page number, and the report writer will automatically replace the symbol with the correct number on each page when the report is created. If you enter the date symbol, the current date will be inserted, which will change if necessary each time you produce the report.

It is common to use the footer to show running totals up to and including the current page, in addition to page numbers and other similar details such as dates or report titles.

A sample of the resulting report is shown in Figure 7.12.

19 April 2004
13:26:25

Client Allocations Report

client_nbr		921	*client_fax*	0327 981111
client_name		Great Arwoods Plc.	*client_telephone*	0327 989127
client_address		18 New Parlie St, Edinburgh, EH87 9QQ		

| *van_reg* | *capacity* | | | |
| D842 YSA | 36 | | | |

| *removal_nbr* | *removal_date* | *removal_time* | *rental_cost* |
| 3 | 24/02/2004 | 11:30 | £150.00 |

| *van_reg* | *capacity* |
| KY51 AFZ | 16 |

removal_nbr	*removal_date*	*removal_time*	*rental_cost*
8	27/02/2004	08:30	£100.00
1	23/02/2004	09:30	£100.00

| *van_reg* | *capacity* |
| P385 ASA | 11 |

removal_nbr	*removal_date*	*removal_time*	*rental_cost*
7	26/02/2004	09:30	£90.00
2	24/02/2004	08:30	£90.00

rental_total £530.00

running_total £530.00

Page 1

Figure 7.12 Report with group header and footer

Title or report header

The start of a report can contain the report header. This will often include the title of the report, the date and perhaps other relevant information about the report such as who compiled it, the company contact details, business logos, etc. Depending on the nature of the report, the report header can be anything from one or two lines to several pages long.

Summary or report footer

The end of a report can contain summary information about the report – data such as overall totals, analysis of the report results such as charts and graphs, and summary text to explain the report's results. As with a report header, the report footer can be anything from one or two lines to several pages long depending on the requirements of the report produced.

The following report layout contains both a Title band and a Summary band. The Title band, in this case, contains text and a graphic and the Summary band contains some text and a chart.

Figure 7.13 Report layout with title (Report Header) and summary (Report Footer) bands

Report functions

Additional fields can be created with a report to carry out calculations based on the report data. These calculations can range from simple arithmetic operations to complex mathematical formulae. Most report writing software applications have a number of in-built functions that allow such operations to be completed relatively simply.

SUM function

Probably the most popular function in any database report is the SUM function. The SUM function takes all of the values in each of the specified fields and totals their values. This can be applied to any report band to give a total for a band, to produce an overall total or to produce a running total.

The following report (Figure 7.15 shown on page 130) uses the SUM function in a variety of ways. The report writing software is used to set additional properties for each SUM function field so that it calculates the sum for the current band, the Group band or the report overall. The properties of the field can also be set so that it carries the total forward from the previous Group band or starts a new calculation from zero.

The report layout in Figure 7.15 produces the report shown in Figure 7.16.

Reed and Co Removals Ltd
Unit 15
17 Regent Quay
Leith
EH18 9UT

CLIENTS AND VAN JOBS

client_nbr	921	client_fax	0327 981111
client_name	Great Arwoods Plc.	client_telephone	0327 989127
client_address	18 New Parlie St, Edinburgh, EH87 9QQ		

van_reg	capacity				
D842 YSA	36				

removal_nbr	removal_date	removal_time	rental_cost
3	24/02/2004	11:30	£150.00

van_reg	capacity
KY51 AFZ	16

removal_nbr	removal_date	removal_time	rental_cost
8	27/02/2004	08:30	£100.00
1	23/02/2004	09:30	£100.00

van_reg	capacity
P385 ASA	11

removal_nbr	removal_date	removal_time	rental_cost
7	26/02/2004	09:30	£90.00
2	24/02/2004	08:30	£90.00
		rental_total	£530.00

client_nbr	2711	client_fax	0312 123199
client_name	West Homes Ltd	client_telephone	0312 123198
client_address	14 Argos St, Glasgow, G23 9UU		

van_reg	capacity
KY51 AFZ	16

removal_nbr	removal_date	removal_time	rental_cost
5	24/02/2004	08:30	£100.00

van_reg	capacity
P385 ASA	11

removal_nbr	removal_date	removal_time	rental_cost
4	23/02/2004	09:30	£90.00

van_reg	capacity
YT71 7YE	28

removal_nbr	removal_date	removal_time	rental_cost
6	24/02/2004	09:30	£125.00
		rental_total	£315.00

Title or Report Header

Group headers and detail of report

The overall figures for this report are encouraging as can be seen from this overall graph.

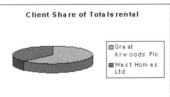

Client Share of Totals rental
- Great Arwoods Plc.
- West Homes Ltd

Summary or Report Footer

Figure 7.14 *Report with title (report header) and summary (report footer) bands*

AVERAGE function

The AVERAGE function finds the average of the field or fields selected. It simplifies adding all of the indicated field values in the report together and dividing by their total number.

As with most functions, the average can be taken of a number of values in the detail or group bands, of a number of consecutive values from rows or grouping level, or for values for the overall report.

This report field is set to produce a running total for [Cost of Hire] for each line of the current detail band..

This report field is set to produce a running total for [Cost of Hire] for each line of the detail band. The total is continued to the next detail band and therefore shows the running total of all [Cost of Hire] fields..

The SUM function produces a running total for [Cost of Hire] for the report overall. The total is carried forward for the next grouping band..

This SUM function produces a total for [Cost of Hire] for each grouping band in this report.

This SUM function calculates the overall total for [Cost of Hire] for the whole report.

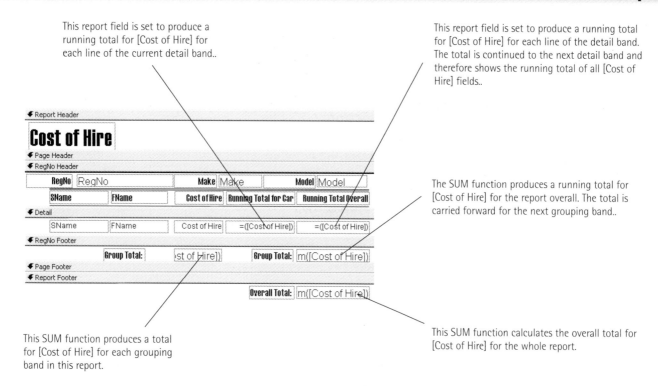

Figure 7.15 *Report layout using the SUM function*

Cost of Hire

RegNo P335SXC		Make Ford		Model Fiesta
SName	FName	Cost of Hire	ing Total for Car	ning Total Overall
French	Tommy	£25.00	£25.00	£25.00
Roberts	Gary	£175.00	£200.00	£200.00
	Group Total:	£200.00	Group Total:	£200.00
RegNo T202FHF		Make Ford		Model Transit
SName	FName	Cost of Hire	ing Total for Car	ning Total Overall
Bell	Bobby	£35.00	£35.00	£235.00
French	Tommy	£245.00	£280.00	£480.00
French	Tommy	£245.00	£525.00	£725.00
	Group Total:	£525.00	Group Total:	£725.00
RegNo T34 BXC		Make Rover		Model 45
SName	FName	Cost of Hire	ing Total for Car	ning Total Overall
Green	Sara	£40.00	£40.00	£765.00
Green	Sara	£160.00	£200.00	£925.00
Johnstone	Brian	£80.00	£280.00	£1,005.00
Roberts	Gary	£280.00	£560.00	£1,285.00
	Group Total:	£560.00	Group Total:	£1,285.00
RegNo V111BBB		Make Audi		Model A5
SName	FName	Cost of Hire	ing Total for Car	ning Total Overall
Cooper	Alice	£50.00	£50.00	£1,335.00
Smith	Janet	£100.00	£150.00	£1,435.00
	Group Total:	£150.00	Group Total:	£1,435.00
RegNo V919RFV		Make Ford		Model Mondeo
SName	FName	Cost of Hire	ing Total for Car	ning Total Overall
McLean	Elizabeth	£225.00	£225.00	£1,660.00
Murray	Kerry	£45.00	£270.00	£1,705.00
Smith	Janet	£90.00	£360.00	£1,795.00
	Group Total:	£360.00	Group Total:	£1,795.00
			Overall Total:	£1,795.00

Figure 7.16 *Report using the SUM function*

MAX and MIN functions

The maximum (MAX) and minimum (MIN) functions find the maximum or minimum values of fields in a report band.

COUNT function

The COUNT function does exactly as it says: it counts the occurrences of a field in a report band.

Date/time functions

There are many different date and time functions which are available in most report writing applications. A range of example date functions are shown in Figure 7.17.

These are just a few possible date functions. Your report writer software may use some of these functions or may have alternatives which carry out the same or similar operations.

Function	Meaning
ADDTIME(expr1,expr2)	Adds time in hours, minutes and seconds to a set date/time.
CURDATE()	Returns the current date.
CURTIME()	Returns the current time.
NOW()	Returns the current date and time.
DATEDIFF(expr1,expr2)	Returns the number of days between the start date expr1 and the end date expr2.
DAY(date)	Returns the day in word form, i.e. Monday, Tuesday, etc. based on the date.
DAYOFWEEK(date)	Returns the day of the week for date, in range 1 to 7.
DAYOFMONTH(date)	Returns the day of the month for date, in range 1 to 31.
DAYOFYEAR(date)	Returns the day of the year for date, in the range 1 to 366.
LAST_DAY(date)	Takes a date value and returns the corresponding value for the last day of the month.
MONTHNAME(date)	Returns the full name of the month for date.
TIME(dateandtime)	Extracts the time part from a *dateandtime* expression.
TIMEDIFF(expr1,expr2)	Returns the time between the start time expr1 and the end time expr2.
WEEKOFYEAR(date)	Returns the calendar week of the *date* as a number in the range from 1 to 53.
YEAR(date)	Returns the year for date, in the range 1000 to 9999.

Figure 7.17 Example date and time functions

Types of report

The reports generated from a database can be classed in two general groups. These groups reflect the complexity of the report and the answer table on which it is built.

Basic reports

A basic report uses a single base table or a simple answer table. A simple answer table would be based on a query which uses no more than two base tables. This non-complex collection of data can be reported on relatively easily.

A basic report has one row per answer table record plus an optional Group band for summary information.

Complex reports

A report which is based on a query with more than two base tables and/or uses multiple grouping bands is a complex report. This type of report brings together data from multiple tables so that it can be presented in an easily understood format.

Report layouts

Reports can be given default layouts. Examples of these are columnar and tabular. Each layout is appropriate for different uses depending on the type of data being viewed, the size of the fields and the requirements of the report such as the target audience.

Columnar

A columnar report shows the fields from the answer table's rows in a vertical format, grouped by record (Figure 7.18).

As you can see, the columnar report provides a view of each record's data but, because of the report layout, comparisons between records and field values are difficult. It is not possible to scan down a column of the same field value to make comparisons.

This style of report is often used for more formal reports where the details from individual records are important rather than an overview of all the

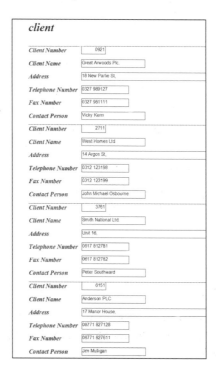

Figure 7.18 Columnar report

data. The details in Figure 7.18 could be used by the customer services manager of Reed and Co. when he or she visits individual clients. The customer services manager is concerned with individual client's details and not the overview of the clients for this purpose.

Tabular

A tabular report displays the records in rows and uses columns to identify the fields from the answer table. This layout has the advantage that comparisons between field data are relatively simple because the values for each field are in vertical columns.

client_nbr	client_name	client_address	client_telephone	client_fax	contact_person
921	Great Arwoods Plc.	18 New Parlie St, Edinburgh, EH87 9QQ	0327 989127	0327 981111	Vicky Kenn
2711	West Homes Ltd	14 Argos St, Glasgow, G23 9UJ	0312 123198	0312 123199	John Michael Osbourne
3761	Smith National Ltd	Unit 16, Cults Industrial Estate, Aberdeen, AB15 9SA	0617 812781	0617 812782	Peter Southward
6151	Anderson PLC	17 Manor House, Dollar, FK87 8YJ	08771 827128	08771 827611	Jim Mulligan

Figure 7.19 Tabular report

Scoping out a report

When constructing a report there are a number of items which need to be considered prior to using the report writing software.

Report information

What information should the report contain? Will it be a list of data for particular tables and summary statistics (simple report)? Will it show trends over time, across an organisation's divisions or for a range of values?

It is important to think carefully about the underlying data required for the report and how that data is best extracted from the database using an appropriate query or collection of queries.

Once you have decided on the required source data, create a query to produce an answer table holding the required data. Remember, the underlying data in an answer table can often be modified directly in the table rather than having to open up a form or base table, which can be useful for quickly editing specific data. Also, if you have multiple reports which require the same source data you can use the same query as the source for each report.

You should confirm that the answer table created by your query contains the data you require for your report.

Report organisation

Having produced the data required for the report you should now consider how the report should be organised. Which report bands will be required and how will the data be laid out on the report?

Will there be:

- a simple tabular or columnar representation
- grouped/sorted bands by specific values
- page headers/footers
- title/summary bands
- a requirement to make the report landscape or portrait?

Having considered this you should create the initial layout of the report. This should contain the required report bands.

Report presentation

What will be the report's look and feel? The typefaces to be used will depend partly on how formal or informal the report is. Generally, for more formal reports use a serif font (such as Times New Roman) whereas for informal reports use a sans-serif font, such as Arial. A 'serif' is the small line that is found at the ends of letters in a serif font (such as the stroke at the bottom and top of the capital letter 'I').

The size, colour and spacing of the text on the report all need to be considered. Many report writers also have the capability of adding graphics to the report such as images, lines, grids, etc. These can be used to enhance the presentation of a report.

Report purpose

How will the report be used? Is it to produce a one-off output for a specific purpose or is it to be used regularly, such as weekly or monthly?

Once you have considered the organisation, presentation and purpose of the report you should add the report fields to produce a report prototype for inspection by the user. The user can then ensure that the data is correct, that the look and feel of the report are acceptable, and, perhaps, identify alternative ways to arrange the data for the report. The report can be revised, using the report writer application, until it meets the user's needs.

Questions

1. What is the purpose of a report writer?

2. Describe the purpose of each of the following:
   a detail band
   b group header/footer
   c page header/footer
   d title
   e summary.

3. Explain how identical SUM functions in a report can produce different results depending on their location in report bands.

4. Describe the difference between tabular and columnar report styles.

5. What does the COUNT function do in a report?

Questions

User Interface Design

What is the user interface? The user interface is normally defined in terms of the screen-based interfaces to an information system. An essential part of the development of a database system is the development of the means of communicating with the database – the user interface.

Establishing interaction

The first step in developing a user interface is to identify exactly where user interaction is required in the database system. One technique adopted to do this is to show all the data inputs and outputs that the database system requires and use these to identify user interface elements. For each human-related input or output, at least one user interface element will be required.

An input or output is any event where the user is responsible for initiating an operation by the computer system. The user, for example, enters a new record, requests a report or deletes a record. All of these are examples of inputs to or outputs from the database system and require user interfaces to be designed to specifically meet their requirements.

Using context diagrams

Context diagrams, also known as **Level 0 DFDs (data flow diagrams)**, are a relatively simple method of recording the data that flows into and out from a database system. A context diagram represents the entire database system being designed. The diagram is drawn to illustrate the data which flows from the user (or users) into the system and back out to the user(s) (Figure 8.1).

The components of a context diagram are shown in Figure 8.1. The database system is shown as a single system (a process), connected to external entities (in this case one entity) by data flows.

An external entity (not related in any way to database entities which we looked at earlier) is a source or destination of a data flow and is outside the database system. Only those entities which originate or receive data are represented. The symbol used is an oval containing a meaningful and unique identifier such as *Customer* or *Pupil*, or in this case *Manager*.

The context diagram clearly shows the interfaces between the system and the external entities with which it communicates. Therefore, whilst it is often conceptually trivial, a context diagram serves to focus attention on the flow of data into and out from the system.

Note, that communications involving external entities are only included where they involve the 'system' process. Whilst the manager would communicate with others, for example his drivers or removal workers – these data flows are outside the 'system' process and so are not included on the context diagram.

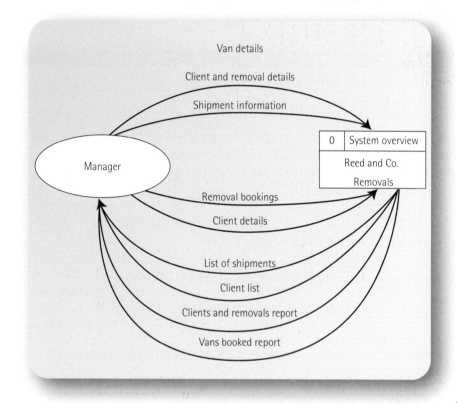

Figure 8.1 Context diagram

Context diagram/data flow diagrams guidelines

First, draw and name a single process box that represents the entire system.

Next, identify and add the external entities that communicate directly with the process box. Do this by considering the origin and destination of the data flows, or in short, who enters data and who receives it. Draw an oval for each external entity and give each an appropriate name.

Finally, add the data flows to the diagram. Each data flow should be given the name of the data that is moving between the external entity and the 'system' process.

In drawing the context diagram you should only be concerned with the most important information flows. These will be concerned with issues such as how client details are received, how bookings for removals are made and how specific reports are communicated to the user. Minor related processes, such as making a request for a specific report, may or may not be shown depending on the complexity of the data flows.

Each data flow will require an element of the user interface to be created for it. A list of the required user interface elements can be drawn up once the context diagram has been produced. This involves taking each data flow in turn and deciding how the data is to be handled as it enters or leaves the 'system' process.

For the system shown in Figure 8.1. there are nine data flows and each data flow requires some kind of related user interface so that the user can enter or receive data.

Listing the user interface elements

Before creating the user interface we need to list the user interface elements based on the context diagram. To do this we consider each data flow in turn and consider their requirements.

	Functionality required of user interface	Type of element?
Van details	Create, amend, delete and browse van details.	
Client and removal details	Create, amend, delete and browse client details and related removals.	
Shipment information	Create, amend, delete and browse shipment details.	
Removal bookings	Create, amend, delete and browse removal records.	
Client details	Create, amend, delete and browse client records.	
List of shipments	Display and print list of shipments report.	
Client list	Display and print client list.	
Clients and removals report	Display and print a report detailing all clients and related removals after a specific date.	
Vans booked report	Display and print a list of all vans booked on jobs for a particular day.	

Figure 8.2 User interface specification

Before we can complete the table the type of user interface required has to be identified for each user interface element.

Types of user interface

There are four main styles of user interface that are common to database applications.

Forms

A form is a user interface for data entry and data retrieval. A form contains a set of fields laid out on a screen, or more often in a window area. Fields are labelled with field names to identify them and there is a facility for displaying error messages either on the form or via an additional form or dialogue box. Forms may also have header and footer areas for additional information. A sample form from the Reed and Co. removals system is shown in Figure 8.3.

client_nbr	client_name		
921	Great Arwoods Plc.		
client_address			
18 New Parlie St, Edinburgh, EH87 9QQ			
client_telephone	client_fax	contact_person	
0327 989127	0327 981111	Vicky Kenn	

Figure 8.3 Form interface

Menus

A menu interface consists of a range of choices displayed in some way on the screen. Menus can be shown as a single level of items or as a number of items grouped logically in a pull-down style. To make a selection from the list the user either moves the mouse cursor to the required option and clicks the mouse button, or uses some combination of keys from the keyboard.

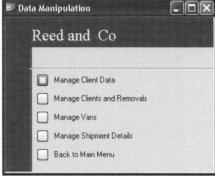

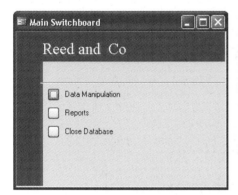

Figure 8.4 Simple menus from a database switchboard

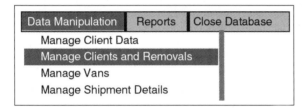

Figure 8.5 A pull-down menu from a database application

Switchboards

Switchboards, illustrated in Figure 8.4, are very common in database applications. Microsoft Access makes the construction of switchboards relatively simple because it includes a wizard which automates the process.

A switchboard is a window which contains a number of menu items. When an item is selected, one database object is activated or an additional switchboard is displayed. The object activated might be a form for data entry; a report to extract data from the database; or a macro or script (a collection of program instructions which tell the database system to carry out specific operations).

Command line

A command line interface (CLI) is rarely found in modern desktop applications but is more common on server applications. A command line interface requires users to know command words which are used to carry out operations.

There is little design required for a command line interface as the functionality is defined by the software being used rather than the user. An example of a command line interface is that available with the free MySQL database engine.

When the software is loaded it presents the user with a command line prompt. At this prompt SQL commands can be entered to control and modify databases managed by the software (Figure 8.6).

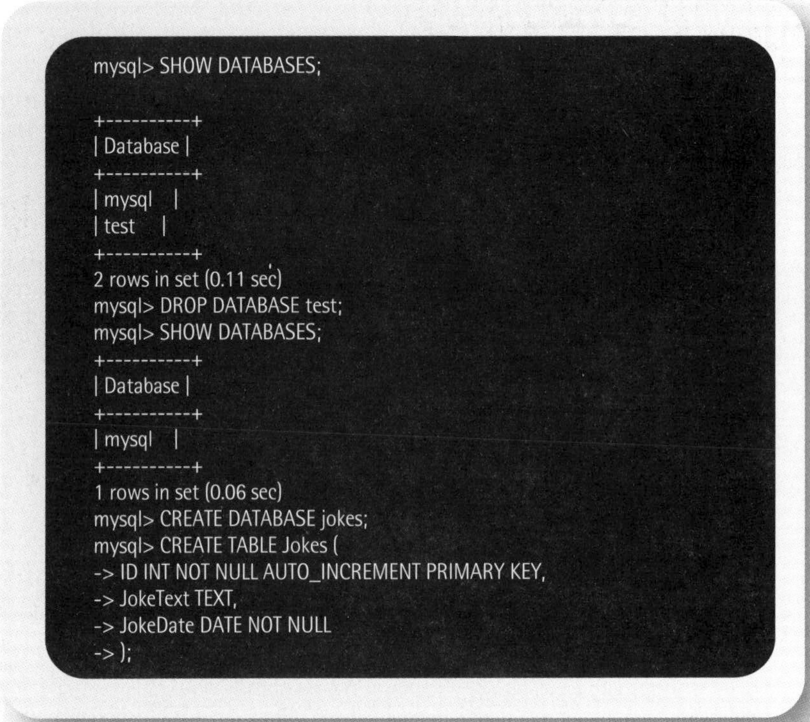

```
mysql> SHOW DATABASES;

+----------+
| Database |
+----------+
| mysql    |
| test     |
+----------+
2 rows in set (0.11 sec)
mysql> DROP DATABASE test;
mysql> SHOW DATABASES;
+----------+
| Database |
+----------+
| mysql    |
+----------+
1 rows in set (0.06 sec)
mysql> CREATE DATABASE jokes;
mysql> CREATE TABLE Jokes (
-> ID INT NOT NULL AUTO_INCREMENT PRIMARY KEY,
-> JokeText TEXT,
-> JokeDate DATE NOT NULL
-> );
```

Figure 8.6 Command line interface

Command line interfaces are commonly used by skilled computer users because of the speed at which the software responds to command line instructions, however this type of user interface is not appropriate for the average computer user because it lacks the graphical user interface elements which make software easier to use.

Direct manipulation

This type of interface is associated with graphical, windows-based systems. The term 'direct manipulation' is used because the user causes events to occur by manipulating graphical objects using the mouse. Currently, direct manipulation interfaces are by far the most common.

In the example in Figure 8.7, the user has selected a form from the switchboard menu by placing the cursor over the menu item and selecting it with the mouse button. This action causes the data entry form shown to appear in a window on the screen. A pull-down menu, within the form, is used to select a value for *van_reg*.

Completing the list of user interface elements

The types of user interface elements required for the database system can now be specified. Direct manipulation is often used when parts of a form are related to tables in the database or when fields are restricted to specific values.

For such interfaces, a 'lookup' can be used to find the related values and offer them, as a choice from a list, to the user. Other interactive elements, such as buttons, can also be used to set field values.

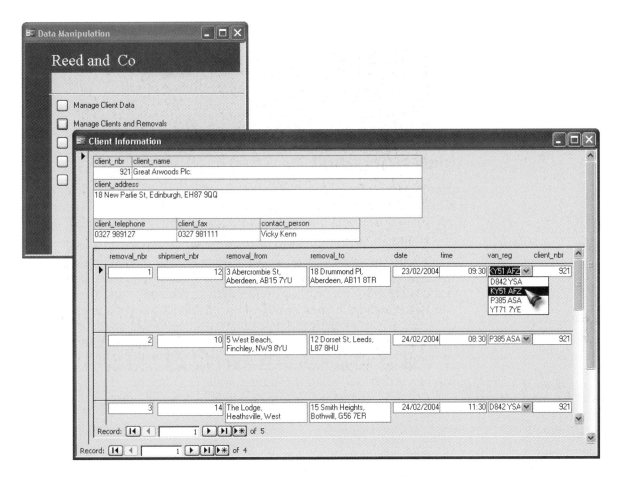

Figure 8.7 Direct manipulation

Forms are used for data manipulation, for example when records need to be created, amended or deleted. Forms can also be used to browse the database instead of examining the base tables. The interface provided by a form is far more user friendly than the equivalent representation using a database table.

	Functionality required of user interface	Type of element?
Van details	Create, amend, delete and browse van details.	Form
Client and removal details	Create, amend, delete and browse client details and related removals.	Direct manipulation (form)
Shipment information	Create, amend, delete and browse shipment details.	Form
Removal bookings	Create, amend, delete and browse removal records.	Direct manipulation (form)
Client details	Create, amend, delete and browse client records.	Form
List of shipments	Display and print list of shipments report.	Menu item (linked to report)
Client list	Display and print client list.	Menu item (linked to report)
Clients and removals report	Display and print a report detailing all clients and related removals after a specific date.	Menu item (linked to a form to allow user to enter date for query as basis of report)
Vans booked report	Display and print a list of all vans booked on jobs for a particular day.	Menu item (linked to a form to allow user to enter date for query as basis of report)

Figure 8.8 User interface specification – complete

Menus are used to navigate the database system, and output functions, such as 'produce a report', are often linked to individual buttons on the menu. Some reports are based on criteria which are entered by the user, such as a report which shows details after a specific date. In this case, the date is entered into a form and the value used in a query to produce the data for the report.

Macros/scripting

User interfaces for database systems are often driven by sets of computer instructions called **macros** or **scripts**. Both macros and scripts carry out the same operations but the terminology is different depending on the RDBMS which is used.

Many programs allow you to create macros/scripts so that you can use a single button to perform a whole series of actions. Suppose, for example, that you are editing a record in a form and want to open a form containing a related record from another table. Using your RDBMS you can create a list of commands that opens the new form based on values on the initial form and then closes the initial form. For examples, see Figures 8.9 and 8.10.

The macro/script can be attached to a button and the sequence of actions will be carried out when the button is clicked. Equally, the macro/script

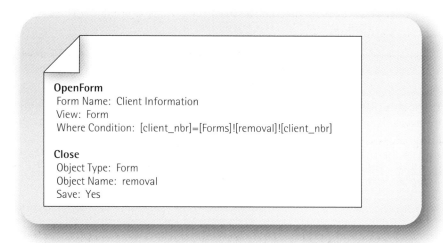

Figure 8.9 Macro documented from Microsoft Access

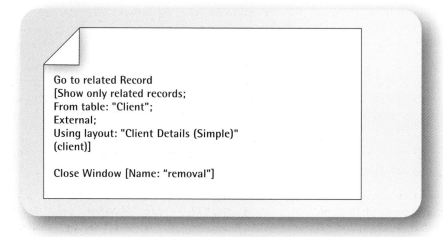

Figure 8.10 Script from FileMaker Pro

could be attached to a pull-down menu or a specific combination of key presses (a keyboard shortcut).

In a way, macros are like simple programs. Some RDBMSs support sophisticated macros that allow you to use variables and flow control structures such as loops and selection, but these are beyond the scope of this course.

Guidelines for user interface design

Regardless of which type of user interface is required, the following guidelines are established good practice for interface design:

- Use consistent and meaningful methods throughout your user interface. For example, if a menu-driven interface is chosen:
  - use a consistent method of selecting the menu options (buttons or keyboard characters)
  - don't switch between pull-down menus and switchboards because it will confuse the user
  - give every menu a title
  - align menu options in the same way (to the left, right or centred)
  - try to have no more than seven options per menu (more than seven often confuses people)
  - organise menus logically so that users can easily navigate between options
  - have a consistent method of displaying error messages or additional information for users.
- Design a different user interface for each distinct group of users. Users with little knowledge of computer systems will require a different user interface from those who are experts.
- Provide suitable feedback to users. When the user completes an operation, provide an indication that this has been successful, if appropriate.
- Have simple and meaningful error messages.
- Avoid information overload. Don't put too much information into one form or one menu. Don't clutter up the screen!

Rapid application development – user interfaces

Rapid application development is a programming system that enables programmers to build working programs quickly. In general, RAD systems provide a number of tools to help build graphical user interfaces that would normally take a large development effort.

The vast majority of modern database applications include a number of RAD tools to allow complex user interfaces to be developed. This allows the programmer to move very quickly from producing a context diagram to producing a working user interface for the underlying database.

Both Microsoft Access and FileMaker Pro have such tools and developers make good use of these to shorten the amount of time required to develop the user interface for a particular database product.

However, care should be taken to ensure that a user interface designed using RAD tools conforms to the guidelines for user interface design given above. A common problem with user interfaces designed using RAD tools is that they are over-complex with too many objects placed on each application form or window. Try to avoid this by considering your user interface design carefully.

User interface controls

User interfaces developed using RAD tools normally consist of a number of standard controls. These controls are linked to the underlying data in the database, to navigation/record browsing commands or to pre-written database instructions (such as macros or scripts). The following is a list of common controls used in most database applications.

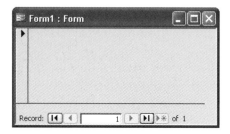

Figure 8.11 Microsoft Access form

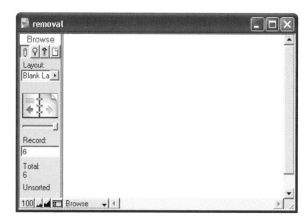

Figure 8.12 FileMaker Pro layout

Form/layout

A **form** (as it is known in Microsoft Access) or a **layout** (as it is known in FileMaker Pro) is the area within which other controls are placed. Forms are used primarily for data entry and manipulation but they are also used for user navigation of the database system. A switchboard is a form/layout which contains a number of buttons that carry out database operations.

A form should always be named beginning with the letters *frm* to identify it as a form object, e.g. *frmuserdetails*.

Command button

A command button (or just 'button') is a control which, when selected, carries out a specific operation. Buttons are most commonly used to help a user navigate the database system and are often linked to macros/scripts which carry out navigation, such as open a specific form when the command button is clicked.

A command button should always be named beginning with the letters *cmd* to identify it as a command button object, e.g. *cmdNextCustomer*.

Label

A label is an area of text on a form which is not used for data entry. Labels are most often used to 'label' areas of a form/layout which are used for data entry.

A label should always be named beginning with the letters *lbl* to identify it as a label object, e.g. *lblLastname*.

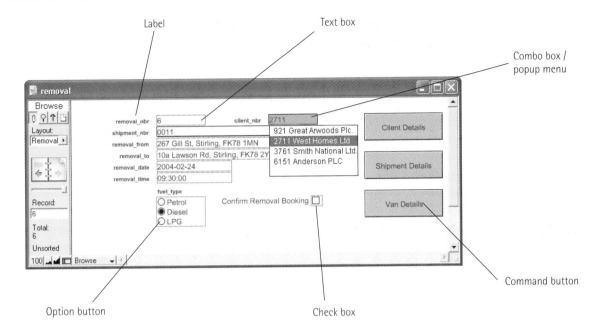

Figure 8.13 *User interface controls*

Text box

A text box is an area of text on a form which is most often used for data entry. In database systems, the text box is normally linked to a field in a table to allow the underlying data to be manipulated.

A text box should always be named beginning with the letters *txt* to identify it as a text box object, e.g. *txtHouseName*.

Combo box/pop-up list

A Microsoft Access combo box is a control which provides the user with a list of possible values for data entry via a menu. Depending on the requirements of the database system, the user's choices may or may not be restricted to the values that appear on the menu. FileMaker Pro calls this control a *pop-up list*.

A combo box should always be named beginning with the letters *cbo* to identify it as a combo box object, e.g. *cboCountry*.

Option button

An option button is an object which normally appears in groupings of at least two. Normally, only one button in the group can be selected because each button represents a value which will be stored in the database. Selecting an option button automatically deselects all others in the group. Option buttons are also known as radio buttons.

An option button should always be named beginning with the letters *opt* to identify it as an option button object, e.g. *optMale*.

Check box

A check box is a means of entering Boolean values. Boolean values have two states, i.e. yes/no, true/false, male/female, etc. If the box is checked then the *true* state is set or, if the box is unchecked, the *false* state is set.

A check box should always be named beginning with *chk* to identify it as a check box object, e.g. *chkConfirm*.

List box

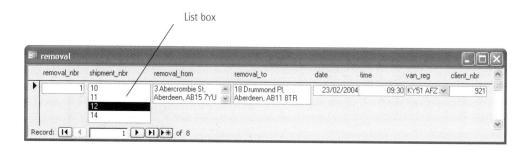

Figure 8.14 *List box control*

List box

A Microsoft Access list box is a control which displays a range of valid values and allows the user to select these from the box. The contents of the box can be scrolled up or down. The box does not disappear once a selection is made and the selected value is highlighted.

A list box should always be named beginning with the letters *lst* to identify it as a list box object, e.g. *lstShipment_nbr*.

Questions

1. What is a user interface?

2. Name and describe one technique for identifying the interaction required by a database system.

3. Paul has written a database to keep track of his MP3 files. He has three tables in his database: artists, albums and songs. He now wishes to create a user interface for his database.

He wants to create, amend and delete data from all three tables and print out the following reports:

- specific artist with their albums
- specific artist and their songs
- list of songs in a specific style, i.e rock, pop, punk, etc.

a Create a context diagram for the above system.

Hint: Paul will have to provide the system with the 'specific' artist etc. required.

b Detail the user interface required by listing the forms and menu items required as a user interface specification.

4. What is a macro/script and how might it be used in a database system?

5. Describe each of the following controls:

a command button

b text box

c label

d combo box/pop-up menu.

6. Amrita is a software developer who also plays squash for her local club. The club uses a database system to manage bookings for the squash courts. The database has three tables: members, bookings and courts.

Each of these tables has to be maintained and the following reports are required:

- current members
- bookings for the current week.

Amrita has been asked to produce a user interface for the club database.

a Create a context diagram for the above system.

b Detail the user interface required by listing the forms and menu items required as a user interface specification.

Data and Information

Chapter 1 gave an overview of data, information and knowledge. Information is the key part of any information system; without information the system is worthless.

Data, information and knowledge

Each of these items is summarised below:

Data

Data can be coded and structured for processing, generally by a computer system. The symbols used to represent the data are meaningless until they are placed in the correct context. The data then becomes information. The subtle difference between data and information is that information is in context, data is not.

Information

Information is data that is presented in context. Computer systems are not capable of understanding the data that they hold, therefore a human is required to interpret the data by placing it in an appropriate context. When the data is interpreted it becomes information.

Knowledge

Combining information with existing knowledge generates more knowledge. Whether something is information or not depends on how we perceive it; information is subjective. Information must always be set in a context that is meaningful to the person who requires it. Also, different people, depending on their existing knowledge, may interpret the same information in different ways.

An example

The characters **A1092** and **A1101** are stored in a data file on a computer hard disk. A route-finder computer program accesses this data to construct a route for John, who is travelling from Cavendish to Lowestoft. The program provides John with a choice of route – via the **A1092** or the **A1101**. This choice of route is presented as *information* because it is in *context*.

John has just finished listening to the traffic report on the radio, which said that there was a road accident on the **A1101** which was causing long delays. The information from the radio has provided John with *knowledge* about the **A1101**. John combines this knowledge with the information presented by the route-finder and selects the route via the **A1092** because it is free from delays.

Data about data – metadata

The most common definition of metadata is 'data about data'. A more helpful definition is that it is structured information about a resource. For example, a catalogue selling household items gives the following metadata about each one: the brand, price, colour and capacity. A library catalogue contains metadata relating to books: their titles, authors, publishers, etc. Metadata enables a resource to be found by describing the characteristics of the resource and how it can be accessed with a series of structured descriptions.

A data dictionary, created to aid the construction of a database, contains a description of the data in the database (Figure 9.1). A meta tag in a web page contains information about the contents of the web page (Figure 9.2).

Entity set	Name	Type	Size	Validation	Index/key
customer	customer_nbr	Integer		> 0, required	Yes, Primary key
customer	customer_name	Text	50	required	No
customer	customer_address	Text	255	required	No
customer	customer_postcode	Text	8	any valid postcode format	No
customer	customer_tel_nbr	Text	22		No

Figure 9.1 Sample data dictionary

```
<META NAME="AUTHOR" CONTENT="Perfect Papers">
<META NAME="COPYRIGHT" CONTENT="Copyright (c) by Perfect Papers">
<META NAME="KEYWORDS" CONTENT="Prelims, Information Systems, Computing,
Biology, Physics, English, Mathematics, SQA, Examination, Standard Grade">
<META NAME="DESCRIPTION" CONTENT="The very best prelim papers for SQA
National Qualifications and Standard Grade">
```

Figure 9.2 Sample metadata from a web page (http://www.perfectpapers.net)

In its broadest sense, metadata can be used to describe data structures, such as the technical specification of a file or the method of connecting to a database. Each element contains information relating to a particular aspect of the information resource, e.g. 'title' or 'creator'.

Why is metadata important?

Metadata is important because it can allow multiple programs to access the same data resource. If the program can interpret the structure of the data or the description of the content from the metadata, then the resource can be accessed.

Metadata makes it easier to manage or find information, be it in the form of web pages, electronic documents, paper files or databases.

For metadata to be effective, it needs to be structured and consistent across organisations. The UK government has developed a standard for metadata which allows government databases to be linked together. The system also allows private databases to be linked to government ones.

The UK government Department for Transport plans to link the national vehicle register with insurance company databases to identify uninsured vehicles and to introduce fines for people who ignore insurance renewal reminders. The Department for Transport system will require the metadata for each of the insurance company databases with which it plans to connect. This metadata will enable the Department for Transport software to access the insurance databases to check customer details.

Categorisation of information

In order to understand information we categorise it. This categorisation allows us to make judgements about the information which impact on how we use it. Information can be categorised in many different ways.

Source

This refers to the *origin* of the information – where it came from. Depending on the source of the information, people make judgements about the information's reliability or completeness.

Primary

All information originates from a primary source. To use a well-known phrase, information from a primary source is 'straight from the horse's mouth!'. Examples of information from a primary source would be a paper order form completed by a customer which is then entered into an order processing information system, or an electronic order form completed by a customer via a website. The source of the information in these examples is the customer and, because the order originates directly from the customer, is a primary source.

Normally, information that originates directly from the primary source will contain fewer errors because it has not been exposed to misinterpretation or incorrect processing by an intermediary (a secondary source).

Secondary

A *secondary* source of information essentially relays information from a primary source. The secondary source may change the format of the information or process it in some way before passing it on.

Any source which is not a primary source is a secondary source. Errors are more likely to occur in data from a secondary source than a primary source because secondary data has been processed. This means that the data has been changed in some way, and it is possible for errors to be introduced as part of the process.

An example of a secondary source could be an order form completed by a telesales operator in response to a telephone call by a customer. The customer, the primary source, is not completing the order form. The telesales operator is processing the customer's order and completing the form based on that processing. The information, the completed order form, has originated from a secondary source, the telesales operator.

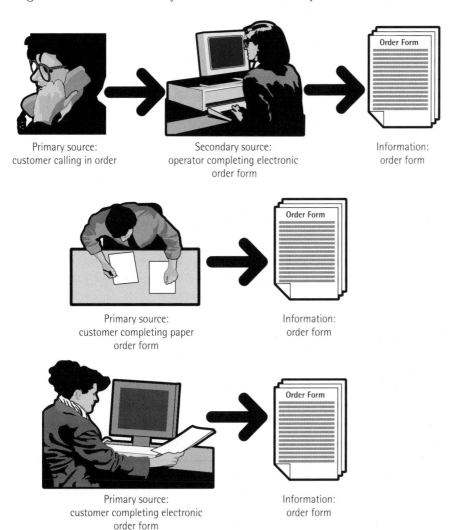

Primary source:
customer calling in order

Secondary source:
operator completing electronic
order form

Information:
order form

Primary source:
customer completing paper
order form

Information:
order form

Primary source:
customer completing electronic
order form

Information:
order form

Figure 9.3 Primary and secondary sources of information

In addition to coming from a primary or secondary source, information can originate within or outside the organisation in which it is processed.

Internal

All organisations generate a substantial amount of information relating to their operation. This information is vital to the successful operation of the organisation. Any information which originates and is processed within an organisation is classed as *internal*.

Marketing and sales reports, production and operational information, financial records and information held on local area networks within an organisation are all examples of information which would originate within the organisation.

External

Any information which originates from outside an organisation but is processed by it is classed as *external*. An order form completed by a customer is from an external source. The customer, who is the source of the order, is outside the company processing the order, and is therefore external.

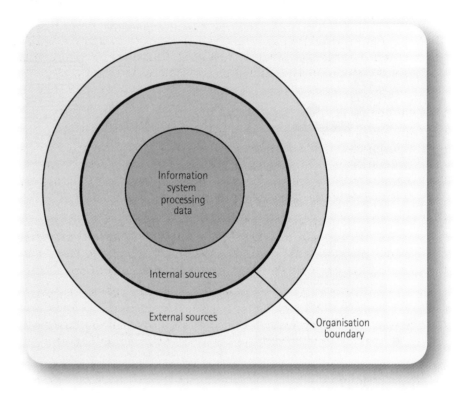

Figure 9.4 *Internal and external sources of information in relation to an organisation*

Nature

The nature of the information refers to whether the information is formal or informal, quantitative or qualitative.

Formal

Formal information is official and authoritative. It is meant to be taken seriously and is presented in a formal manner. It is usually prepared and verified more carefully than informal information, and its accuracy and reliability are also expected to be higher. Examples include a company's annual report to shareholders or a head teacher's message in a school magazine.

Informal

Informal information is more casual, less authoritative, less formally presented and possibly less reliable than formal information. A company chairman's off-the-cuff comments over a cup of coffee with colleagues would be informal. A quick e-mail to a friend giving them some advice would be informal.

Quantitative

Quantitative information is numerical data like test scores, numbers, statistics gathered with the use of survey instruments and check boxes, scales, etc. It is not meant to be open to personal interpretation, or influenced by opinion or experience.

Quantitative information gives objective, unbiased, hard facts about something. For example, the number of pupils achieving an A pass in Higher English in 2005.

The word 'quantitative' should remind you of the word 'quantity'. Qantities are measured, and this is how quantitative information is often gathered. Generally, if you can measure something objectively, you should do so.

Qualitative

Qualitative information is individuals' narrative reports of their experiences. Qualitative information is gathered with methods that are personal, direct and open-ended, with minimal constraints on what the answers to the questions may be. These methods include personal interviews, case studies, formal focus groups, participant observation, etc.

Qualitative information can enrich and enliven evaluations, for example with reports of common individual experiences. But, equally important, qualitative methods can allow the emergence, or discovery, of new, unanticipated information relevant to an organisation's operation.

Qualitative information can take the form of opinions and personal experience; it can help you understand people's perceptions and interpretations of circumstances and events. For example, a user's report on how easy it was to place an order on a company's website would be qualitative.

Some things, such as emotions, opinions and human reactions, cannot be measured objectively, so in these cases qualitative methods such as interviews, rather than quantitative methods of data collection, are used.

Level

The *level* of information refers to the level, within an organisation, at which the information is processed. This reflects the nature of the operations which are carried out. The level can be strategic, tactical or operational.

Strategic

The *strategic* level of an organisation is the top level of management. This level uses information to set aims and objectives for the long term, normally for the next three years or more.

Information used at the strategic level is mostly of a summary nature, so it usually contains less detail than information used at lower levels. However, because the information summarises the operations of the entire organisation, it is usually of greater scope than tactical and operational information.

At the strategic level, managers use a significant amount of external information because they are planning and making decisions about how the organisation will progress and function in the outside world. In order for strategic managers to make long-term decisions, they need to use forecasts of future conditions. These forecasts are created by processing historic and current information. For example, the board of a charity organisation that helps homeless people uses government projections about homelessness to

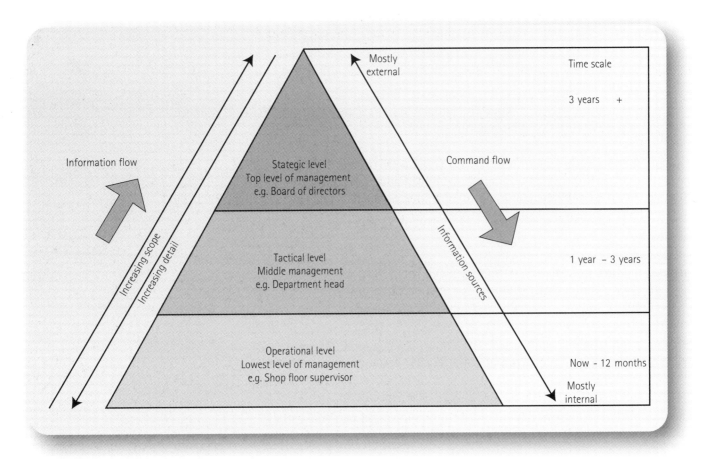

Figure 9.5 *Levels within an organisation*

assist its planning for the next three years and more. This information helps it decide where and when resources are required in order to assist people.

Information used at a strategic level will normally:

- originate from mostly external sources
- be summarised, containing less detail than information used by lower levels of an organisation
- deal with long timescales
- be used to set the aims and objectives of a whole organisation
- be related to large sections of an organisation's operation
- be synthesised from both past and present information.

Tactical

The *tactical* level of an organisation normally consists of middle-level managers. These managers are responsible for implementing the aims and objectives set by the strategic level of management. These aims and objectives are achieved by making plans for and decisions about what activities are to be carried out at an operational level (see below).

Middle-level managers, such as department heads, need information from internal and external sources. The information will be more detailed than that used by the strategic level and will allow the managers to make decisions which affect the company in the medium term, normally from one to three years.

Examples of information used by the tactical level of an organisation might be information about performance, productivity, current markets and resources.

Information of a tactical level will normally:

- originate from external and internal sources
- contain a reasonable amount of detail, but be less detailed than information used at the operational level
- deal with medium timescales
- be from both the past and the present time period
- be used to implement the aims and objectives of a whole organisation
- be related to a specific section of an organisation's operation.

Operational

Information at the *operational* level is used to complete the short-term and day-to-day operations of an organisation. Operational staff require very clear instructions to complete their work. The information used at this level is mostly internal, such as schemes of work, timesheets, etc., with little opportunity for the information to be misinterpreted.

Operational information contains a greater amount of detail than that used at the levels above because it refers to specific events, specific individuals or specific operations, e.g. James Watt, in technical support, has worked 48 hours this week. Similarly, because the information refers so closely to individual objects, it is very tightly scoped, i.e. for one specific purpose or task'.

Information of an operational level will normally:

- originate from mostly internal sources
- contain a large amount of detail
- be from the current time period only
- deal with short timescales
- be used to implement plans and decisions made at the tactical level
- be related to specific individuals, events or operations within specific areas of an organisation.

Level	Types of problems tackled	Time frame	Information needs
Senior management	Strategic e.g. 'We want to be the best at customer service'	Months–years	Highly summarised
Middle management	Tactical e.g. 'We will improve staff training'	Weeks–months	Summarised
Operational management	Operational e.g. 'We will hire motivational speaker John Mitchell to talk to staff on Friday'	Hours–days	Raw or slightly processed

Note that the timescales in Figure 9.6 above are relative and still cover the long, medium and short term.

Figure 9.6 Examples of the levels within an organisation

Time

All information is time-based to some extent.

Historic

Historic information is gathered and stored over a period of time. It allows comparisons to be made between an organisation's past and present positions and activities. Historic information can be used to identify a wide range of issues, including previous errors and successes and trends over time.

An example of historic information would be a report detailing sales made in the previous 12-month period.

Present

Information relating to the current operating time period of an organisation is classed as *present*. If a company produces a work schedule for each day, then a list of deliveries for the current day would be categorised as present. If the work schedule related to a weekly period, then a list of deliveries for Friday would also be categorised as present. The time frame within which information is categorised as 'present' depends on the organisation's working practices.

Future

Historic and present information can be processed to produce forecasts or predictions of possible future outcomes. Weather forecasters use information about current weather conditions and historic information about the climate to predict what the weather will be tomorrow, the next day and so on. The weather forecast is information which would be categorised as *future*.

Frequency

Frequency refers to when information becomes available, or to the interval between updates of the information being available.

Continuous

Information which is always available in real time is *continuous*. An example of this would be the statistics report created for a website. The report is created from all the data available until the moment the report was requested.

Any system which can generate reports based on the data gathered to the time of the report's creation is categorised as 'continuous'.

Periodic

Systems which make data available at specific intervals are categorised as *periodic*. These systems produce reports at a range of intervals such as:

- hourly
- daily
- monthly
- annually
- other time interval (e.g. every 12 hours)
- random (created by an event – such as a customer placing an order causing an order-fulfilment report to be created).

Use

Information can be used for various purposes, but generally these can be placed into one of three categories.

Planning

Planning provides a framework which defines the tasks to be completed by an organisation. It involves deciding, in advance, what tasks must be completed and how they are to be completed. The primary purpose of planning is to provide the guidelines necessary for decision making and follow-on actions, throughout an organisation. Planning provides opportunities to construct a sequence of activities that, when executed, will achieve the required aims and objectives of the organisation.

Planning involves decisions by management about:

- what is to be done in the future
- how to do it
- when to do it
- who is to do it and what resources are required.

Control

Control is the process of monitoring the operation of an organisation and taking the necessary action if the outcome of the monitoring is unsatisfactory.

Control involves comparing actual output with a standard. The standard could be a plan, a quality level or some other measurement of performance. For example, a plan is created for building a new house. The time, resources and funding allocated to each stage of the house building (foundations, walls, etc.) match the actual time, resources and funding used until the plumbing work for the house is started. Due to technical problems, the time spent on the plumbing is greater than that planned.

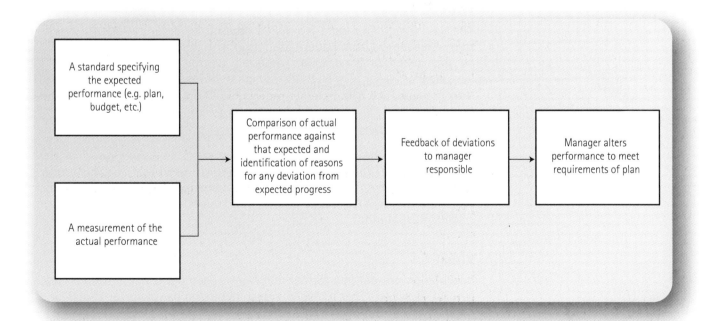

Figure 9.7 The control process

The extra time spent on the plumbing is detected because the actual progress is compared with the planned progress and found to be different. In order to control the situation, extra resources and funding are allocated to the electricians so that the electrical work is finished sooner, therefore bringing the project back on schedule.

Decision making

Decision making is the process of selecting an action or actions from those possible based on information available. Decision making involves working out the available options and then evaluating each option in turn. After this evaluation, a choice is made as to which option is to be executed, and finally the chosen option is carried out.

All levels within an organisation carry out planning, control and decision making to a greater or lesser degree. At higher levels, planning and control are closely linked. Management are concerned with monitoring progress against the company's plan, assessing the suitability of the plan and predicting future conditions. For example, a middle manager has a sales target to meet, but sales have been poor in the first two weeks of the month therefore she is working longer hours to try to meet the target.

At lower levels, management is concerned with the execution of the plan rather than control. For example, a supervisor at a bakery has been told to produce 200 loaves of bread. He tries to ensure that he and his staff complete the task as planned but it is not his responsibility to employ more staff to ensure that the required number of loaves are made. It is the responsibility of the level of management above to exercise control in this situation.

Form

Information can be created in a variety of forms, classified as written, aural or visual.

Written

The vast majority of data is created or used by organisations in *written* form. This ranges from paper-based reports to the tables of data presented on the screen of a computer monitor. Written information requires a language and a set of written characters in order for it to be recorded and read.

Aural

Information in the form of sound is categorised as *aural*. Speech is the most common form of aural information used by organisations. Examples of this include voice mail, conversations with customers, mobile phone text messages converted to speech and the spoken part of a sales presentation.

Visual

Information present in a format that can be seen but is not written is categorised as *visual*. This includes video, photographs, pictures, charts and graphs.

Type

Information types are based on the quantity of information given or the statistical basis on which they are constructed.

Detailed

The amount of *detail* in the information used within an organisation decreases as the levels of management are ascended. At the operational level the information used is very detailed and exacting. At this level it states exactly what is required or what has been completed, e.g. *'Today 210 loaves, 300 pancakes and 120 doughnuts were baked and shipped to our stores.'*

At the strategic level this information might be mentioned in a report only as *'Levels of production are in line with requirements.'* The top level of management doesn't need to know the number of pancakes baked; it only needs to know that production is as required.

Sampled

Information can be a *sample* of the total amount of information available. For example, an insurance company wishes to find out about the insurance requirements of potential customers. Rather than asking every potential customer, which would be costly, time consuming and unrealistic, the company commissions a survey of a sample of the potential customers.

Sampling is most often used for information which is required for processing at tactical or strategic levels.

Aggregated

Summarising information in terms of totals and statistics is an example of *aggregation*. This is vital for reports used at tactical and strategic levels. Managers at these levels only require an overview of the operation of the organisation; this can be provided by aggregated information.

An example of aggregated information is a report detailing the average sales per month over a two-year period.

Information characteristics

The quality of the information available can be influenced by a number of factors. For information to be of value to an organisation it must have certain characteristics which are appropriate for the information's intended use.

Relevance (or appropriateness)

Information should be *appropriate* for its intended purpose. For example, there is little point in using a report which details the most popular types of car sold by a company in a meeting about pay increases for the following year. The information about cars is irrelevant to the requirements of the meeting. Information about average salaries and the total wage bill *would* be relevant for the meeting.

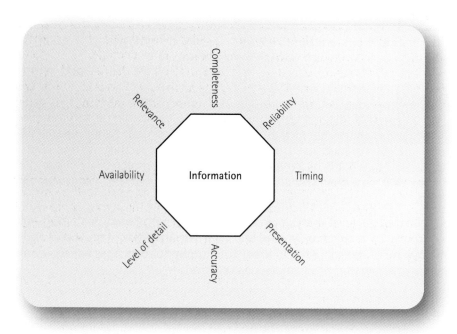

Figure 9.8 The characteristics of information

Accuracy

Information should be accurately recorded and stored. If not, then decisions based on it may be incorrect. For example, if government statistics from a census incorrectly show an increase in births within an area, plans may be made to build schools and construction companies may invest in new housing developments which are not actually needed.

The use of data recorded and held by information systems normally improves the accuracy of the stored information. Fewer errors are introduced during processing and checks can be made during data entry to reduce possible errors.

Completeness

Information used by management should be complete. Omissions may cause it to be flawed and therefore not suitable for its intended purpose. If incomplete information is used as the basis for selecting a course of action, then it is possible that the action is incorrect or inappropriate and that a different one should have been selected.

For example, if an organisation is given information regarding the costs of supplying a fleet of cars to its salesforce, and service and maintenance costs are not included, then costings based on the incomplete information will be considerably less than the actual cost of operating the cars.

Reliability (or objectivity)

If information is to be trusted and used for the purposes of planning, control and decision making, it must be reliable. *Reliable* or *objective* information should be factual and not influenced by personal emotions or prejudices. Much of the information on the World Wide Web appears to be useful for many organisations, but the reliability of some websites is, at times, questionable.

Timing

Timing refers to when information is available in relation to its purpose. Information received too late is irrelevant. For example, a company requires information about a trade fair to allow it to display and demonstrate a new product line. The information arrives two days after the final date for booking a place at the fair. The timing of the information is such that it cannot be used by the company.

Level of detail (or conciseness)

The level of detail in information should be appropriate to the task for which it's to be used. Too much detail and a significant amount of time will have to be spent interpreting the information before a decision can be made. Too little detail and there will be insufficient information for a decision to be made, or it may be made incorrectly.

For example, a safety manager for a chemical manufacturer has been given one week to upgrade the factory area to match new legislation on safety measures. The information relating to the new legislation is contained in three books. It may not be possible for the manager to extract relevant details in time to alter the procedures. The information may be complete, available now, of little cost and obtained legally, but it is not concise enough to allow any necessary changes to be made in the required timescale.

Presentation

The way that information is presented will impact on the quality of the information. If it is poorly presented it may be illegible or difficult to interpret. *Presentation* refers to the visual qualities of information rather than the level of detail. For example, a marketing report that includes graphs of statistics produced by a computer program would normally be of higher quality than a report containing hand-drawn graphs (see Figure 9.9).

Availability

Information must be available for use when required. Equally, the source data on which the information is based should also be available when the information is created. For example, a report is to contain an interview with a key member of staff about a new business customer, but the key member of staff is not available to complete the interview.

The value of information

It is possible for information to cost nothing but to be extremely valuable to an organisation. Equally, it is possible to use large sums of money to gather information which is of very little value to an organisation.

For information to be of value it must meet the organisation's information requirements and have the necessary characteristics to fulfil its intended purpose.

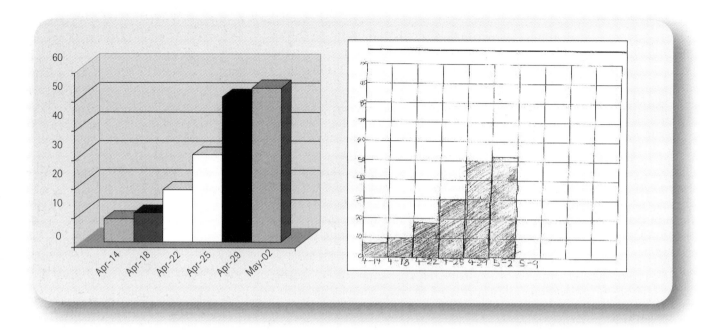

Figure 9.9 *Presentation and information quality*

Examples

Mary wishes to open a mail order business and commissions a survey of the people in her town to help her decide on the type of business she will operate. The survey is carried out on one Saturday afternoon and covers a total of 178 people, of which only 124 surveys were fully completed. The survey cost Mary over £700.

Charlie also wishes to open a mail order business and creates a survey which is completed on the World Wide Web to help him decide what type of business he will operate. Everyone who fully completes and submits a survey form is entered into a prize draw with the chance to win £200. At the end of the month, Charlie has received completed survey forms from 1078 people from all over the country, and the survey has cost him just over £200, including the prize!

In both these examples, information of value to the individual is collected, however the cost of the information in the first example is far greater than that in the second. The second set of information is more valuable because it covers a greater geographical area and number of people.

Questions

1. Describe how data becomes information and then knowledge.

2. What is metadata? Give two examples.

3. What is the main advantage of using a primary information source over a secondary information source?

4. Describe the difference between internal and external sources of information.

5. Discuss the advantages and disadvantages relating to information of a formal or informal nature.

6. What is quantitative information?

7. What is qualitative information?

8. State the main features of information which is used at a strategic level.

9. Give an example of information which would be used at an operational level rather than a tactical or strategic level.

10. Give an example of how historic and current information can be used to produce *future* information for an organisation.

11. What is meant by the *frequency* of information?

12. What is planning?

13. *Completeness*, *availability* and *presentation* are three characteristics of information. Name three other characteristics of information and describe how each would be considered when information is being prepared for a meeting of the strategic level of an organisation.

14. The DVD Company is an online retailer specialising in the sale of DVDs. At the start of each year the management of the company set sales figures for each month. The company has tools such as discount promotions, banner advertising, search engine adverts, e-mail newsletters and traditional magazine/newspaper advertising which can be used to advertise products available on the company's website.

   a Define the terms *data* and *information* using examples from above to illustrate your answer.

   b The DVD Company use the above targets principally as part of *control*.

     Explain why activities relating to the above targets are likely to be classed as *control* and give examples of the tasks that this control would consist of.

   c Compare the table and the chart in terms of *level of detail*.

Month	Website hits (000)	Sales revenue (000)
Jan	40	67.9
Feb	46	78.1
Mar	48	81.5
Apr	44	74.7
May	49	83.2
Jun	50	84.9
Jul	46	78.1
Aug	45	76.4
Sep	50	84.9
Oct	52	88.3
Nov	60	101.9
Dec	67	113.8

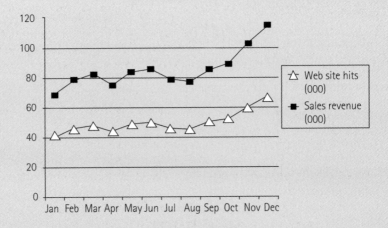

15. Compare a report which contains detailed information with one which contains information which has been aggregated.

Identify the levels for which each report would be more suitable.

16. What is meant by the *form* of information?

Organisational Information Systems

What are organisational information systems?

An organisational information system (OIS) is a collection of information systems which function across the operations of an organisation. The OIS in any organisation is a collection of subsystems, each processing data. Some of these systems are completely independent but most are interconnected. These interconnected systems can share data with the other information systems in the OIS.

Organisational information systems range in complexity, from those which simply replace human administrative staff by carrying out the same tasks using computer software, to complex intelligent systems which analyse and process data 'intelligently' to assist senior managers in the organisation.

In order for these systems to share data they need to be interconnected using communications technology. They also require data storage which permits secure and reliable simultaneous multi-user data access.

These systems are of four main types:

- data processing systems (DPS)
- management information systems (MIS)
- decision support systems (DSS)
- executive information systems (EIS).

Data processing systems (DPS)

Data processing systems are primarily concerned with processing numerical data, and function at the operational level within an organisation.

Organisations produce a significant amount of data on a daily basis. Each event which creates data is a **transaction** which should be recorded to ensure the effective and efficient operation of the organisation. Transaction data is essential to the operational, tactical and strategic levels of management and provide each level, when processed appropriately, with the information required to successfully manage the operations of the organisation.

The data from these transactions is stored in a database to be recalled later for processing, if required.

A data processing system:

- serves the most elementary day-to-day activities of an organisation
- supports the operational level of an organisation
- is often critical to the survival of an organisation
- is used mostly for predefined, structured tasks

- can have strategic consequences (e.g. airline reservation system)
- usually has high volumes of input and output
- provides data which is summarised into information by systems used by higher levels of management
- needs to be fault tolerant.

A typical data processing system is that found in nearly every supermarket.

Example

All goods in a supermarket have barcodes printed on them. When a customer takes items to the checkout, each item's barcode is passed over a laser scanner built into the POS (point-of-sale) terminal. This reads the barcode and sends it to the main computer.

The computer stores a database containing information about all the products the supermarket sells. The computer sends the price and a description of the item back to the POS terminal. The price is added to the customer's bill.

The price and the description are displayed on a small monitor. They also get printed onto the customer's receipt. The computer also notes that one of this item has been sold and will reduce the stock level for this item by one in the database. This way the computer always has a record of exactly how many of each item is in the supermarket. This is called automatic stock-taking.

At the end of each day, the computer sends out requests for more of those items which are running low.

A point-of-sale terminal in a supermarket

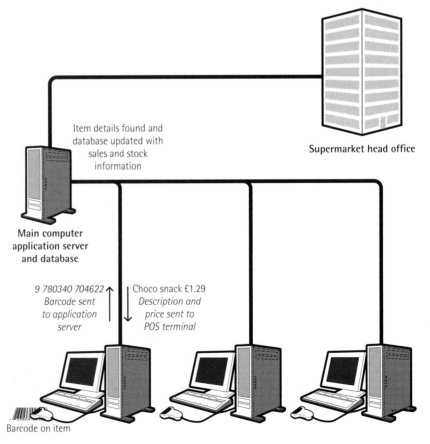

Item details found and database updated with sales and stock information

Supermarket head office

Main computer application server and database

9 780340 704622
Barcode sent to application server

Choco snack £1.29
Description and price sent to POS terminal

Barcode on item

Point-of-sale terminal   Point-of-sale terminal   Point-of-sale terminal

Figure 10.1 Point-of-sale system

The customer can pay his or her bill using EFT (Electronic fund transfer). A credit card or debit card is swiped through a card reader to read the customer's account details. These details and the amount of the bill are sent through the telephone system to the bank's computer system.

The correct amount of money is transferred, by the computer system, from the customer's account to the supermarket's account.

Types of data processing systems

Manufacturing and production systems

Manufacturing and production systems supply data to operate, monitor and control production processes in manufacturing or industrial settings. For example, purchasing and receiving raw materials or parts, shipping manufactured items, controlling robotic systems, keeping an inventory of parts and stock, quality control, etc.

An example is a manufacturing and production system concerned with quality control in a factory:

- gets information from measuring samples of products
- does statistical analyses of samples
- shows when operators should take corrective action.

Sales and marketing systems

Sales and marketing systems support the sales and marketing functions of an organisation by assisting the movement of goods and services from producers to customers.

Examples include:

- sales support – keeping customer records, follow-up
- telemarketing – using the phone for selling
- order processing – processing orders, producing invoices, supplying data for sales analysis and inventory control
- point-of-sale – capturing sales data at the till using an electronic scanner.

Finance and accounting systems

Finance and accounting systems maintain records concerning the flow of funds in an organisation and produce financial statements, such as balance sheets and income statements for budgeting, cost accounting, accounts receivable/payable, payroll, etc. Systems of this type were among the earliest systems to be computerised due to the prescriptive and repetitive nature of the tasks involved.

Human resources systems

Human resources systems deal with recruitment, placement, performance evaluation, compensation and career development of an organisation's workers. Examples include personnel record keeping, applicant tracking, job vacancies and positions, training and skills, allocation and monitoring of employee benefits.

Management information systems (MIS)

Management is all about planning, leading, organising and controlling. Accomplishing any of these tasks is difficult without information. Generating the right kind of information and being able to access it at the correct time are very important for accomplishing any of these tasks.

A management information system converts the data from one or more data processing systems into the information needed for carrying out the tasks mentioned above. The transactions recorded in data processing systems are analysed and reported on by an MIS. Management information systems use large quantities of input data and they produce summary reports as output.

It is common for each operating area within an organisation to use a dedicated management information system which has been customised to meet the requirements of that area, e.g. an inventory-related MIS will operate in the warehouse area of a company, but the accounts area will operate a finance and accountancy-related MIS.

Management information systems do not predict future events or scenarios. Executive information systems (EISs), which service the strategic level of an organisation, use the output from MIS systems as input.

For example, an MIS created for a supermarket collects past transactions from the data processing system, then summarises them to show total sales volume for each item on sale. The manager can then make decisions about which items to discontinue and which to increase in stock.

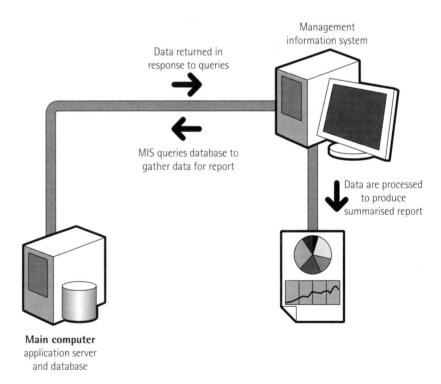

Figure 10.2 Supermarket management information system

A management information system:

- supports the tactical (middle management) level of an organisation
- is often dedicated to a particular area of an organisation
- uses large quantities of input data to produce summarised outputs
- allows users to develop their own custom reports to meet specific criteria

- does not predict or deduce
- is good for producing reports for repetitive routine problems, e.g. '*What are the current stock and reorder levels?*'
- produces output which is used by executive information systems.

Types of MIS reports

- fixed format, standard reports, hard-copy (on paper) and soft-copy (on screen) reports
- summary reports such as trends and totals
- exception reports – report out-of-the-ordinary events or values
- periodic reports – regularly scheduled (such as weekly, monthly, etc.)
- on-demand reports – response to unscheduled demand

Decision support systems (DSS)

A decision support system (DSS) is an interactive computer-based system intended to help managers make decisions. A DSS helps a manager retrieve, summarise and analyse decision-relevant data, normally at the tactical level of an organisation.

A DSS helps managers answer questions relevant to a decision situation. The questions may be sophisticated and complex, or basic and even simplistic. For example, a manager might query a database to ask questions like '*what are total sales for each of the last five years? What items have been out of stock for more than five days in a month? Which customers had the most orders (£ value) in 2005?*'. Managers may also ask questions like '*Are we meeting profit targets? Which salespersons are meeting their sales goals?*'.

A decision support system:

- is an interactive system
- supports, primarily, the tactical level within an organisation
- provides models, information and data manipulation
- assists unique and non-recurring, generally unstructured decisions
- supports analytical work
- assists multiple decisions and what-if analysis of data

Case Study

Water pollution in Egypt is increasing all the time. Pollutants to the water system come from several sources. One of the major sources is the disposal of untreated or semi-treated domestic sewage into water bodies. The low level of sanitation service, especially in rural areas (7 per cent at most), makes nearby streams (either canals or drains) the perfect places for inhabitants to dispose of their waste.

Many of the industrial establishments do not comply with the law, dumping their waste water, untreated, into surface water bodies as well as injecting it into ground water. Extensive drainage re-use within the Nile delta and direct drainage spillage into the River Nile, along the valley, increase the effect of agricultural pollution as well.

Current plans show that more land will be reclaimed and more industrial areas will be constructed, which will add more pollutants to the system if the effluents from these areas are not treated.

A Decision Support System for Water Quality Management (DSSWQM), developed by Delft Hydraulics (http://www.wldelft.nl), was applied to the River Nile to provide answers about the cost-effectiveness of possible measures to improve the Nile water quality inside Egypt.

Alternatives were considered, including treatment at pollution source (e.g. at an industrial site), raising the capacity/efficiency of existing treatment plants, and treatment before consumption (i.e. treating water before it is used as drinking water or for some other purpose).

The DSS results on costs and water quality indicated, amongst other things, that treatment at pollution source would not be cost-effective if applied to only some of the pollution sources along the Nile. On the other hand, if applied to all sources, treatment would be very costly. Alternative measures were therefore combined in different ways to form different tactical options.

Therefore, the output from the decision support system helped planners to investigate the best combination of treatment at pollution source and treatment before consumption measures.

Executive information systems (EIS)

Executive information systems provide executives with information in a readily accessible, interactive format. They are a management information system for use by executives at the strategic level. EISs are designed to analyse, compare and identify trends and outcomes to help an organisation to develop. This requires access to external information, such as changes to tax laws introduced by the government, and access to summarised information produced by internal data processing, management information and decision support systems.

Executive information systems let the chief executive officer, or other senior manager, access all levels of the organisation by producing summaries over the entire organisation, and also by allowing *drill down* to specific levels to obtain more detail.

Executive information systems are designed specifically to reduce the time required to produce information for strategic management purposes. They use new computer technology, in the form of data sources, hardware and programs, to place data in a common format, and they provide executives with fast and easy access to information.

They focus on helping executives assimilate information quickly in order to identify problems and opportunities. In other words, EISs help executives track their critical success factors. Each system is tailored to the needs and preferences of an individual user, and information is presented in a format which can be readily interpreted.

The presentation of such information requires a high level of graphics (such as charts and graphs) which can provide simplified representations of complex data. EISs are very expensive to run and require extensive staff support to operate due to their individuality and customised options.

An executive information system:

- supports the strategic level within an organisation
- provides highly graphical, summarised output
- can access internal and external sources of information
- allows drill-downs in detail to levels below
- requires a high level of technical support
- draws on summarised data from DPS, MIS and DSS.

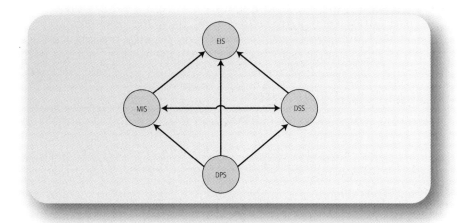

Figure 10.3 *Input/output inter-relationships between information systems*

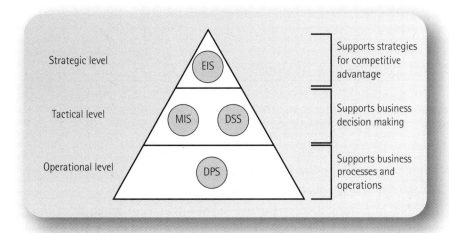

Figure 10.4 *Information systems and operating levels*

Expert systems

Expert systems are computer applications which perform tasks that would otherwise be performed by human experts. For example, there are expert systems that can diagnose human illnesses, make financial forecasts, and schedule routes for delivery vehicles.

Some expert systems are designed to take the place of human experts, while others are designed to aid them. Expert systems are part of a general category of computer applications known as **artificial intelligence**. To design an expert system, one needs a **knowledge engineer**. This is an individual who studies how human experts make decisions and translates this into terms that a computer can understand.

Components of an expert system

A typical expert system consists of three parts:

- A problem-domain-specific **knowledge base** that stores the encoded knowledge to support one problem domain, such as diagnosing why a car won't start. In a rule-based expert system, the knowledge base includes the if–then rules and additional specifications that control how it is used.

- An **inference engine** that implements the reasoning mechanism and controls the process. The inference engine might be generalised so that the same software is able to process many different knowledge bases.

- The **user interface** requests information from the user and outputs intermediate and final results. In some expert systems, input is acquired from additional sources such as databases and sensors.

Operation of an expert system

1 The user requests information via the user interface. This is normally in the form of a question.

2 This is taken as input to the expert system and is passed to the inference engine for processing.

3 The inference engine interrogates the knowledge base to identify the data required.

4 The resulting information is passed to the inference engine for further processing.

5 Once the query is complete the results are passed to the user interface for output.

Expert systems in a business context

Analysing business data requires significant skills. If this expertise can be captured in a computer program which can be used by less-experienced users, then there are significant benefits for the business.

Businesses have great interest in expert systems for the following reasons:

- to preserve expertise that might be lost through the retirement, resignation or death of an acknowledged expert

- to store information in an active form – to create an organisational knowledge base

- to create a mechanism that is not subject to human failings such as fatigue, worry and crisis

- to eliminate routine and unsatisfying jobs currently done by people

- to enhance the organisation's knowledge base by suggesting solutions to specific problems that are too massive and complex to be analysed by human beings in a short period of time.

Expert systems can generate economic benefits in many areas of a business: the speed-up of professional (and semi-professional) work; cost savings on operations; return on investment; improved quality and consistency of decision making; new products and services; captured organisational know-how; improvements in the way the company does its business; crisis management; and the stimulation of innovation.

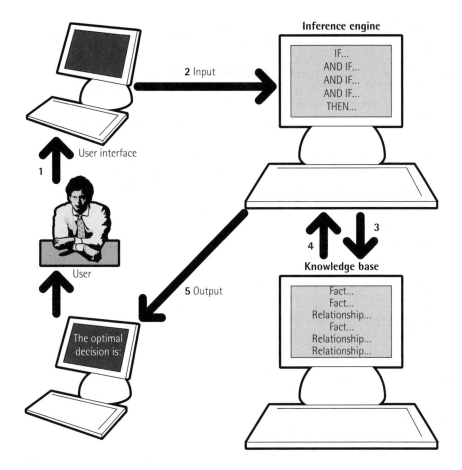

Figure 10.5 A basic expert system

Problems with expert systems

Only certain classes of problems can be solved using expert systems. Virtually all successful expert systems deal with problems of classification in which there are relatively few alternative outcomes and in which these possible outcomes are all known in advance. Many expert systems require large, lengthy and expensive development efforts. In the long run, hiring or training more experts may be less expensive than building an expert system.

The knowledge base of expert systems is limited; it cannot learn or change over time by itself. Keeping the knowledge base up to date is a critical problem. Expert systems can also only deal with limited forms of knowledge.

Organisational information system management strategies

Organisations working with information systems require strategies to allow them to control access to data, to protect their systems and data from unauthorised access, and to improve and update their information systems in response to changes in working practices or technology.

There are five key areas which organisations must consider as part of the development and operation of organisational information systems. These are:

- network strategy
- security strategy
- backup strategy
- upgrade strategy
- software strategy.

Network strategy

A network strategy allows an organisation to manage how data is distributed across the enterprise. In order for an organisation to function correctly, information must be available in the required location to facilitate management functions. This information is communicated via networked communications.

What is a network?

A network exists where any group of two or more computer systems are linked together. There are many types of computer networks, including:

- local-area networks (LANs): The computers are geographically close together (that is, in the same building)
- wide-area networks (WANs): The computers are farther apart and are connected by telephone lines or radio waves
- campus-area networks (CANs): The computers are within a limited geographic area, such as a campus or military base
- metropolitan-area networks (MANs): A data network designed for a town or city
- home-area networks (HANs): A network contained within a user's home that connects a person's digital devices such as computers, media devices (television, mp3 player, etc.) and network-enabled domestic appliances.

The most common of these are LANs and WANs.

In addition to type, networks are also classified according to their topology, protocol or architecture.

Topology

The way that the workstations are connected to the network through the actual cables that transmit data, the physical structure of the network, is called the **topology**.

Bus

A bus topology consists of a main run of cable with a terminator at each end (Figure 10.6). All networked devices (nodes) are connected to the cable. Ethernet and LocalTalk, which are two popular styles of small network, use a bus topology.

Advantages of a bus topology

- The bus topology is easy to implement and extend because all that is required is a **back-bone** cable into which the various nodes are attached (normally nodes are attached by means of a **drop cable**).
- Bus topologies are well suited for temporary networks that must be set up in a hurry and where costs are to be kept to a minimum (bus topology networks are the least expensive to implement).
- If one node fails then this does not cause the network to fail because data flows along the bus rather than through individual nodes.

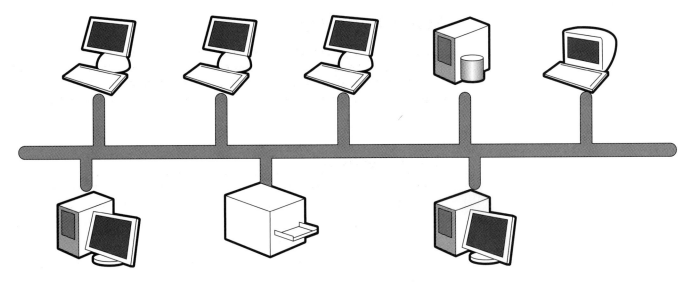

Figure 10.6 A bus topology

Disadvantages of a bus topology

- The entire network shuts down if there is a break in the back-bone cable. Data cannot 'jump' the break because there is no other physical connection along which it can travel.

- Bus topology networks require **terminators** at both ends of the backbone cable to indicate the physical end of the network. The terminator absorbs network signals so that they do not reflect back down the backbone and interfere with network traffic.

- If the network does have a failure it is very difficult to identify the problem due to the nature of the bus. Sometimes, the only way to discover the location of the network fault is to move the terminator along the bus, effectively shortening the length of the network, until the network functions again. When the network functions return, the point of the error should be immediately behind the terminator.

Bus topologies are not meant to be used as a stand-alone solution in large buildings or complexes because of these disadvantages.

Star

A star topology is designed with each node connected directly to a central node. The central node can be a network hub or switch.

The central node offers a common connection for all other nodes on the network. Each network device has its own direct cable connection to the central node. In most cases, this means more cable is required than for a bus topology. However, this makes adding or moving computers a relatively easy task; simply plug them into a cable outlet on the wall.

Data on a star network passes through the central node before continuing to its destination. The central node manages and controls all functions of the network. It also acts as a repeater for the data flow by boosting the network signal before sending it on to its destination.

Advantages of a star topology

- It is relatively easy to install and wire a star network because the construction of the network only involves running a cable from each network device to the central node. Each device on the network has its own connection to the central node therefore there are no disruptions to the network when connecting or removing devices.

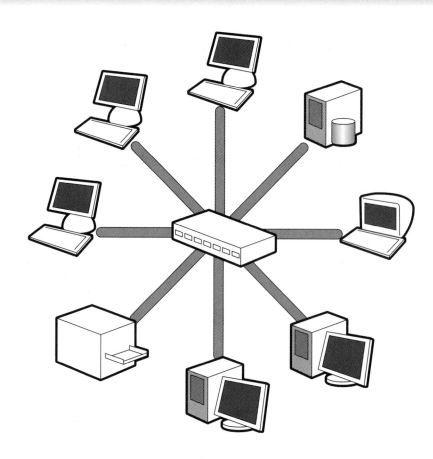

Figure 10.7 A star topology

- It is relatively easy to detect faults and to remove parts because if an error occurs it should only affect one node on the network, therefore making fault finding easier.

Disadvantages of a star topology

- Significantly more network cabling must be used to create a star network in comparison with a bus network.
- If the central node fails, all other nodes attached to it are disabled and unable to communicate with any other node on the network.
- Star networks are more expensive than bus topologies because of the cost of the hub or switch that is needed to function as the central node.

Ring

A ring topology consists of a set of nodes connected serially by cable. In other words, it is a circle or ring of computers. There are no terminated ends to the cable; the signal travels around the circle in a clockwise direction.

Under the ring concept, a signal is transferred sequentially via a 'token' from one station to the next. When a station wants to transmit, it 'grabs' the token, attaches data and an address to it, and then sends it around the ring. The token travels along the ring until it reaches the destination address. The receiving computer acknowledges receipt with a return message to the sender. The sender then releases the token for use by another computer.

Each station on the ring has equal access but only one station can talk at a time.

In contrast to the 'passive' topology of the bus, the ring employs an 'active' topology. Each station repeats or 'boosts' the signal before passing it on to the next station.

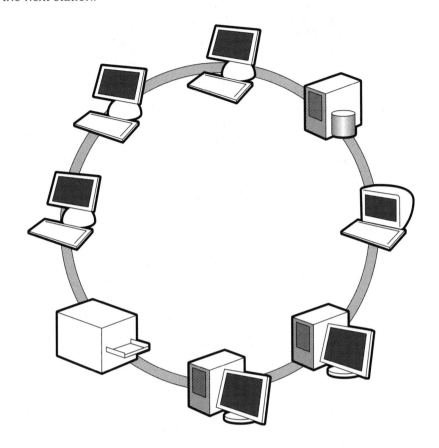

Figure 10.8 A ring topology

Advantages of a ring topology

- Networks based on a ring topology can grow without significantly impacting on the performance of the system.
- All stations on the network have equal access to communication because of the use of the token.

Disadvantages of a ring topology

- Ring networks require specialist hardware to function which makes them one of the most expensive topologies to implement.
- It is possible that the failure of one computer may impact on others in a clockwise direction around the ring.

Mesh

Mesh is a network topology in which devices are connected with many redundant interconnections between network nodes. In a true mesh topology every node has a connection to every other node in the network; this is called a fully connected mesh. In a partially connected mesh, there are still multiple connections but all nodes are not connected.

Full mesh topology occurs when every node has a circuit connecting it to every other node in the network. Full mesh is very expensive to implement but yields the greatest amount of redundancy, so in the event that one of the nodes fails, network traffic can be directed to any of the other nodes. Full mesh is usually reserved for back-bone networks.

A partially connected mesh topology is less expensive to implement and yields less redundancy than a fully connected mesh topology. With partially connected mesh, some nodes may be organised in a fully connected mesh but others are only connected to one or two nodes in the network.

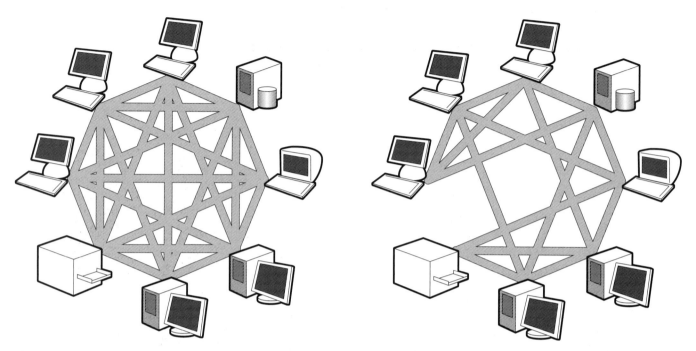

Figure 10.9 A mesh topology. Fully connected mesh (left) and partially connected mesh (right)

Advantages of a mesh topology

- Mesh topologies provide multiple physical paths along which data can travel. If one of the network connections is cut there will normally be another route available along which the data can travel to reach its destination.

Disadvantages of a mesh topology

- Mesh topologies are expensive to implement because of the multiple physical connections required to link each node on the network. These physical connections are difficult to install because of the sheer number involved.

- The complexity of the mesh makes it difficult to manage. Keeping track of the network data cables and their connections and routes becomes a very difficult task with such a complicated network.

- If an error occurs it can be difficult to detect, given the sheer number of network cables involved.

Tree

A tree topology is like a series of interconnected star topology networks. Tree topologies allow for the expansion of an existing network, and enable organisations to configure new networking to meet their needs.

Advantages of a tree topology

- Additional nodes can be added easily to individual segments, and segments can be added easily to the main central node.

- It is relatively easy to install and wire a tree network. Construction of the network involves simply running a cable from each network device to the central node in each segment, and then connecting the segments.

- Each device on the network has its own connection to the central node in the segment, and therefore there are no disruptions to the network when connecting or removing devices.

- It is relatively easy to detect faults and to remove parts. This is because if an error occurs it should only affect one node or segment on the network.

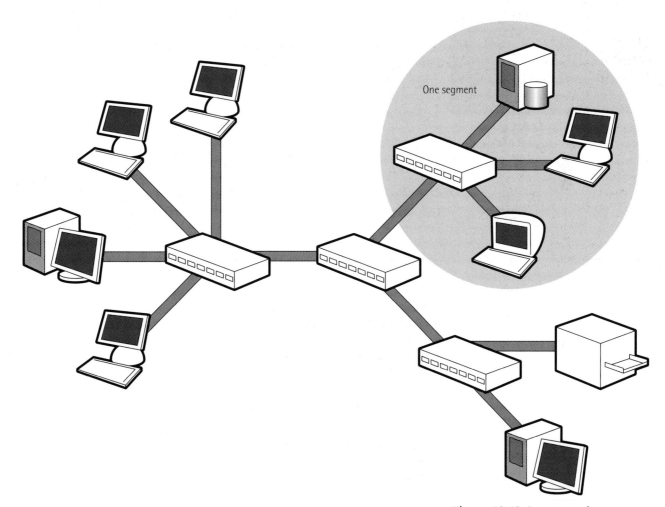

One segment

Figure 10.10 A tree topology

Disadvantages of a tree topology

- The overall length of each segment is limited by the type of cabling used. Again, the network fails if the central connecting node fails, and individual segments fail if the segment central node fails.

- Overall, the tree topology is more difficult to configure and wire than other topologies.

Protocol

A **protocol** is a set of rules and signals that governs communication between the computers on a network. These rules include guidelines that regulate the following characteristics of a network: access method, allowed topologies, types of cabling, and speed of data transfer.

All networks require a protocol to operate. One of the most popular protocols for LANs is called Ethernet. Another popular LAN protocol for PCs is the IBM token-ring network.

Ethernet

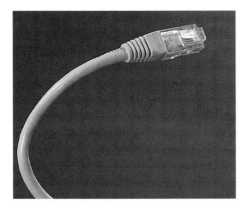

Cable such as this uses the Ethernet protocol to transmit data at high speeds

The Ethernet protocol is by far the most widely used. Ethernet uses an access method called CSMA/CD (Carrier Sense Multiple Access/Collision Detection). This is a system where each computer 'listens' to the cable before sending anything through the network. If the network is clear, the computer will transmit. If another node is already transmitting on the cable, the computer will wait and try again when the line is clear. Sometimes, two computers attempt to transmit at the same time. When this happens a collision occurs. Each computer then backs off and waits a random amount of time before attempting to re-transmit.

With this access method, it is normal to have collisions. However, the delay caused by collisions and re-transmitting is very small and does not normally affect the speed of transmission across the network.

The Ethernet protocol allows for bus, star or tree topologies. Data can be transmitted over a variety of media at speeds from 10 Mbps up to 1000 Mbps.

To allow for an increased speed of transmission, the Ethernet protocol has developed a standard that supports 100 Mbps. This is known as Fast Ethernet. The most recent development in the Ethernet standard is a protocol that has a transmission speed of 1 Gbps. Gigabit Ethernet is primarily used for back-bones on a network but is, increasingly, being deployed to the desktop to allow video conference and high-quality voice communications amongst other applications.

Architecture

Networks can be broadly classified as using either a peer-to-peer or client/server architecture.

Peer-to-peer

Peer-to-peer networking (often referred to simply as peer-to-peer, or abbreviated to P2P) is a type of network in which each node has equivalent capabilities and responsibilities in terms of communication on the network. No one node on the network stores all the files or controls the data traffic on the network.

Peer-to-peer networks are generally simpler than client/server networks, but they usually do not offer the same performance as client/server networks under heavy loads. Peer-to-peer networks are commonly found in homes or small business situations where only two or three machines are networked.

Client/server

In client/server architectures some computers are dedicated to serving the others. These computers, called servers, can be file servers, database servers, web servers and so on. The nodes on the network, the clients, access the server for data. The server then sends the data to the client in response to the request.

Wide-area networks

A wide-area network is a computer network that spans a relatively large geographical area. Computers connected to a wide-area network are often connected through public networks, such as the telephone system. They can also be connected through leased lines or satellites. The largest WAN in existence is the Internet.

The main purpose of a WAN is to provide reliable, fast and safe communication between two or more nodes with low delays and at a relatively low cost. WANs enable an organisation to have one integral network between all its departments and offices, even if they are not all in the same building or city, providing communication between the organisation and the rest of the world.

In principle, this task is accomplished by connecting the organisation to the network nodes by different types of communication media and applications. Since WANs are usually developed by the telecommunications companies of each country, their development is influenced by each country's own strategies and politics.

Distributed networks

A distributed network is a computer network on which processing is shared by many different parts of the network. Processing may be shared by client computers, file servers, print servers and application servers such as database servers.

Distributed processing enables the most efficient use of processing power because available processors can be dynamically assigned as either general or job-specific processors, depending on the type of work to be done and the existing workload. Distributed processing also enables duplication and distribution of key services, such as directory services which locate and identify resources on the network, so that full services remain available regardless of the failure of individual parts of the network.

Network hardware

A wide variety of hardware devices are required for the correct operation of a computer network.

Server

A **server** is a computer or device on a network that manages network resources. For example, a file server is a computer and storage device dedicated to storing files. Any user on the network can store files on the server.

A print server is a computer that manages one or more printers, and a network server is a computer that manages network traffic. A database server is a computer system that processes database queries.

Servers are often dedicated, meaning that they perform no tasks other than their server tasks. Multiprocessing operating systems allow multiple programs to run at the same time. A server, in this case, could refer to the program that is managing resources rather than the entire computer.

Hub

Hubs are commonly used to connect segments of a network. A hub contains multiple ports. When a block of data (a packet) arrives at one port, it is copied to the other ports so that all segments of the LAN can see all packets.

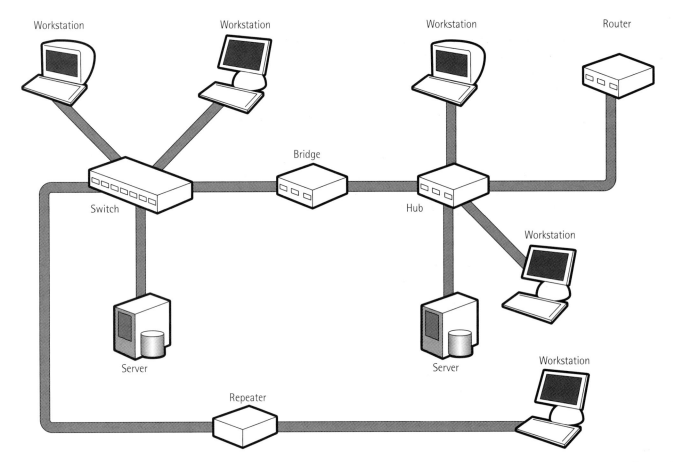

Figure 10.11 Network hardware

Hubs repeat everything they receive and can be used to extend the network. However, this can result in a lot of unnecessary traffic being sent to all devices on the network. Hubs pass on traffic to the network regardless of the intended destination; the PCs to which the packets are sent use the address information in each packet to work out which packets are meant for them. In a small network repeating is not a problem, but for a larger, more heavily used network, another piece of networking equipment (such as a switch) may be required to help reduce the amount of unnecessary traffic being generated.

Switch

A **switch** acts very much as a hub, however a switch can interpret the destination of data packets and will route packets only to their intended destination. This increases the capacity of the network because the incoming data is not repeated to every node.

Switches control the flow of network traffic based on the address information in each packet. A switch learns which devices are connected to its ports (by monitoring the packets it receives), and then forwards on packets to the appropriate port only. This allows simultaneous communication across the switch, improving bandwidth.

This switching operation reduces the amount of unnecessary traffic that would have occurred if the same information had been sent from every port (as with a hub).

Switches and hubs are often used in the same network; the hubs extend the network by providing more ports, and the switches divide the network into smaller, less congested sections.

An Ethernet switch in a busy office

Repeater

A network device used to regenerate or replicate a signal on a network is a **repeater**. Repeaters are used to regenerate or boost signals distorted by transmission loss. An example of transmission loss would be when a workstation to be placed on the network is a considerable distance from the nearest hub or switch. In such a case, a repeater would be required to boost the network signal due to the length of the cable linking the workstation to the hub/switch.

A repeater can also relay messages between segments of networks that use different protocols or cable types. Hubs can operate as repeaters by relaying messages to all connected computers. A repeater cannot do the intelligent routing performed by bridges and routers.

Router

A **router** is a device which forwards data packets along networks. It is normally connected to at least two networks, often two LANs or WANs or a LAN and an internet service provider's network. Routers are located at gateways, the places where two or more networks connect.

Routers use headers and forwarding tables to determine the best path for forwarding the packets, and they use protocols to communicate with each other and configure the best route between any two points on the networks. A router typically links networks which use different transmission protocols.

Bridge

A **bridge** is a device that connects two local-area networks (LANs), or two segments of the same LAN that use the same protocol. A bridge essentially joins together the two networks, allowing data transmission between them.

Network adapter

A **network adapter**, also known as a network interface card (NIC), is a computer circuit board or card that is installed in a computer so that it can be connected to a network. The network adapter encodes and decodes network transmissions.

Personal computers and workstations on a local area network (LAN) typically contain a network interface card specifically designed for the LAN transmission technology, such as Ethernet, adopted by the network. Network interface cards provide a dedicated, full-time connection to a network.

Structured cabling

Structured cabling is the only cabling that needs to be installed to meet the needs of telephone and data communications, now and in the future. It is a system that provides a very *structured* approach to the entire cabling system. Structured cabling creates a single mixed-media network, a network which uses a mixture of wireless, cabling and other transmission media, and which handles all information traffic, e.g. voice, data and video.

Structured cabling divides the entire network system into manageable blocks and then integrates these blocks to produce high-performance networks. The implementation of structured cabling means that the user's investment in network technologies is protected because the network is 'future-proof'. This means the network can be expanded as required, and new technology introduced as it becomes available.

In addition to investment protection, structured cabling also has administrative and management capabilities. All the cables originating from the various work locations are terminated on patch panels in network cabinets. Simple labelling and colouring of the cables provides a quick and easy way to identify network nodes. This means that all the administrative and management requirements of the network are located at a single point.

Network architecture keeps changing over time and the cabling architecture should be able to change with minimal inconvenience. The provision of central patch panels provides the flexibility to make additions, moves and changes to the network. The changes can be made simply by switching over the network cables. Structured cabling is also technology independent.

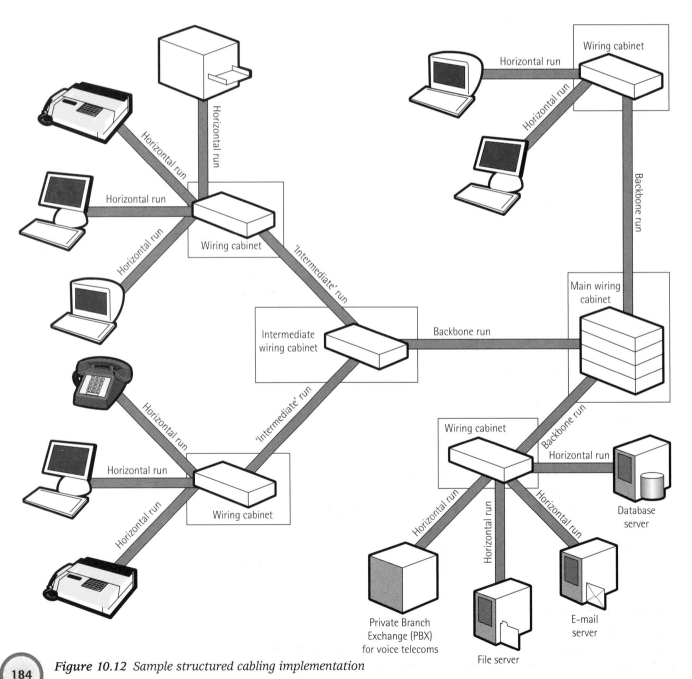

Figure 10.12 Sample structured cabling implementation

Another primary advantage of structured cabling is fault isolation. By dividing the entire infrastructure into simple manageable blocks, it is easy to isolate and test specific points in order to find faults and correct them with minimal disturbance to the network. A structured approach in cabling helps reduce maintenance costs too. Structured cabling systems are now the norm for small, medium and large networks.

Advantages of structured cabling

- **Consistency** – A structured cabling system means the same cabling system is used for data, voice and video.
- **Support for equipment** – A standard-based cable system will support applications and hardware even with 'mix & match' manufacturers.
- **Simplify moves/adds/changes** – Structured cabling systems can support any changes within the system.
- **Simplify troubleshooting** – Problems are less likely to down the entire network, easier to isolate and easier to fix.
- **Support for future applications** – Structured cabling systems support future applications like multimedia, video conferencing, etc. with little or no upgrade problems.

Disadvantages of structured cabling

- **Cost** – There are significant additional hardware costs when installing a network which uses structured cabling.
- **Required expertise** – The planning and design of structured cabling is a highly skilled job which requires specialist expertise for which an organisation may have to pay.

Network software

All computer networks require software in order to function. Computers and other devices connected to the network must be **network-enabled**. This means that these devices must run a network operating system. In addition, networks often require management tools which assist in the monitoring and administration of the network.

Network operating systems

A **network operating system** is any operating system product which has device drivers and communication software which allow connection to network services.

Network operating systems have existed for more than 30 years. The UNIX operating system was designed from the beginning to support networking. In its early forms, Windows did not support networking, so Novell NetWare became the first popular network operating system for the personal computer (Windows 95 and Windows for Workgroups were Microsoft's first network operating system products).

Today, nearly any consumer operating system qualifies as a NOS due to the popularity of the Internet and the need to support basic Internet Protocol (IP) networking.

Network management systems

Network management systems are a collection of tools (often referred to as subsystems) which allow the performance, setup, security and functionality of the network to be controlled and managed.

Network management systems normally consist of a main application and an associated central database which collects data, in the form of logs, from small programs, called **agents**, which run on or monitor the network and the computers and other devices attached to it. Agents store data in their own databases and supply them proactively or reactively to the central database.

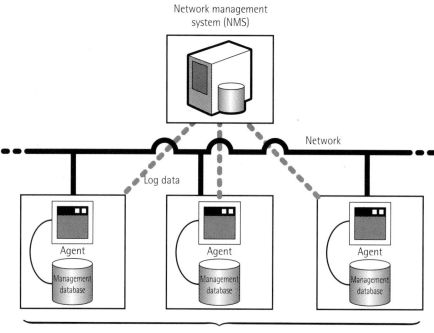

Figure 10.13 *Network management system*

The information gathered by these agents is used to monitor and control network performance, network configuration, network faults and network security.

Performance management

The goal of performance management is to measure and control network performance so that it can be maintained at an acceptable level.

Performance tools analyse the network to establish current performance and to set tolerances for how much that performance can fluctuate before action is required. When a performance threshold is exceeded, an alert is generated and sent to the network management system so that suitable action can be taken by the network administrator.

Configuration management

Configuration management monitors the configuration of the network and devices attached to the network. The effects of different items of hardware and software on network operation can be logged and managed using configuration management software.

When a problem occurs, the log created by the configuration management software can be searched to help identify the nature of the problem and possible solutions.

Fault management

Fault management detects, logs, notifies users of, and, if possible, automatically fixes network problems to keep the network running effectively.

Fault management involves determining the symptoms of the problem and then isolating the problem so that it can be remedied. The problem is then fixed and the solution is tested. Finally, the detection and resolution of the problem is recorded.

Security management

Security management provides control of access to network resources, according to local guidelines, so that the network cannot be sabotaged (intentionally or unintentionally) and sensitive information cannot be accessed by those without appropriate authorisation.

A security management subsystem, for example, can monitor users logging onto a network resource and can refuse access to those who enter inappropriate passwords.

Security management subsystems allow network administrators to identify sensitive network resources (including systems and files) and determine which users are allowed access. They also monitor access to sensitive network resources and log inappropriate access to these resources.

Network accounting and statistical systems

Network accounting systems measure network use so that individuals or groups of users on the network can be regulated appropriately. Such regulation reduces network problems (because network resources can be allocated according to availability or capacity) and maximises the fairness of network access across all users.

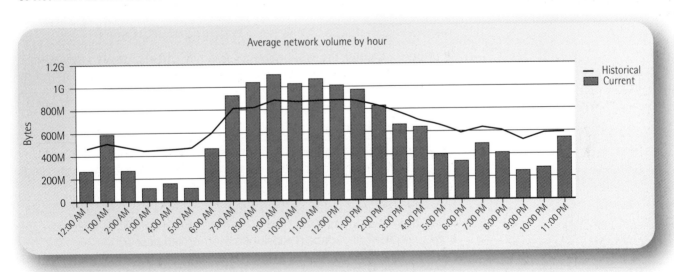

As with performance management, the first step toward appropriate account management is to measure the current use made of network resources (file servers, printers, etc.) by users. Analysis of these results provides information about current usage patterns, and limits can be set for the amount of any resource that a user can make use of. These limits are called **quotas**.

Figure 10.14 Example report from a network accounting system

For example, a user may be allocated a quota of 300 Mb on the main file server. Once this quota is reached the user will be prohibited from using additional storage.

Each user has an account which contains the user name, passwords, quotas and other information which the user requires to access the network. This account is often stored in a database and is maintained and accessed by the account management software and the network operating system.

Developing a network strategy

The network strategy details the types of networking currently used by an organisation and the requirements for future networking developments. These requirements can be broken down into five main areas:

- **Data transfer (traffic):** How much data will be moving across the network and what are the projections for the future? Is the network carrying voice, data and video?
- **Distribution/coverage:** Where is the network to be located? Which areas of the organisation will be granted access and to what extent? Is structured cabling being used?
- **Access and security:** What precautions prevent unauthorised access to the computer systems and data?
- **Facilities:** What applications and tools are available to process data on the network? What future applications are required?
- **Storage capacity:** What is the current capacity for data storage on the network and what are the projected requirements for storage?

The network strategy of the organisation sets out the current position for these areas and indicates how future development will be undertaken.

Security strategy

All organisations suffer from potential breaches of security. These can range from innocent attempts to access restricted resources to deliberate and prolonged attacks on computer systems and networks.

In order to counter the wide range of security threats, organisations must consider the precautions they need to take and how they will respond in the event of a security problem or attack.

Security of data

Data security refers to the level of protection data stored within the organisation has from unauthorised access, and potential data loss due to failure of hardware and/or software.

Unauthorised access can be from within or from outside the organisation, intentional or unintentional. There are a number of methods which can be used to prevent or reduce the risk of unauthorised access.

Access rights

An organisation can protect sensitive data from unauthorised access using a system of security access rights or privileges which are allocated to users. Access to data is then restricted to only those users who have been allocated the appropriate security access rights.

Also access rights can be allocated to specific network devices therefore limiting access to sensitive data from those devices regardless of the access rights of the individual user.

These access rights differ depending on the operating system being used, but some of the rights involve:

- read – authority to read specific data
- write – authority to write data (i.e. create, modify and delete)

- create – authority to create data but not to modify or delete it
- delete – authority to delete data
- modify – authority to make changes to data
- execute – authority to run programs on a particular computer.

Network administrators will have the highest level of access so that they can control and maintain the network. The level of access given to other users will depend on the nature of their work and the data access needs of their position in the organisation.

Password protection and guidelines

Computer and network accounts normally make use of a user name to uniquely identify the users, and a password for verification of the user's identity. Many hackers make use of the fact that many computer users use insecure passwords which can be easily guessed using a variety of methods to gain access to systems.

Password construction guidelines

Poor, weak passwords are easily cracked, and put an organisation's network at risk. Therefore strong passwords are required. It also helps if the passwords can be remembered easily. Some general rules to help construct strong, almost unbreakable passwords are:

- Passwords should not be based on well-known or easily accessible personal information.
- Passwords should contain at least 8 characters.
- Passwords should contain at least 5 upper-case letters (e.g. N) or 5 lower-case letters (e.g. t) or a combination of both.
- Passwords should contain at least 2 numerical characters (e.g. 5).
- Passwords should contain at least 1 special character (e.g. £).
- A new password should contain at least 5 characters that are different from those found in the old password which it is replacing.
- Passwords should not be based on users' personal information or that of his or her friends, family members, or pets. Personal information includes user name, name, birthday, address, phone number, National Insurance number or any variations of this information.
- Passwords should not be words that can be found in a standard dictionary (English or foreign) or are well-known slang or jargon.
- Passwords should not be trivial, predictable or obvious.
- Passwords should not be based on publicly known fictional characters from books, films, and so on.
- Passwords should not be based on an organisation's name or geographic location.

Password protection guidelines

1 Passwords should be treated as confidential information. No member of an organisation should give, tell, or hint at their password to another person, including IT staff, administrators, superiors, colleagues, friends or family members, under any circumstances.

2 Passwords should not be transmitted electronically over the unprotected Internet, such as via e-mail. However, passwords may be used to gain

remote access to an organisation's resources via a secured virtual private network or SSL-protected website.

3   Users should not keep an unsecured written record of passwords, either on paper or in an electronic file. If it proves necessary to keep a record of a password, then it must be kept in a controlled access place if in hardcopy form, or in an encrypted file if in electronic form.

4   If possible, don't use the same password to access multiple systems. Change passwords for different network accounts.

5   Compromised passwords should be reported to the organisation's network administrator and the password changed immediately.

Encryption

Encryption is the process of changing data into a form that can be read only by the intended receiver. To decipher the message, the receiver of the encrypted data must have the proper decryption key. In traditional encryption schemes, the sender and the receiver use the same key to encrypt and decrypt data.

Public-key encryption schemes use two keys: a public key, which anyone may use, and a corresponding private key, which is possessed only by the person who created it. With this method, anyone may send a message encrypted with the owner's public key, but only the owner has the private key necessary to decrypt it. PGP (pretty good privacy), DES (data encryption standard) and SSL (secure sockets layer) are three of the most popular public-key encryption schemes.

Secure sockets layer is a technology used on the Internet to secure web pages and transactions by means of public-key cryptography. A digitally secure communications channel is established between the server and the client after which all data is encrypted. The message is certified as genuine

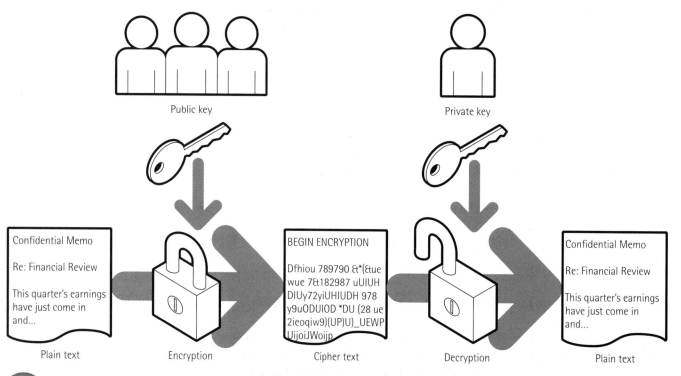

Figure 10.15 An example of public/private key encryption

through the use of a digital signature, and trust in an individual or a website is ascertained by using digital certificates which are signed by a certificate authority acting as a 'trusted third party'.

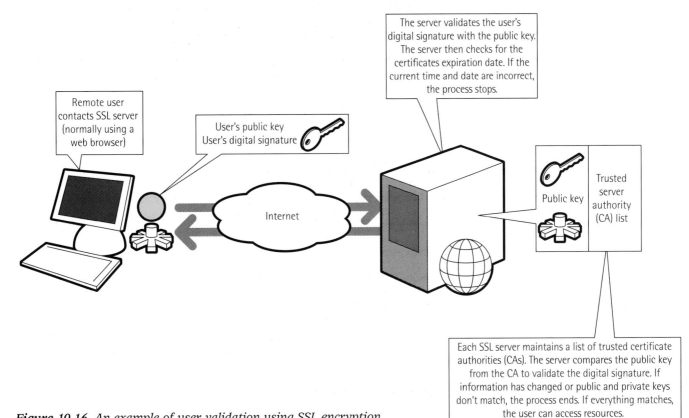

Figure 10.16 *An example of user validation using SSL encryption*

Virus, Trojan and worm protection

There is an ever increasing array of computer programs which can attack an organisation from within or from outside.

Virus

A virus is a program or piece of code that, without your knowledge, is loaded and run on your computer. Viruses can also replicate themselves, normally by attaching themselves to existing program files.

A simple virus that can make a copy of itself over and over again is relatively easy to produce and **virus development kits** can be freely downloaded from the World Wide Web for malicious coders and hackers to use.

Even a simple virus is dangerous because it will quickly use all available memory and bring the system to a halt. An even more dangerous type of virus is one capable of transmitting itself across networks and bypassing security systems.

While there are thousands of variations of viruses, most fall into one of the following six general categories:

- **Boot sector virus:** Replaces or implants itself in the boot sector. The boot sector is an area of the hard drive (or any other disk) accessed when you first turn on your computer. This kind of virus can prevent you from being able to start your computer.

- **File virus:** Infects programs. These infected programs then spread the virus by infecting associated documents and other programs whenever they are opened or run.

- **Macro virus:** Written using a macro programming language, these viruses affect Microsoft Office applications, such as Word and Excel, and account for about 75 per cent of viruses found in the wild. A document infected with a macro virus generally modifies a pre-existing, commonly used command (such as Save) to trigger its payload upon execution of that command.

- **Multipartite virus:** Infects both files and the boot sector. A double attack that can reinfect your system dozens of times before it's caught.

- **Polymorphic virus:** Changes code whenever it passes to another machine; in theory these viruses should be more difficult for antivirus scanners to detect, but in practice they are usually not that well written.

- **Stealth virus:** Hides its presence by making an infected file appear not to be infected, but doesn't usually stand up to antivirus software.

Trojan

A Trojan horse (often referred to just as a Trojan) is a destructive program that pretends to be a helpful application or file. Unlike viruses, Trojan horses do not replicate themselves but they can be just as destructive.

Once installed, a Trojan can allow hackers to gain access to your computer system and files. A common use of Trojan horses is to allow spammers (junk e-mail senders) to send thousands of e-mails from another computer. The benefits to the spammer are that they can increase the number of e-mails being sent by using additional computer power, and that the e-mails cannot directly be traced back to them. This allows the spam e-mail to by-pass some of the anti-spam software which many people use to protect themselves from spam e-mail.

A particularly prominent type of Trojan horse is **spyware**. Spyware refers to any software that secretly gathers user information through the user's Internet connection without his or her knowledge, usually for advertising purposes. Spyware applications are typically bundled as a hidden component of freeware or shareware programs that can be downloaded from the Internet; however, it should be noted that the majority of shareware and freeware applications do not come with spyware. Once installed, the spyware monitors user activity on the Internet and transmits that information in the background to someone else. Spyware can also gather information about e-mail addresses and even user names/passwords and credit card numbers.

Once an attacker obtains user names and passwords, systems believed to be secure become vulnerable. Attackers may then access sensitive information, or in the case of Valve Software, corporate intellectual property.

In September 2003, attackers broke into the e-mail of Valve founder Gabe Newell. In a deliberate attack, they installed Trojans on many of the computers at the game developer's studio to capture source code. The Trojan used logged the keystrokes made on the keyboards of the computers.

'This [keystroke] recorder is apparently a customized version ... created to infect Valve (at least it hasn't been seen anywhere else, and isn't detected by normal virus scanning tools)', said Newell in a message board posting in October 2003.

The source code for Half-Life 2 was stolen, delaying the release of this highly anticipated PC game and costing Valve and Vivendi Universal Games an inestimable amount of revenue.

Worm

A worm is a self-replicating program that reproduces itself over a network, using the resources on one machine (processor time, memory, hard disk, network connection, etc.) to attack other machines. A worm is not quite the same as a virus, which is normally a piece of program code that inserts itself into other programs.

The most impressive example of a worm is the Internet worm which struck on 3 November, 1988, a day now known as Black Thursday. Network administrators around the world came to work on that day and discovered that their networks of computers were suffering under a huge processor load. If they were able to log in and generate a system status listing, they saw what appeared to be dozens or hundreds of 'shell' (command interpreter) processes. If they tried to kill the processes, they found that new processes appeared faster than they could kill them. Re-booting the computer seemed to have no effect and within minutes, after starting up again, the machine was overloaded by these mysterious processes.

These systems had been invaded by a worm. The worm had taken advantage of lapses in security on systems that were running particular versions of the network operating system UNIX. These lapses allowed it to connect to machines across a network, bypass their security, copy itself and then proceed to attack still more machines. The massive system load was generated by multitudes of worms trying to propagate the epidemic.

The Internet had never been attacked in this way before, although there had been plenty of speculation that an attack was in store. Most network administrators were unfamiliar with the concept of worms and it took some time before they were able to establish what was going on and how to deal with it.

Antivirus software

An antivirus utility searches a hard disk for viruses and removes any that are found. Most antivirus programs also offer a level of protection against Trojans and worms.

Most antivirus programs include an auto-update feature that enables the program to download profiles of new viruses so that it can check for the new viruses as soon as they are discovered. All computer systems, and particularly those which are connected to the Internet, should have antivirus software installed to provide protection from malicious code.

Intrusion detection

Intrusion detection involves a set of system tools designed to recognise unauthorised and malicious entry into a network or computer system, including monitoring for suspicious network data packet traffic, tracking intruders and identifying where the security hole is.

Many intrusion-detection tools can also detect a variety of misuse originating from inside the network in addition to attacks from outside.

Denial of service

A 'denial-of-service' attack, or DoS, is characterised by an explicit attempt by attackers to prevent legitimate users of a service, such as a website, from using that service. Examples include:

- attempts to 'flood' a network or server, thereby preventing legitimate network traffic
- attempts to disrupt connections between two machines, thereby preventing access to a service
- attempts to prevent a particular individual from accessing a service
- attempts to disrupt service to a specific system or person.

The most common type of DoS attack is one which floods a network or server with data. This type of attack involves a massive stream of information sent to a target with the intention of flooding it until it crashes or can no longer take legitimate traffic. Unlike most other hacking attacks, it does not involve the attacker gaining access or entry into the targeted server or network.

The attacker sends network data in the form of 'pings' – small packets of data used as a signal between computers. If the attacking computer (the pinger) lies about its real address, the target computer can't return the ping to make the connection. In this case, the target waits and finally gives up. Eventually, this can overwhelm a server.

Other types of attack may include a denial of service as a component, but only as part of a larger attack. Illegal use of resources may also result in denial of service. For example, an intruder may use an organisation's anonymous file transfer area as a place to store illegal copies of commercial software, consuming disk space and generating network traffic as other hackers access the area to download the software.

Firewall

The original meaning of firewall was 'a wall constructed to prevent the spread of fire'. Computer firewalls are constructed to prevent unwanted intrusions from the Internet or other network into a PC or network. A firewall is required because threats arise when an attacker exploits a combination of a PC's unique IP (Internet Protocol) address and one or more of the thousands of TCP (Transmission Control Protocol) and UDP (Universal Datagram Protocol) ports that are used for communications over the network.

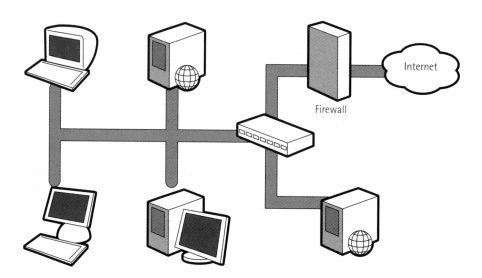

Figure 10.17 An example of a firewall protecting a nework

Firewalls watch these thousands of ports, which are present in both dial-up and broadband Internet connections, and deny access to unauthorised traffic. Hardware-based firewalls are usually integrated into router and gateway products and sit between your PC or network and a cable or DSL modem. Software-based firewalls run on your PC or network server.

More important than the router's actual firewall, however, is the fact that it usually incorporates a NAT (network address translation) server that hides the IP addresses of the network computers (and therefore, their existence) from anyone outside the local network.

Hardware maintenance

To prevent loss of data it is important that standard maintenance routines are completed at regular intervals. These include:

- taking backups of important files
- scanning the hard disk for malicious software
- running disk-checking tools to test for defects on the hard disk and other storage
- running antivirus software
- checking server logs for unauthorised activity.

These operations help maintain data security and reduce the risk of unauthorised access.

Disaster recovery

Disaster recovery involves a series of actions to be taken in the event of major unplanned outages (computer or network failures) to minimise their adverse effects. Disasters can result from events such as:

- hacker attacks
- malicious computer code (including viruses, Trojans and worms)
- electric power failures
- underground cable cuts or failures
- fire, flood, earthquake and other natural disasters
- mistakes in system administration.

The related concept of business continuity involves insuring that an organisation's critical business processes, including those utilising IT systems, can be maintained in the event of a disaster.

Why is disaster recovery important?

When executed well, disaster recovery procedures save large sums of money. Disaster recovery can also improve the quality of human life, and it may even save lives.

The terrorist attacks of 11 September in the US, for example, caused large-scale network outages. Among the affected systems were some of the fibre optic telecommunications services provided by Verizon (a US telecommunications company). Besides the financial impact to Wall Street firms from lost data networks, the loss of voice contact with friends and family greatly affected many individuals on that day.

Disaster recovery planning

The best approach to disaster recovery focuses primarily on planning and prevention. While the damage resulting from the events of 11 September could not have been anticipated, many other more typical disaster scenarios can be analysed in detail.

For those events that can't be prevented, a computer/network disaster recovery plan takes into account the need to:

- detect the outages or other disaster effects as quickly as possible
- notify any affected parties so that they can take action
- isolate the affected systems so that damage cannot spread
- repair the critical affected systems so that operations can be resumed.

Disaster recovery techniques

All good computer/network disaster recovery plans consider the three main components of operations: data, systems and people.

Most organisations rely on some form of additional capacity (extra servers, computer systems, hard disk storage, IT staff, etc.) to make possible the recovery of data and systems. The additional capacity allows secondary data or system resources to be pressed into service on short notice should primary resources fail or otherwise become unavailable.

The use of backup strategies, for example making copies of critical data at a given point in time so that they can be restored later if needed, is vital in restoring systems. Organisations may also choose to replicate servers, by creating backup images of them, and other critical hardware at multiple locations to guard against any single point of failure.

Integrity of data

Data integrity refers to the accuracy of the data stored by an organisation. Data can become inaccurate in some of the following ways:

- **Error in data collection:** Mistakes in collecting data.
- **Transmission errors:** Errors which occur when data is changed during transmission due to a hardware failure. For example, files being sent across the Internet from one computer to another may become corrupt through sending, which would make them unusable.
- **Read errors:** When data is misread.
- **Transcription errors:** Errors that are made when data is entered, for example a typing error by a data entry operator.
- **Unauthorised modification:** Errors introduced by unauthorised access to a computer system or network.

Inaccurate data can have serious consequences for the operation of an organisation and, if inaccurate personal data is held, can lead to prosecution under the terms of the Data Protection Act.

Privacy of data

Privacy is an individual's right to be secure from unauthorised disclosure of information about them stored in documents and computer files. Organisations have a duty to protect the privacy of data which they hold about members of the public and their staff, and to process this data only in the manner for which it was intended.

Within the European Community privacy of electronic data is protected by The Directive on Privacy and Electronic Communications. This details how electronic information can be used in a variety of circumstances, including SMS messaging, internet cookies, spam, etc.

Within the UK, the Data Protection Act also provides security against data which is erroneous or being used for a non-approved purpose. Within the UK, organisations which store data of any kind must abide by the Act and its principals, which are detailed in Chapter 12.

Policies and procedures

Most organisations have a range of policies or procedures associated with the operation of their computer systems. These policies and procedures are essentially rules which organisations set down for employees to follow when accessing information systems.

Professional associations, such as the British Computer Society, are expected to follow a set of procedures or policies in relation to the minimum standards of competence, conduct and behaviour.

British Computer Society – code of ethics

The British Computer Society's code of ethics sets out the professional standards required by the Society as a condition of membership. It applies to members of all grades, including students and affiliates, and also non-members who offer their expertise as part of the Society's Professional Advice Register.

Figure 10.18 The British Computer Society logo (http://www.bcs.org)

Within this code of ethics, the term 'relevant authority' is used to identify the person or organisation which has authority over the member's activity as a professional. If the member is a practising professional, this is normally an employer or client. If the member is a student, this is normally an academic institution.

The code governs a member's personal conduct as an individual member of the BCS, and not the nature of the relevant authority's business or their ethics. It will therefore be a matter of the member exercising his or her personal judgement in meeting the code's requirements. Any breach of the code of conduct brought to the attention of the Society will be considered under the Society's disciplinary procedures. Members should also ensure that the Society is notified of any significant violation of the code by another BCS member.

The code is separated into four sections, as detailed below. The full code can be downloaded from *http://www.bcs.org/BCS/Join/WhyJoin/Conduct.htm*

The public interest

1 You shall carry out work or study with due care and diligence in accordance with the relevant authority's requirements, and the interests of system users. If your professional judgement is overruled, you shall indicate the likely risks and consequences.

2 In your professional role you shall have regard for the public health, safety and environment.

3 You shall have regard to the legitimate rights of third parties.

4 You shall ensure that within your professional field/s you have knowledge and understanding of relevant legislation, regulations and standards, and that you comply with such requirements.

5 You shall conduct your professional activities without discrimination against clients or colleagues.

6 You shall reject any offer of bribery or inducement.

Duty to relevant authority

7 You shall avoid any situation that may give rise to a conflict of interest between you and your relevant authority. You shall make full and immediate disclosure to them if any conflict is likely to occur or be seen by a third party as likely to occur.

8 You shall not disclose or authorise to be disclosed, or use for personal gain or to benefit a third party, confidential information except with the permission of your relevant authority, or at the direction of a court of law.

9 You shall not misrepresent or withhold information on the performance of products, systems or services, or take advantage of the lack of relevant knowledge or inexperience of others.

Duty to the profession

10 You shall uphold the reputation and good standing of the BCS in particular, and the profession in general, and shall seek to improve professional standards through participation in their development, use and enforcement.

11 You shall act with integrity in your relationships with all members of the BCS and with members of other professions with whom you work in a professional capacity.

12 You shall have due regard for the possible consequences of your statements on others. You shall not make any public statement in your professional capacity unless you are properly qualified and, where appropriate, authorised to do so. You shall not purport to represent the BCS unless authorised to do so.

13 You shall notify the Society if convicted of a criminal offence or upon becoming bankrupt or disqualified as Company Director.

Professional competence and integrity

14 You shall seek to upgrade your professional knowledge and skill, and shall maintain awareness of technological developments, procedures and standards which are relevant to your field, and encourage your subordinates to do likewise.

15 You shall not claim any level of competence that you do not possess. You shall only offer to do work or provide a service that is within your professional competence.

16 You shall observe the relevant BCS Codes of Practice and all other standards which, in your judgement, are relevant, and you shall encourage your colleagues to do likewise.

17 You shall accept professional responsibility for your work and for the work of colleagues who are defined in a given context as working under your supervision.

Backup strategy

A backup is a copy of files on a second medium (a disk or tape) as a precaution in case the first medium fails. One of the cardinal rules in using computers is 'Back up your files regularly'. Even the most reliable computer will break down eventually. Many professionals recommend that organisations and individuals make two, or even three, backups of all their files.

To be especially safe, one of these backups should be kept in a different location from the others. Backups can be created using operating system commands, or organisations can buy special-purpose backup utilities and software. Backup programs often compress the data so that backups use less storage capacity.

Selecting backup media

When developing a backup strategy an organisation must determine what backup platform (hardware) it will use for data protection. Many choices exist, from extensive data-replication systems that create off-site replicas to traditional tape-based systems. Budget and expertise will determine which method (or combination of methods) is best for any one organisation. Tape systems are generally the least expensive and least technologically demanding. Other choices include hard disk and RAID mirror systems amongst others.

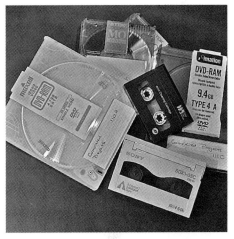

Before a system administrator can determine a backup strategy, he or she must first determine how much data the organisation will be protecting. This information will help determine what type of system is required: from single-tape drives through to large hard disk systems.

The process of determining what will be protected goes beyond summing up the total of all data on the organisation's servers, since much of this data is likely to be non-mission-critical to the organisation's operation. Good examples of non-critical files are programs and applications (which are easily restored from the original media) and users' personal files, such as MP3s.

Tapes and disks used as backup media

Once the system administrator knows the amount of data requiring protection, he or she can determine which type of device best suits the needs of the organisation.

Backup methodology

It is vital to select the best methodology for backing up an organisation's data based on the nature of the organisation and its processing requirements. The most common methodologies are:

- **Full:** This methodology transfers a copy of all data within the scope of the backup to the destination media (tape or disk), regardless of whether the data has changed since the last backup was performed.

- **Differential:** This methodology backs up all files changed since the last full backup, regardless of whether they have been changed since the last backup operation of any kind.

- **Incremental:** Here, only those files that have changed since the last backup operation of any kind (full, differential or incremental) will be transferred.

Essentially, the method chosen will depend on the storage capacity of the backup medium and the organisation's need for speedy disaster recovery. For example, by running a full backup daily, a very large amount of storage capacity will be required, but only the last backup will be needed to restore all data.

Conversely, using a full backup once a week with an incremental daily backup uses much less storage capacity, but a recovery would require the last full and each incremental backup to be fed back onto the servers. Most organisations will use a combination of methodologies that allow them to conserve tape space while still allowing data to be restored quickly. Using weekly full backups with daily incremental backups is generally considered the strategic norm.

Media rotation and storage

A backup strategy requires media rotation and storage to be considered. Unfortunately, most organisations store physical backup media within about a metre of the servers they protect. As recent physical disasters have shown, this is not a good way to protect data since the backup media stands a very good chance of being lost with the servers in a disaster. Physical media needs to be stored off-site in a secure location from which it can be retrieved quickly, if needed.

To reduce costs for both media and off-site storage, a good media-rotation scheme is essential. By re-using media after a predetermined period of time, media rotation schemes ensure that a minimum number of backups are stored off-site. There are a variety of possible rotation schemes which include grandfather-father-son and Tower of Hanoi.

Grandfather-father-son (GFS)

The most commonly used media rotation schedule is **Grandfather-father-son**. This scheme uses daily (son), weekly (father) and monthly (grandfather) backup sets.

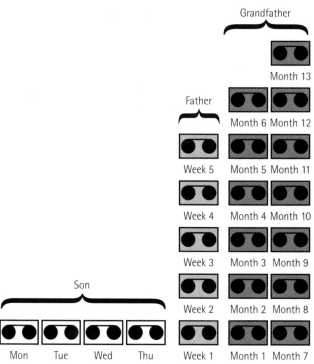

Figure 10.19 Grandfather-father-son (GFS) rotation system

The GFS scheme begins with the daily backups. Typically, four backup media are labelled for the day of the week each backs up; for example, Monday through Thursday. Each media is recalled for use on its labelled day. If only a one-week version history of files is maintained, then each media is overwritten each week. In order to maintain a three-week version history of files (recommended), more media are required. For example this week's Monday media will not be overwritten for three weeks.

Weekly backups follow a similar scenario. A set of up to five weekly backup media is labelled 'Week1', 'Week 2', and so on. Full backups are recorded weekly, on the day that a 'son' media is not used. Following the example above, these would be 'Friday' media. This 'father' media is re-used monthly. Five weekly tapes are required in order to maintain a one-month history of files, as some months have five weeks.

The final set of three media is labelled 'Month 1', 'Month 2', and so on, according to which month of the quarter they will be used. This 'grandfather' media records full backups on the last business day of each month. If the backup schedule follows a corporate financial calendar, then the monthly media will take the place of the Week 4 or Week 5 weekly father tape, depending on the month. If the backup schedule follows calendar months, then the monthly backup will vary throughout the year, replacing a daily or weekly tape. Typically, monthly tapes are overwritten quarterly or yearly (recommended), depending on version history requirements.

Each of these media may be a single tape, a set of tapes, removable hard disk or hard disk unit, depending on the amount of data to back up and the type of backup used (incremental or full). Weekly and/or monthly media are generally stored as archives.

GFS rotation schemes allow for the monthly backups to be immediately stored in a secure location, while the most current weekly full and incremental backups are housed for immediate use in restoration, then allowed to sit off-site in case of a catastrophic failure. While there is some limited liability inherent in this system (an organisation could lose up to one week of data if struck by a fire or some other disaster), this system offers the highest security with the lowest cost.

Developing a backup strategy

A backup strategy is developed by determining:

- which data needs to be protected
- which media to use for that protection
- how to protect the media itself.

A system administrator can create and maintain a reliable backup system for an organisation by considering these factors, and this system will ensure operational continuity in the event of a disaster.

Upgrade strategy

As organisations develop over time, additional hardware and software resources are required and older resources require replacement. An organisation's upgrade strategy determines how these new and replacement resources will be provided, developed and tested.

There are a number of issues which must be considered as part of any upgrade strategy:

- future proofing
- compatibility and integration testing
- support for legacy systems.

Future proofing

If possible, all new resources deployed by an organisation should be future proof. Future proofing involves selecting hardware and software resources which will have a lifespan generally of three to five years.

Computer and communication technology develops at an incredible rate, and future proofing requires an organisation to attempt to anticipate future developments in order to secure resources which will be compatible with them. An example of future proofing would be ensuring that a new computer system can be upgraded with additional memory and storage if required. If upgrades or additional resources are to be used with existing systems, it is important that these resources and systems are tested for compatibility.

An organisational information system consists of many different sections, often each with its own hardware and software. It is important that upgrades to one area within the organisation do not impact negatively on another area.

Compatibility testing

Compatibility testing checks for unintended interactions that disrupt normal operation or decrease any other functional or non-functional properties of the system. An example of compatibility testing would be ensuring that an upgrade version of a computer's operating system was compatible with the organisation's main applications.

There are several interrelated elements of computer systems which require testing when a new item of hardware or software is introduced to an existing system. These are shown in Figure 10.20.

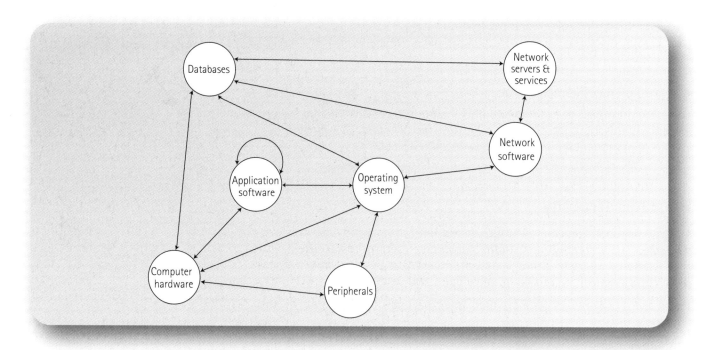

Figure 10.20 Compatibility testing

It is possible that one small incompatibility between any two items may cause operational problems which prevent a new system from being implemented. In this case, the system would need to be modified to address the incompatibilities and then tested again to ensure that the modifications did not cause further incompatibilities.

Integration testing

Integration testing is a type of testing in which software and/or hardware components are combined and tested to confirm that they interact according to their requirements. Integration testing can continue progressively until the entire system has been integrated.

An example of integration testing would be if a new stock control system were to be introduced in a large supermarket. The system would first be tested for compatibility with existing systems within the stock control area. Then the new system would be tested to ensure that inputs and outputs from and to other information systems, such as point-of-sale and ordering, functioned correctly. This ensures that the new stock control system is fully integrated into the functions of the organisation.

Support for legacy systems

Legacy systems are the systems which are in existence and either deployed or under development at the start of an upgrade program. All legacy systems will be affected by upgrading, to a greater or lesser extent.

Some systems will become transitional systems before they are retired. This means they continue in their original function until the new upgrade system is ready to take over. Other systems will simply be retired as their functions are assumed by upgraded systems. Still others will be abandoned only when they become obsolete.

Issues of cost make it important to support legacy systems as part of any upgrade strategy. Many effective and vital business applications were developed for mini and mainframe computer systems. These systems are costly to replace. Often the cost of developing new software to replace these applications is higher than the cost of purchasing new hardware.

An upgrade strategy will normally include some kind of support for allowing these legacy applications to be accessed or run on modern hardware. This may involve some hardware or software **emulation**.

Emulation

Older applications can still be important for an organisation when it upgrades its systems. The common scenario is a program, such as stock control, which is key to the business operation, and was written for a mini computer system and multiple dumb terminals. The hardware used to run the system is well beyond its useful life and is no longer supported by its manufacturer. The organisation has decided to purchase new hardware in a move to modernise all of its operational systems. A way must be found to continue to run the stock control application even when the hardware for which it was written is not available. The solution to this problem is emulation.

Emulation requires an emulator. An emulator is a product designed to imitate one system while running on another. The emulator accepts the same data, executes the same programs, and achieves the same results as the system it is emulating. The concept was invented by IBM systems engineer Larry H. Moss in 1964 to describe how the new IBM System/360 would provide support for programs that had been designed to work with older IBM mainframes.

There are three basic types of emulator:

- **Firmware emulator** – All in hardware, such as the hardware emulator built into the PlayStation 2 – PSX2 which supports PlayStation 1 games
- **Combo emulator** – Part hardware, part software, such as the Mac Houdini board which provides support for PC operating systems on the Apple Mac platform
- **Software emulator** – Coded entirely in software, no special hardware required for operation, such as the Xeon emulator which allows Xbox software to be played on Windows PCs.

Emulators allow applications which might not otherwise be available to run on the current processing platform. It is also possible to use an emulator to move data across platforms (i.e. from one platform to another) when the platforms are otherwise incompatible.

The down side of using an emulator is that often (but not always) the performance of the emulator may be slower than the native platform, and it is possible that the emulator will not fully support modern hardware which was not supported by the emulated platform.

Data migration

Large and medium-sized organisations will have a great deal of centralised data which will be accessed by a number of legacy systems. If an organisation updates its central storage system it will have to amend legacy systems to function with these updated data stores.

Equally, it is vital that the data held centrally are *migrated to* (copied to) the new storage system. This is often a difficult task due to the incompatibilities of older hardware in comparison with more modern systems.

Software strategy

An organisation requires a strategy to guide the acquisition, installation, support, training and evaluation of software for business use. If there is no clear strategy, then the organisation can encounter serious difficulties caused by incompatible applications, lack of staff expertise and software unfit for the required purpose.

Example

Ireland's leading bank, Allied Irish Bank (AIB), has developed a software strategy which has removed the company's original dependence on Microsoft operating systems and application software.

The bank replaced its Windows-based desktop systems, used by tellers in the banks, with Linux-based desktop systems. The key features of the bank's strategy were:

- to reduce costs
- to produce a secure computing environment
- to produce application software customised to banking needs.

The costs of developing banking applications on Windows systems were greater than the equivalent costs for Linux. Linux is an open-source operating system which greatly reduces the purchase costs for desktop computer systems. The cost of the operating system represented a significant saving for AIB (Windows XP Professional retails for more than three times the price of RedHat Linux).

The new software is customised to meet the bank's needs and the tellers use only one or two desktop applications during the working day. These applications were written specifically for AIB. The Linux software allows the bank complete control of desktops and is configured to provide the maximum security for business applications.

The cost of keeping the Linux-based systems free of viruses and other malicious code is less than the price of doing so for Microsoft Windows PCs, and the recent high profile viruses and worms were not designed to target Linux systems. Linux also tends to be more secure because it is open-source; the source code for the software is under constant peer review. This collaborative work finds problems in the operating system before hackers can exploit them.

A software strategy has to address several areas, such as the appropriate route for upgrading software, evaluation of software to identify possible options, support for staff in terms of training, and more general user support.

Upgrading

The key factors to consider when upgrading any organisation information system are described below.

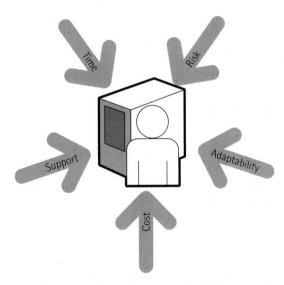

Figure 10.21 Key factors to consider when upgrading

Cost

All organisations have to consider the merits of upgrading systems against the costs. Often, an organisation may find that the benefits of upgrading a particular system are negated by the costs involved.

Even upgrading a desktop systems to the latest version of a particular operating system can have significant implications. There will be the cost of the new operating system, possible hardware upgrades such as additional memory or hard disk storage, possible application upgrades (because older applications don't run, or don't run as efficiently, on the new OS) and so on. Added to this is the cost in terms of technical support to install and maintain the operating system software, and the cost of support for users' questions and problems.

With larger, customised solutions the cost implications are greater. The cost to develop, install and support a new custom application must be considered. Add to this the expense of porting existing business data to the new platform and the costs can be considerable.

These costs must be measured against the benefits of upgrading the system to ensure that the upgrade is a positive step for the organisation.

Time

Any upgrade of an organisational information system will have time implications. There will be the time needed to develop and test the new system, the time required to install the system and the time required to train staff to operate the system.

Each time requirement will divert resources from the core operation of the organisation. For example, staff will not be performing their normal functions if they are being trained to operate a new system. This may mean a reduction in revenue from business activities, or frustrated customers because they cannot contact staff for service.

Risk

There is always an element of risk in the introduction of a new system. The new system will undoubtedly contain errors which were not detected during testing. These errors mean there is a serious risk of losing data, and the system may need to be shut down while debugging and fixing is carried out. This unexpected downtime may impact significantly on the operations of the organisation.

Ultimately, the potential risk to customer relationships must be considered when deciding whether or not to upgrade. Customers demand short turn-arounds and high degrees of accuracy throughout. Shipping mistakes and other customer service errors that can result from glitches in the upgrade process can cost an organisation dearly in lost customers and revenue.

Adaptability

It is a serious mistake to assume that any software upgrade, no matter how comprehensive it may seem during the initial implementation, can provide all of the functionality that an organisation will need for the foreseeable future. That is why adaptability is so crucial. A system upgrade that does not meet new operation or business requirements forces an organisation to develop additional customised systems, which puts the organisation at a competitive disadvantage as it diverts capital and resources away from other core goals.

In the end, an organisation will bear unnecessary expense and jeopardise operations in meeting the changing demands of customers if its systems are not adaptable. It is therefore important that new information systems can be easily adapted to meet a variety of changing organisational needs.

Support

Any new information system will require support from some source. This source will be either in-house technical support or outside support from an IS developer or vendor. The quality, cost and speed of response from this source of support will be a vital component in the success of the new system.

If there are doubts about the level and quality of the support available then an organisation will have to carefully consider if an upgrade of a system is an appropriate step to take.

Evaluation of software

A software strategy requires that an organisation identifies the best software available, based on cost and functionality, that meets its operational requirements. Applications from the desktop to the server can be evaluated to ascertain their suitability for the organisation. This evaluation will be carried out against certain criteria. These are described below.

Functionality

In relation to information systems, functionality (from the Latin *functio* meaning 'to perform') is what a product, such as a software application or computing device, can do for a user.

When evaluating software, you are essentially summarising the features of the software in relation to your organisation's requirements. It is estimated that only 20 per cent of the functionality of most modern applications is utilised by their users. Many applications contain features which will not be used by the majority of users. Too much functionality wastes resources (memory, backing storage, money) and places additional stress on an organisation.

Alternatively, insufficient functionality may not meet the requirements of the organisation and will require additional software to address the functionality gap.

Essentially, evaluating functionality is about ensuring that the software being evaluated will meet the operational needs of the organisation.

Performance

Performance is a statement of the speed at which a computer system works. Essentially, it is a means of comparing different computer applications running on the same hardware.

Ideally, benchmark tests should be used to evaluate the performance of an application in different situations. Benchmarks for software determine the efficiency, accuracy or speed of a program in performing a particular task, such as recalculating data in a spreadsheet. The same data is used with each program tested, so the resulting scores can be compared to see which programs perform well and in what areas.

Usability

There are generally three types of usability evaluation methods: testing, inspection and inquiry.

In the **usability testing** approach, users work on typical tasks using the software and the person or persons performing the evaluation (the evaluators) use the results to see how the user interface supports the users to do their tasks.

In the **usability inspection** approach the evaluators examine usability-related aspects of the user interface of the software. This is done without observation of or comments from the system's proposed users and depends on the evaluators' expertise in usability design.

Usability inquiry requires that the evaluators obtain information about users' likes, dislikes, needs and understanding of the system by talking to them, observing them using the system in real work (not for the purpose of usability testing), or letting them answer questions verbally or in written form.

The purpose of usability evaluations is to ensure that the user interface of the proposed software will allow the required functionality of the software to be accessed by the users. If the user interface is too complex it may prevent users from making the most of the functionality of the software.

Compatibility

Application software can be evaluated in terms of its compatibility with existing systems. Compatibility evaluation should consider the specifications of the systems currently available within the organisation and the minimum requirements of the software being evaluated.

Elements of compatibility include:

- **Processor and operating system** – Does the software use the same processor and operating system as the organisation? Examples of popular processor/OS combinations include: Intel Processor and Windows OS, Apple iMac and Mac OS X Panther, and Intel Processor and RedHat Linux.
- **Memory** – What is the minimum memory required to run the software? How does this compare with the memory available on the target computer system on which the software will run?
- **Peripherals** – What additional devices are required by the software? CD-ROM, modem, graphics cards, etc. are often required by certain items of software.
- **Backing storage capacity** – What are the installation and operating requirements of the software? How much storage is required for the software and how much storage does it require when it is running? Is there sufficient space available on the target machine?

In addition to the hardware elements mentioned above, it is also possible that clashes between two or more software packages may cause an item of software to malfunction. These possible incompatibilities should be carefully examined when evaluating software.

Data migration

Software can also be evaluated in terms of the ease of data migration. It is essential for any organisation that the data from legacy systems is available for future processing and archiving. The ease of data migration from one software application to another is a critical factor when considering new software for an organisation.

Reliability

Reliability is the ability of an item of software to perform a function when required. It is vital to the success of an organisation that the software tools which it uses will function as expected when required to do so.

Resource requirements

In addition to the hardware requirements discussed under 'Compatibility', any program uses the resources of the computer system on which it is running. These resources include processor time, memory and, often, bandwidth. Evaluations of software applications should, if possible, include details of the resources used by the application. Benchmarks will often report on the use of computer resources by particular applications.

Portability

When used to describe software, **portable** means that the software has the ability to run on a variety of computers. 'Portable' and 'machine independent' mean the same thing – that the software does not depend on a particular type of hardware.

An item of software can be evaluated on the degree to which it or its data files are portable across a variety of computing platforms used within the organisation.

Support

Software can also be evaluated on the level of support there is available for it. Software support can be a critical factor in the successful deployment of a new application within an organisation. The differing levels of support provided by in-house services or by software companies can all form part of the evaluation.

In addition to support services, the on-line support, such as on-line help, and paper-based support, in the form of printed manuals and tutorials, can be evaluated in terms of their ability to assist the user with the operation of the software.

Training

A software strategy needs to not only address how software is to be acquired, developed and deployed. It must also provide support for how the user will be helped to operate software. Some consideration must therefore be given to providing training for users so that they are more able to operate the organisation's information systems.

This training can be delivered in a number of different ways (see below).

On-the-job training

The user is trained to use the system as part of his or her normal working activities. The user will normally be shown how to use the system by a colleague and will then use the system as part of his or her work. Questions about the operation of the software will be dealt with on an ongoing basis by colleagues, managers and technical support providing assistance as required.

In-house training

In-house training is delivered by staff within the organisation, normally from an IT department or similar, to groups of users who have been removed from their normal tasks to attend the training. This type of training is more intensive than on-the-job training and more clearly focused on learning how to use the system and its software.

The IT staff will be available to answer questions as the training is delivered to the users.

External courses

If the necessary expertise is not available in-house or the IT staff are not available due to other work commitments, then an external training provider may be contracted to provide the required training.

It is most common for this type of training to be used to deliver skills in popular applications such as those produced by Adobe, Macromedia and Microsoft. External courses may be delivered within an organisation's premises, by the external provider, or at an off-site location prescribed by the training provider.

User support

In addition to training, users can be supported in a number of other ways:

Manuals

Paper manuals like these are becoming less common, with more and more manuals supplied on CD as PDF files

Manuals are printed guides or digital books about how to install and use software. Typically, there are three types of manual supplied with commercial application software: the installation guide; the tutorial guide; and the reference manual.

The installation guide is designed to assist the user in installing and configuring a new piece of software on a specific computer system.

The purpose of a tutorial guide is to introduce the user to the main features of the software. The tutorial is sometimes built into the software as an on-line tutorial.

Reference manuals detail all features of the software and how to use them. Reference manuals are generally weighty volumes, and are now more commonly available as digital books.

It is worth noting that many packages do not have separate manuals for the installation, tutorial and reference guides but contain all three in a single manual with separate sections dedicated to these three guides. In fact, the sale of manuals and software together in large packages has now been separated. Organisations buying multiple copies of the software may choose to buy only one or two manuals to save on costs.

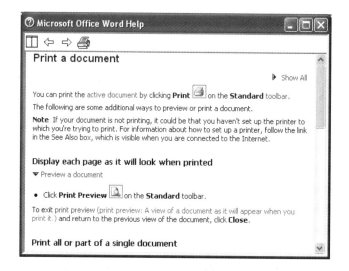

Figure 10.22 Sample help screen from Microsoft Word

On-line help/tutorials

Nowadays many packages make increased use of on-line help rather than using printed documentation. This on-line help can be built into the package as help files, or obtained externally via the Internet.

'On-line' in this sense does not mean on the World Wide Web. The term 'on-line' means that the help is available on the computer rather than via some other medium. The user can access the help without leaving the computer on which he or she is working. The content of the help can be on the computer's hard disk, on CD-ROM, on the WWW or on some other medium.

On-line help systems are becoming increasingly complex. A help system will almost certainly contain a search facility to enable users to locate a specific help topic, and an index to allow browsing by topic.

Context-sensitive help systems are also common. Context-sensitive help is intelligent help that you can access directly from within your software. In a software application with context-sensitive help, each dialogue box typically has a *Help* button. When you click on the *Help* button, the screen displays information designed to help you with that specific dialogue box.

Help desk

A help desk is a source of technical support for hardware and/or software. A help desk is either an in-house provision or outsourced to a third party. Users can contact the help desk if they have specific problems relating to the hardware and/or software used by the organisation.

The help desk is staffed by people that can either solve the problem directly or forward the problem to someone else, such as the software vendor's technical support team. Help desk software provides the means to log in problems and track them until they are solved. It also provides the management with information regarding support activities.

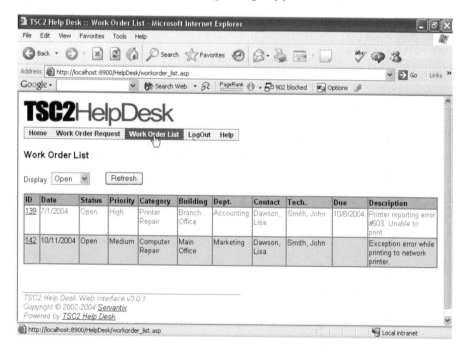

Figure 10.23 Sample screen from TSC2 help desk by Servantix LLC

Newsgroups

Newsgroups allow users to **post** messages (called 'posting'), respond to others' posts, and even download files from the group, all when it's most convenient for the user. If a user has a support question this can be posted to the group and any member of the group can reply with an answer to the problem. The reply could come from help desk personnel, vendor IT support or from another user.

Usenet has tens of thousands of newsgroups, with a significant number of them dedicated to product support. Several conversations, called **threads**, are usually going on at once in any group; participants take these discussions seriously and often respond to anything they see written ('posted') to the group. Newsgroups are an excellent way of gaining high quality technical support at limited cost.

The drawback of using newsgroups is that not all users are experts, and users should exercise some caution when using information posted to the group in response to queries. The response may be technically incorrect, or it may be exactly what the user was looking for! It is useful to examine a number of responses to a posting before deciding on the action to take.

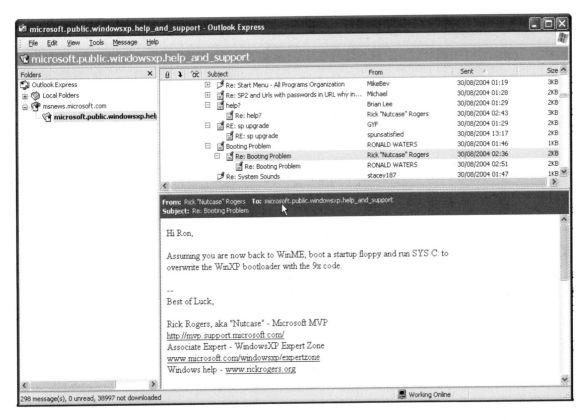

Figure 10.24 Product support newsgroup

FAQs

Frequently asked questions (FAQs) are a popular way of summarising the most commonly asked questions and their answers about a particular subject. It is common for FAQs to be created for popular applications and these FAQs are posted on newsgroups or on websites for users to download (Figure 10.25).

Distributed databases

A distributed database is a database that is stored in more than one physical location. Parts or copies of the database are physically stored in one location and other parts of the database are stored in different locations.

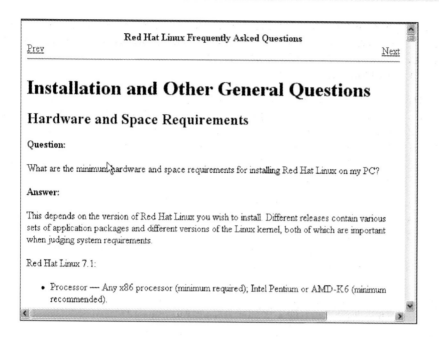

Figure 10.25 A sample online FAQ

Methods of distribution

There are two main ways of distributing a database. The central database can be partitioned or repicated. If the central database is partitioned each remote server has the necessary data on customers to serve only its local area. If the central database is replicated then each remote location has access to a complete copy of all the customer data. Changes in local files can be justified with the central database on a batch basis, often at night.

Partitioning

Partitioning splits the tables of the central database into smaller sections. These sections can be vertically or horizontally partitioned. A *vertical partition* is normally used when the database is being split to improve access speeds (Figure 10.26). Commonly queried fields are grouped into a table and the less frequently accessed data into another. The rows within the split tables will be physically closer together on the backing storage medium and therefore faster to retrieve.

If vertical partitioning is used as a method of dividing the database into distributed locations then the commonly accessed partitioned tables would be in one location or mirrored to multiple locations, with the less frequently used tables held centrally or in fewer locations.

For example, a customer services centre would require speedy access to customer contact details but not to a customer's credit details. The database tables relating to customer data could be vertically partitioned along these lines; the customer contact details could be stored in the customer services department and the credit details stored in the accounts department. The unique ID for customers would be used to reconcile customer data. Changes to the distributed databases would be copied to the central database during a quiet processing time, such as overnight.

Horizontal partitioning involves creating two or more tables with exactly the same structure and splitting the rows between those tables according to some criteria. An example of horizontal partitioning would be when a company is split into multiple regions. The data required by each region are held in partitioned tables according to customer location, e.g. the Stirling office holds all the details for customers from Stirling and Central Scotland.

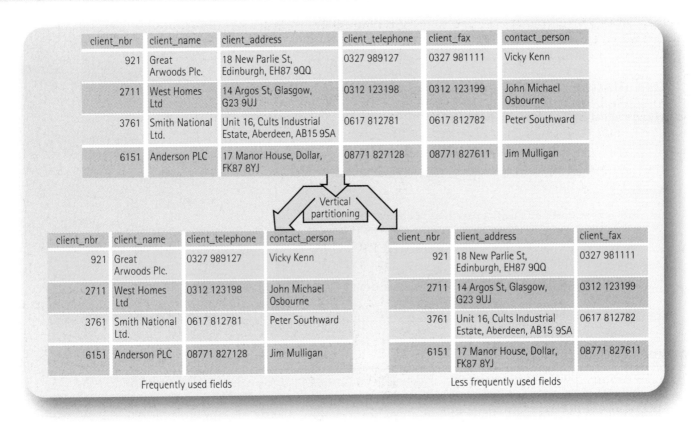

client_nbr	client_name	client_address	client_telephone	client_fax	contact_person
921	Great Arwoods Plc.	18 New Parlie St, Edinburgh, EH87 9QQ	0327 989127	0327 981111	Vicky Kenn
2711	West Homes Ltd	14 Argos St, Glasgow, G23 9UJ	0312 123198	0312 123199	John Michael Osbourne
3761	Smith National Ltd.	Unit 16, Cults Industrial Estate, Aberdeen, AB15 9SA	0617 812781	0617 812782	Peter Southward
6151	Anderson PLC	17 Manor House, Dollar, FK87 8YJ	08771 827128	08771 827611	Jim Mulligan

Vertical partitioning

client_nbr	client_name	client_telephone	contact_person
921	Great Arwoods Plc.	0327 989127	Vicky Kenn
2711	West Homes Ltd	0312 123198	John Michael Osbourne
3761	Smith National Ltd.	0617 812781	Peter Southward
6151	Anderson PLC	08771 827128	Jim Mulligan

Frequently used fields

client_nbr	client_address	client_fax
921	18 New Parlie St, Edinburgh, EH87 9QQ	0327 981111
2711	14 Argos St, Glasgow, G23 9UJ	0312 123199
3761	Unit 16, Cults Industrial Estate, Aberdeen, AB15 9SA	0617 812782
6151	17 Manor House, Dollar, FK87 8YJ	08771 827611

Less frequently used fields

Figure 10.26 *Example of vertical partitioning of a database table*

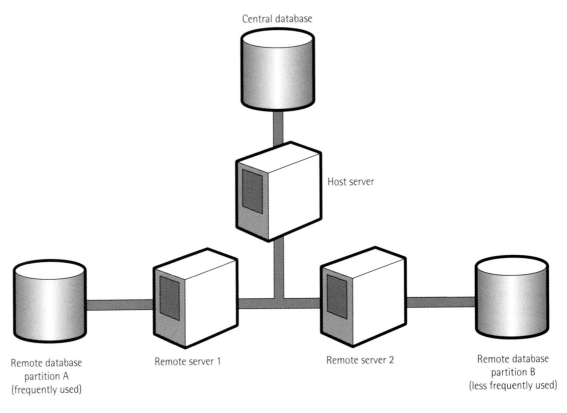

Figure 10.27 *Example of a distributed database – partitioning (vertical)*

The drawback of this horizontal partitioning is when the organisation needs to examine all the data available, such as when compiling end-of-year reports. In these circumstances a special query will be required to pull together the data in the remote databases, or the central database will be updated with the remote data before the report is compiled.

Replication

Another strategy is to replicate the central database at all remote locations. All data is copied to all locations in the organisation. The data is processed locally and updates are made to the locally held database.

Again, these changes are copied to the centrally held database during times of low processor and network load, such as weekends or overnight.

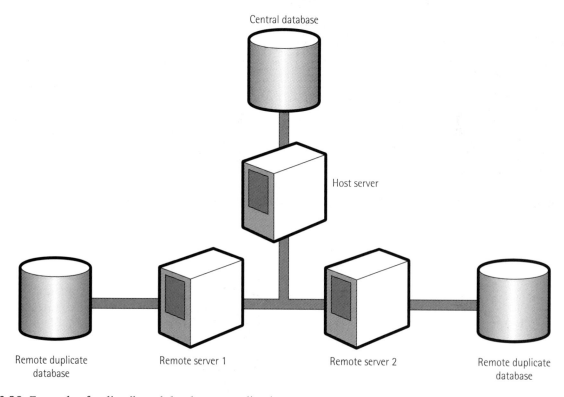

Figure 10.28 Example of a distributed database – replication

Central index

The FBI's National Crime Information Centre database is a distributed database which uses a central index to store the location of records. When a request for data is received the host server interrogates the central index and identifies a location where the complete record requested can be found. This location can then be accessed to retrieve the record.

The advantages of the central index are that the central database does not contain all the available data and therefore is not updated with vast numbers of records every day. The central index only contains the location of the available records, and is therefore only updated should the location of records change, or when records are deleted or created. The amount of processor effort required for this is much less than that required to update an entire centrally held database.

The disadvantage of this approach is that there can be a significant delay in retrieving records from the distributed database according to their location. An interview recording could be stored on a computer nearby or on an office computer system at the other side of the world.

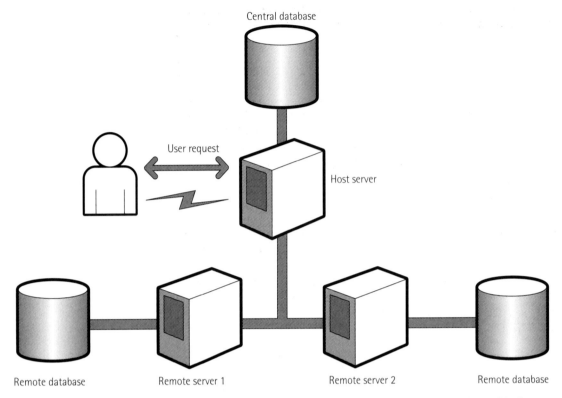

Figure 10.29 Example of a distributed database – central index

Advantages of distributed databases

Distributing databases reduce the vulnerability of an organisation to a single, massive, central catastrophe (such as fire or terrorist attack) by distributing data across the organisation. The power of the information system can be increased because, rather than use powerful super-computers to handle transactions, organisations can invest in many lower-powered machines which, cumulatively, have greater processing power. The distribution of organisational data allows these systems to process data and store that data locally in distributed database tables.

Data warehouses

A data warehouse is a database which holds all of an organisation's data. The warehouse can be distributed over several computers and can contain several databases and information from numerous sources in a variety of formats.

The data warehouse also contains data about how the warehouse is organised (metadata), where the information can be found (distributed locations), and any connections between data (relationships).

Data warehousing is used to overcome the key problem that many organisations face, i.e. how to gather all organisational data together for processing by executive information systems (EISs) and decision support systems (DSSs).

Data warehousing tools are used to extract data from a variety of sources and integrate this data in a centrally held relational database without affecting the data of the source operational or tactical information systems. The data in the warehouse might be updated daily, weekly, bi-weekly or monthly depending on the type of data and needs of the organisation.

Once the data warehouse has been constructed it can be used by EIS and DSS systems to support the work of tactical and strategic management within the organisation.

Data mining

In addition to use by EIS and DSS systems, a data warehouse can be 'mined' for additional information. Data mining looks for hidden patterns in a database that can be used to predict future behaviour or to identify possible business opportunities, such as identifying customer groups for targeted marketing.

A simple example of how data can tell a business about its customers is the case of an existing bank customer who suddenly applies for a joint bank account. If the bank knows this is the customer's first joint account, the bank might conclude that the customer is about to get married. The bank will, therefore, attempt to market life insurance, mortgages and other long-term investments to the customer to save for buying a house, paying child-care costs, preparing for retirement, etc. The bank may also sell this information to a third party to allow that third party to market additional products to the soon-to-be-married customer!

American Express has a database which can store over 500 billion records. These records detail the spending habits of their customers. Data mining can be used to promote services to its customers. For example, a customer who recently used his card to purchase a flight from Edinburgh to Paris might find that he receives a promotional offer for a weekend trip to New York with his next credit card statement.

Questions

1. We encounter data processing systems (DPSs) almost every day. Outline the key features of a data processing system and give an example of a DPS with which you are familiar.

2. Management information systems make use of the output from data processing systems.

    a Describe the purpose of a management information system.

    b Which level of an organisation will make use of a MIS?

    c Describe an example of output from a MIS.

3. Decision support systems assist management decision making.

    a What are the key features of a decision support system?

    b Give an example of a task for which DSS would be used to assist management.

4. Executive information systems are key to the successful operation of large organisations.

    a What are the key features of an executive information system?

    b EIS allow managers to 'drill down' detail levels. Explain the term 'drill down'. You may wish to give an example in your answer.

5. The management of any organisation operates at three different levels: strategic, tactical and operational.

    a Discuss the nature of decisions assisted by information systems at each of these levels, and indicate the types of systems used.

    b Data processing systems are often described as transactional processing systems. What is meant by the term *transaction*?

    c Decision support systems often incorporate an element of *simulation*.

    Explain what this means in the context of information systems.

6. Expert systems can be of use in businesses and other organisations.

    a An expert system consists of three parts. State the name and give a description of each part.

    b Give **three** business reasons for the development of expert systems.

    c Describe **two** drawbacks of using expert systems to support decision making.

7. What is a network and what does the term *network topology* mean?

8. Westfield Business Services has just created a computer network of 50 computers using a star topology.

    a Give **two** advantages of networking the computers.

    b Describe the organisation of a typical star network.

    c Describe **two** advantages of a star network when compared to ring and bus network topologies.

9. Bus networks typically suffer a high failure rate.

a Explain why this might be the case and describe one method of identifying such network failures.

b Give a situation when a bus topology network would be appropriate.

10. Describe the relative advantages and disadvantages of tree and mesh network topologies.

11. Network operating systems use protocols to aid communication across the network.

a What is a protocol?

b The Ethernet protocol uses an access method called CSMA/CD.

i What does CSMA/CD stand for?

ii Describe the operation of CSMA/CD on a typical network.

12. Island Grocers is a small firm with six stand-alone computer systems. The manager of the company decides to convert the computers into a peer-to-peer network.

a The manager is impressed with his new network but is considering buying a server for the network to change it to a client/server network.

List **two** differences between a client/server network and a peer-to-peer network.

b The manager has arranged for Internet access to be made available via the network but he is concerned about unauthorised access to his network from the Internet.

Explain how a *firewall* could be used to prevent this happening.

13. The infrastructure of a typical network uses a variety of devices. Describe, briefly, each of the following devices:

a server

b hub

c switch

d repeater

e router

f bridge

g network adapter (NIC).

14. Structured cabling has significant advantages over non-structured alternatives.

a How does structured cabling contribute to the management of change in a network?

b Give **two** advantages and **two** disadvantages of structured cabling.

15. Network operating systems provide a wide range of features. Network management systems are increasingly used by organisations to manage their networks.

a Describe the purpose of performance management tools within a network operating system.

b Describe the purpose of fault management tools within a network operating system.

16. John is using a computer at his work but is unable to save a file to the network file server. The network administrator tells John that he does not have the correct *access rights* to save the file.

a What are access rights and why are they used?

b Suggest which rights John would have to be given to save the file.

17. Passwords are the most common form of user authentication used by information systems.

a Give an example of a weak password and a strong password.

b Suggest **two** guidelines which should be adhered to for the protection of password security.

18. Encryption is an additional form of security which can be used to encode data for protection purposes.

a What is the purpose of a public key and a private key in a public-key encryption scheme?

b What is SSL and where is it most frequently used?

19. Malicious computer code can be categorised into three main groups: viruses, Trojans and worms.

a Describe each of these security threats.

b What is *spyware* and why does it pose a potential threat to security?

c New malicious programs are constantly being developed by malicious programmers.

How do antivirus software products deal with this ever-evolving threat?

20. Jerry operates a website which allows users to post comments about news and current affairs.

One morning Jerry finds that his website is extremely slow to respond to requests for data. Later that day he checks the site and it performs perfectly.

Jerry checks the server logs for his site and sees that one computer from the Internet was trying to access his site several thousand times a second.

What happened to Jerry's site and why was it so unusable earlier in the day?

21. Disaster recovery is vital for any organisation.

a What are the **four** main areas which a disaster recovery plan should address?

b Give **three** examples of a disaster which might adversely affect the operation of an organisational information system.

c What is *single-point failure* and how can an organisation protect against it?

22. Data backups are essential to protect an organisation from data loss as the result of a disaster.

    a Describe each of the following common backup methodologies: *full*, *differential* and *incremental*.

      Give advantages and disadvantages of each methodology.

    b Pauline works for a small business and she backs up her computer system each night and leaves the backup tape in the drawer next to her computer. Is this a good idea?

      Give a reason for your answer.

    c Grandfather-father-son is a common backup media rotation scheme. Briefly describe how this scheme operates.

23. As an organisation develops it will be required to upgrade its systems. An upgrade strategy is an essential part of this process and details how these upgrade requirements will be met.

    a What is *future proofing* and why is it required?

    b How does compatibility testing differ from integration testing?

    c As systems are upgraded, support for legacy systems becomes increasingly important.

      Describe a method of supporting legacy systems on new hardware.

    d Give **three** key factors which should be considered when considering an upgrade of computer software.

      Explain the possible impact of each of the factors you have given.

24. When choosing software, three factors could be considered to determine the most suitable package: *compatibility*, *functionality* and *support*.

    a Briefly explain why each of these would influence a company's decision to purchase a particular package.

    b State **three** other criteria which can be used to evaluate software.

25. Give **two** advantages to an organisation of providing *on-the-job* staff training as opposed to sending staff on dedicated *external courses*.

26. Many application packages are now supplied with on-line help instead of printed documentation.

    a Give **one** advantage and **one** disadvantage of only providing on-line help.

    b One example of online help is *context-sensitive help*. Describe a typical context-sensitive help system.

27. In addition to printed documentation and online help, information system users can be given additional support in a number of ways.

    Pick any two sources of additional support and give **one** advantage and **one** disadvantage of each as a source of support.

28. Distributed databases are common in large organisations.

Questions

Questions

a What is a distributed database?

b *Partitioning*, *replication* and *central index* are three methods of distributing a database across an organisation.

Briefly describe each of these methods.

29. EasyVan is a van rental company with offices across Scotland. Each office services its local area.

a A distributed database is to be developed for EasyVan which will make use of partitioning of the existing central database.

  i Suggest which type of partitioning will be most appropriate, *vertical* or *horizontal*.

  ii Give a reason for your answer.

b Give **two** advantages of using a distributed database as opposed to a centralised database.

30. What is *data warehousing* and why was it developed?

31. What is *data mining* and how can it assist an organisation?

Information Management Software

What is information management?

Information and information technology play an increasingly important role in our daily lives. Information management focuses on capturing, organising, manipulating and accessing information more effectively.

Information management is a *process*, requiring a means to distribute, access and use information, often among people in a group or organisation. Very often this is achieved through the use of information technology.

Information is important to individuals, but also central to collaborative groups, organisations (businesses, education and government), communities and society generally. Computing and networking have vastly expanded access to information in these areas. Information is now widely distributed, poorly organised and overwhelmingly abundant. It is this prevalence of information which makes information management so important. Good information management can take a previously chaotic situation with poorly organised data and produce well-structured and ordered information which can be easily accessed and processed.

Classes of information management software

Information management software provides a range of tools to capture, organise, manipulate and access information. These tools range from specialist applications, custom designed to meet an organisation's information management needs, to more general application packages commonly used by organisations.

This chapter looks at the more general classes of information management software:

- wordprocessing/desktop publishing
- presentation/web authoring
- spreadsheet/data handling
- project management
- personal information management.

Each of these applications has a specific role to play in managing information for individuals and organisations.

Wordprocessing/desktop publishing

These applications are used to present text primarily for presentation as printed material.

Working with wordprocessing software

Wordprocessing software

Of all computer applications, wordprocessing is the most common. A wordprocessor allows you to create a document, store it electronically on a disk, display it on a screen, modify it by entering commands and characters from the keyboard, and print it on a printer.

The great advantage of wordprocessing over using a typewriter is that you can make changes without retyping the entire document. If you make a typing mistake, you simply back up the cursor and correct your mistake. If you want to delete a paragraph, you simply remove it, without leaving a trace. It is equally easy to insert a word, sentence, or paragraph in the middle of a document. Wordprocessors also make it easy to move sections of text from one place to another within a document, or between documents. When you have made all the changes you want, you can send the file to a printer to get a hardcopy.

Wordprocessors vary considerably, but all wordprocessors support the following basic features:

Insert text	Insert text anywhere in the document.
Delete text	Erase characters, words, lines or pages as easily as you can cross them out on paper.
Cut and paste	Remove (cut) a section of text from one place in a document and insert (paste) it somewhere else.
Copy	Duplicate a section of text.
Page size and margins	Define various page sizes and margins, and the wordprocessor will automatically readjust the text so that it fits.
Search and replace	Direct the wordprocessor to search for a particular word or phrase. You can also direct the wordprocessor to replace one group of characters with another everywhere that the first group appears.
Word wrap	The wordprocessor automatically moves to the next line when you have filled one line with text, and it will readjust text if you change the margins.
Print	Send a document to a printer to get hardcopy.

Wordprocessors that support only these features (and maybe a few others) are called *text editors*. Most wordprocessors, however, support additional features that enable you to manipulate and format documents in more sophisticated ways. The additional features found in most modern wordprocessors usually include the following.

File management

Many wordprocessors contain file management capabilities that allow you to create, delete, move and search for files. The file management tool may allow searches to be carried out on part of a document name or on part of the contents of a document.

Font specifications

Font specifications allow you to change the properties of characters using the wordprocessing software. For example, you can specify bold, italics and underlining. Most wordprocessors also let you change the font size, the typeface and other properties of the font such as colour.

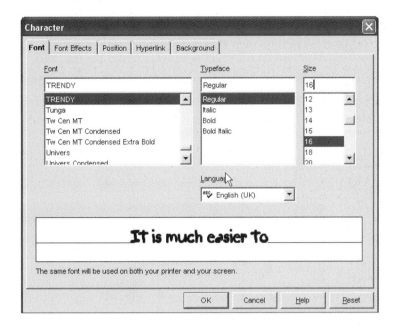

Figure 11.1 *Changing font specifications – Open Office 1.1.3*

Styles

Styles can be defined within a document or a document template (see later). A style is a collection of formatting properties which can be applied in one operation to selected text. For example, the style Normal may set the selected text to Ariel font, size 10 with fully justified alignment.

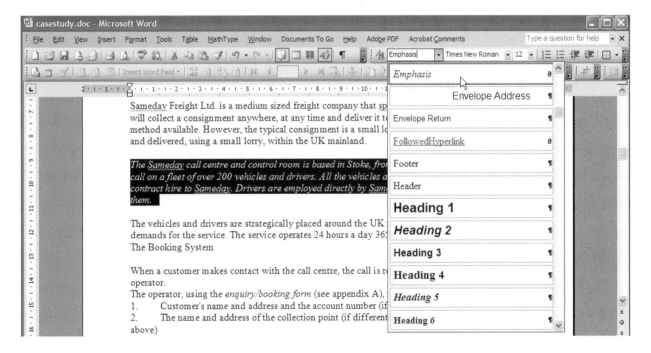

Figure 11.2 *Applying a style – Microsoft Word 2003*

Footnotes and cross references

This feature automates the numbering and placement of footnotes and enables you to cross-reference other sections of the document easily.

Contents

Wordprocesing software may include tools to automatically create a table of contents. A common approach to this is to compile the table of contents for a document from the headings used in the document. Each heading has a heading style applied, perhaps a Heading 1 style for main headings, a Heading 2 style for subheadings and so on.

These headings can automatically be added to a table of contents by the wordprocessing software. The various levels of heading can be arranged in a hierarchical structure (Figure 11.3).

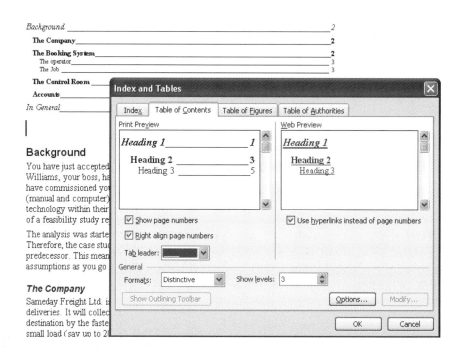

Figure 11.3 Inserting a table of contents – Microsoft Word 2003

Index

An index lists the terms and topics discussed in a document, along with the pages they appear on. To create an index, the index entries in the document are marked using the wordprocessing software and then the index is built.

Normally, an index entry can be an individual word, phrase, or symbol; a topic that spans a range of pages; or a reference to another entry, such as 'Databases. See Software'.

Once index entries are marked, the software allows the user to select an index design and build the finished index. First it collects the index entries and sorts them alphabetically, then it references their page numbers, finds and removes duplicate entries from the same page, and finally displays the index in the document.

Graphics

Tools for inserting or placing graphics allow you to embed illustrations, photographs and/or other graphics into a document. Some wordprocessors include tools to create the illustrations; others allow you to insert an illustration produced using different applications.

Most wordprocessing applications include ClipArt libraries. These contain a number of graphical (and other) multimedia objects which can be inserted in the document as required.

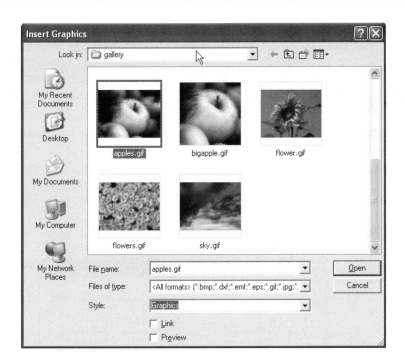

Figure 11.4 Inserting graphics – Open Office 1.1.3

Text wrapping

Text wrapping allows you to specify how text flows around graphics and other objects in a document. Text can commonly be wrapped squarely, tightly and to the top and bottom of an image. Other options, such as placing an image in front of or behind the text, are also possible (Figure 11.5).

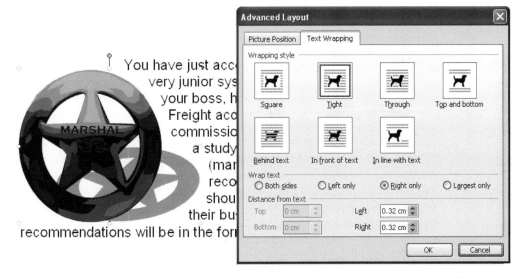

Figure 11.5 Applying text wrapping – Microsoft Word 2003

Headers, footers, and page numbering

Headers and footers can be customised and added to the wordprocessed document. These will appear at the top of each page for a header and the bottom of each page for a footer. The wordprocessor automatically keeps track of page numbers so that the correct number appears on each page. It is normally possible to customise the headers and footers so that they apply to only part of the document. This means that different headers and footers can be created for different sections of the document.

Layout/pagination

Page layout tools allow the user to specify different page margins and orientations (portrait/landscape) within a single document and to specify various methods for indenting paragraphs. *Pagination* is the process of defining where page breaks will occur. This can involve setting page length, paper size, margins and, where required, page numbering.

Columns

The number of columns of text on each page can be specified. This allows a number of different page layouts to appear within one document.

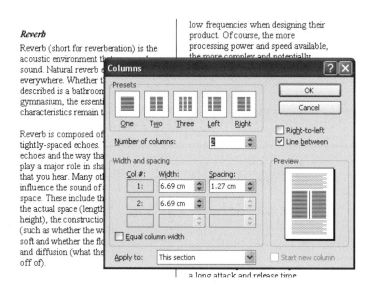

Figure 11.6 Editing text columns – Microsoft Word 2003

Figure 11.7 Thesaurus – Microsoft Word 2003

Page breaks and pagination

When a page is filled with text or graphics, the wordprocessing software inserts an automatic page break and starts a new page. To force a page break at a specific location, a manual page break can be inserted. For example, a manual page break can be used to ensure that a chapter title always starts on a new page.

When editing documents that are several pages in length, it is common to have to continually reset manual page breaks, as their positions change. Instead, it is possible to set *pagination options* to control where the word-processing software positions automatic page breaks. For example, the software can prevent a page break from occurring within a paragraph or ensure that a page break doesn't fall between two paragraphs, such as a heading and the following body text.

Spell checker

A spell checker is a utility that allows you to check the spelling of words. It will highlight any words that it does not recognise. The words which the spell checker can recognise are held in a *dictionary file*. There is one dictionary file for each language available within the software. Each user can, in addition, have his or her own custom dictionary file for words which he or she adds.

Thesaurus

A built-in thesaurus allows users to search for synonyms.

Merges

A merge inserts text from one file into another file. This is particularly useful for generating many documents which have the same format but different data. Generating mailing labels is the classic example of using merges.

Windows

The user can edit two or more documents at the same time in different windows on screen. Each document appears in a separate window. This is particularly valuable when working on a large project that consists of several different files.

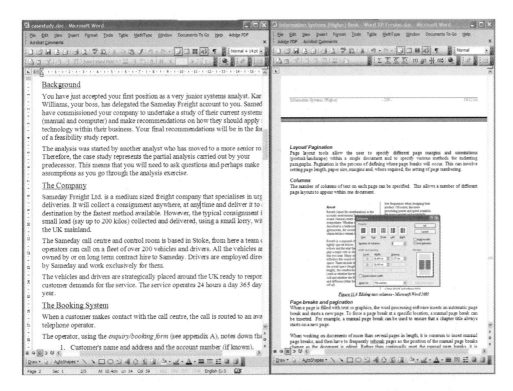

Figure 11.8 Viewing multiple document windows – Microsoft Word 2003

Macros

A macro is a collection of commands which can be executed by the word-processing software. Macros are often associated with a combination of keystrokes. When a keystroke is entered into the computer (such as **Control + Shift + K**) the macro associated with the keystroke is executed. Macros are often used to collect commonly used sequences of operations into one command. Macros can be recorded by the wordprocessing software or written using a special macro scripting language.

Templates

Default documents can be created and saved. These documents will contain a number of text styles which can be applied consistently to the new document. The font used, the paragraph style and all other properties of the document can be applied from the template.

Fonts

All individual letters, punctuation, numerals and symbols are *characters*. The complete set of characters in any one typeface is a **font**. Lower-case refers to small letters and upper-case refers to capital letters. 'Small caps' refers to text in x-height upper-case. (x-height is the height of the letter 'x'.)

A *sans-serif font* is a font where the characters do not have a serif (*sans* is French for without). The characters of a serif font all have a serif.

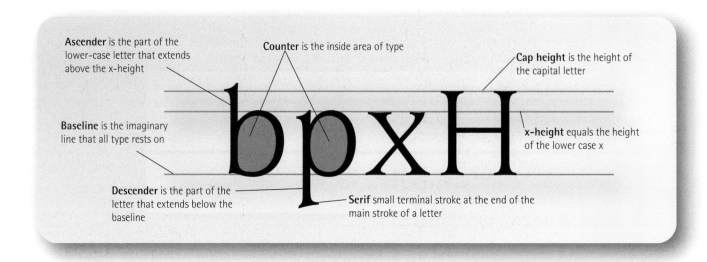

Figure 11.9 A sample typeface (font)

The line dividing wordprocessors from desktop publishing systems is constantly shifting. In general, though, desktop publishing applications support finer control over layout, and more support for full-colour documents.

Desktop publishing

Desktop publishing packages provide a range of features beyond those available in most wordprocessing applications. These tools allow the user to closely control the layout of text and images for printing. Complete control over colour and colour separation for printing are also often features of desktop publishing.

Frames

A frame is a floating and moveable area of the screen into which text or a graphic can be placed. Frames can be layered so elements within them can be placed on top of each other and moved forward and back in the document to change their position relative to the other frames (Figure 11.10).

As with wordprocessing, *text wrapping* can be set for each frame. This will determine how text flows around the frame.

Guides

A guide is a line shown in a document but which does not appear when the document is printed. A guide is used to align frames and other objects that form part of the desktop published document. Often, the software is configured so that objects 'snap' to the guide when they get close to it. Guides may be added to document pages in horizontal or vertical positions (such as by margins or headings) or in other positions as required (Figure 11.11).

Figure 11.10 Layering frames in desktop publishing software

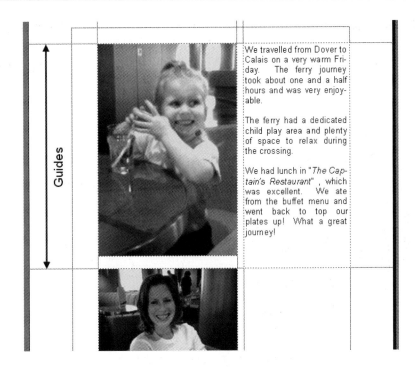

Guides

We travelled from Dover to Calais on a very warm Friday. The ferry journey took about one and a half hours and was very enjoyable.

The ferry had a dedicated child play area and plenty of space to relax during the crossing.

We had lunch in "*The Captain's Restaurant*", which was excellent. We ate from the buffet menu and went back to top our plates up! What a great journey!

Figure 11.11 Guides in desktop publishing software

Kerning

In typography, *kerning* refers to adjusting the space between characters, especially by placing two characters closer together than normal. Kerning makes certain combinations of letters, such as WA, MW, TA and VA, look better.

Only the most sophisticated wordprocessors and desktop publishing systems perform kerning. Normally, you can activate or deactivate kerning for particular fonts.

Leading

Leading is the space between lines of text. Pronounced 'ledding', its name comes from the practice of using metal strips (usually lead) of varying widths to separate lines of text in the days of metal type. Leading is also called line spacing. Setting the leading in desktop publishing allows greater control of line space when compared with traditional wordprocessing applications.

OCTAVE
Before adjusting kerning

OCTAVE
After adjusting kerning

Figure 11.12 An example of kerning

Style sheets

Style sheets are collections of tags, frames, text formats and other information relating to the layout of a page or document. Style sheets determine the appearance of the printed page.

You can use only one style sheet for each document, but style sheets can be switched during the production of a document. This automatically applies the styles from the new style sheet and allows the user to view the document in different presentation styles in order to select the best design.

Style sheets are useful because the user can apply the same style sheet to many documents. For example, one style sheet could be defined for personal letters, another for official letters, and a third for reports. Style sheets can also be thought of as document *templates*.

Widow/orphan control

Orphan is a term used to describe a single word appearing at the bottom of a paragraph or column. A *widow* is a single word or short phrase appearing alone at the top of a page or column.

Most desktop publishing packages have a feature called 'widow/orphan control' which specifies how widowed/orphaned text is to be treated and how it can be corrected. Some applications automatically increase or reduce word spacing in order to bring the widowed/orphaned text back into the main paragraph.

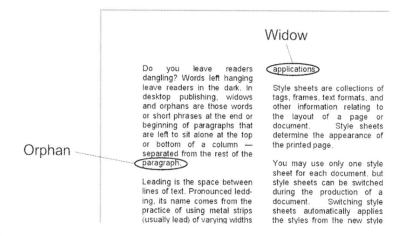

Figure 11.13 Example of an orphan and a widow in desktop publishing

A designer working with desktop publishing software

Wordprocessing/desktop publishing summary

Wordprocessing and desktop publishing applications are the most commonly used applications today. The preparation of text for print is key to managing any organisation, and the various features offered by these applications should be considered carefully before selecting which one to use to prepare a document.

Graphic designers were originally attracted to desktop publishing packages for the software's ability to manipulate text and graphics on screen quickly and easily. This allowed designers to try out new ideas and layouts without having to print them. These features are now readily available in less expensive to use 'trimmed down' DTP packages, which are also easier for novice users to operate.

Software developers are adding more page layout and type control features to their wordprocessing applications – features that were previously the domain of DTP packages. This is one of the reasons why the line between desktop publishing and wordprocessing is blurring.

Presentation/web authoring

Presentation and web authoring software can each be used to present information to an audience. The 'audience' could be a single user viewing the information at a computer terminal, or a collection of individuals watching a presentation. Each of these applications prepares information for digital media, as opposed to wordprocessing and desktop publishing applications which prepare information for printed media.

Presentation

Presentation packages are primarily concerned with presenting information in a linear structure – one page or slide after another. This is the traditional format used for business presentations. Business presentations account for more than 95 per cent of the use of presentation software in the world today, according to Microsoft. Microsoft makes PowerPoint, the world's most frequently used presentation software.

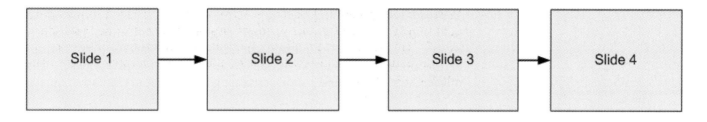

Figure 11.14 *A linear presentation structure*

The tools provided by presentation software allow a number of objects (text, graphics, video, etc.) to be assembled into slides which can be displayed to an audience.

Design for kiosk or design for presentation

Presentation software is primarily used to create presentations which are either printed out onto transparent slides for use with an overhead projector; presented using a digital projector; or, for a small audience, presented on screen.

It is also possible to use presentation software to create an interactive presentation which can be viewed as an *information kiosk*. For navigation, these presentations often use on-screen buttons and text for a branching structure, allowing the user an element of choice as he or she views the presentation, with options or links providing access to a range of content.

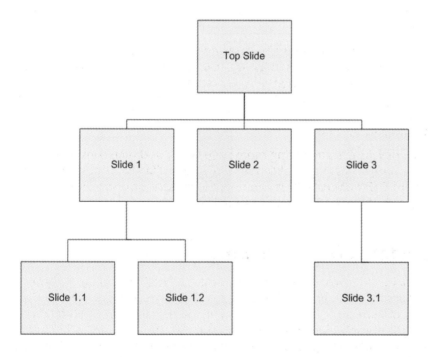

Figure 11.15 *A branch structure for a kiosk presentation*

All presentation packages have a number of common features which are used to generate professional presentations for organisation purposes. These features include the following.

Creating pages/inserting pages

Each complete screen in a presentation is called a *page* or *slide* depending on the software being used. We shall refer to each screen as a 'slide' for simplicity. New slides can be created at any point in an existing presentation or simply added at the end of the presentation.

Master slide

A new presentation can be created as a completely empty file which requires styles and other presentation details to be specified by the user, or the presentation can be based on a *master slide* or *template*. This master slide/template is a slide containing the default presentation details for each slide in the presentation. This can dictate the formatting of text, headings, page numbers, background graphics, etc. These master slides are loaded and then form the basis for every new slide created using the software.

Many presentation applications provide support for a number of master slides. This allows a number of slide styles to be used within one presentation.

In Figure 11.16 the master slide includes details of the text formats to be used and the numbering levels available within the master slide. Each level and heading has its own style. The graphic shown on the master slide will be duplicated on each page of the presentation.

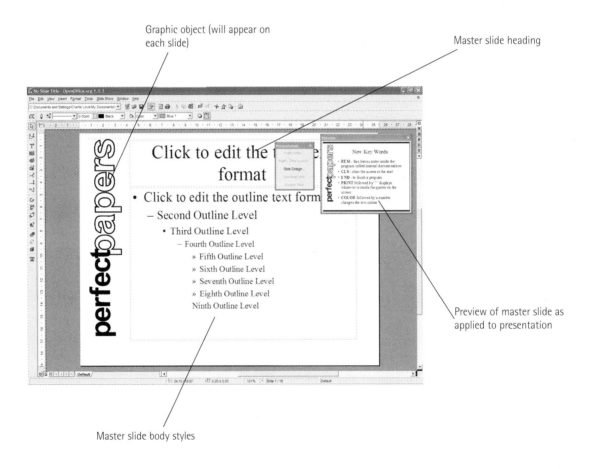

Figure 11.16 A master slide from OpenOffice 1.1.3

House styles can be applied to presentations by using the in-house master slide or template. 'House style' is the term used to describe a set of rules that organisations may adopt to create and maintain a visual consistency in their documents. A house style will dictate how presentations and other digital and printed media should be formatted. A good house style allows an organisation to establish a strong corporate identity, that is, a strong image associated with the company. An example of this would be the Golden 'M' device and colour scheme used by the fast-food chain McDonalds.

Slide sorter/slide view

A *slide sorter* or *slide view* is a common tool which provides an overview of the slides in the presentation. Each slide can be viewed in miniature. The slides are shown in the 'default' order of presentation. The sequence can be altered by dragging and dropping the slides in a different order.

The slide sorter or slide view can be thought of as a slide 'storyboard' which details the default linear structure that the presentation will follow.

Slide transitions

The transition between each slide can be specified in the slide sorter. A *transition* is a visual effect used when changing from one slide to another. Example transitions are:

- **fade to black** – when the screen fades to black and then fades up again with the new slide
- **push right** – when the current slide is pushed from the left of the screen and out the right-hand side by the new slide
- **dissolve** – when the current slide 'dissolves', via pixilation, to a display of the next slide.

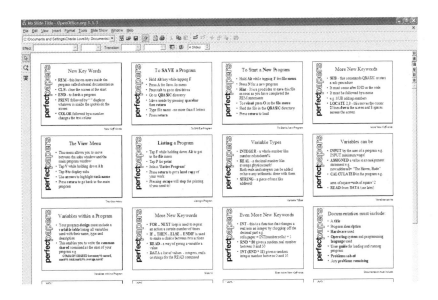

Figure 11.17 Setting a transition in slide view – OpenOffice 1.1.3

Outline view

Outline view in a presentation application allows the user to create slides by entering the text for the slides first. The text is entered as headings and then the content text is added below it. Text can be indented to create bulleted lists and so on.

Figure 11.18 Outline view – Microsoft PowerPoint 2003

Structure (heading, content, etc.)

Typically, each slide in a presentation has a structure. The most common structure for a presentation is a slide which has a heading followed by a number of bullet points. These contain the content of the slide (the information being presented). Most presentation applications have a range of default slide structures or layouts which can be applied. Figure 11.19 displays a number of these from Microsoft PowerPoint.

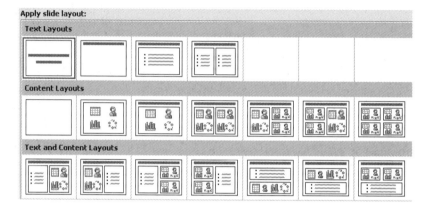

Figure 11.19 Some possible slide layouts from Microsoft PowerPoint

These layouts allow different media elements to be inserted into the presentation. These elements include charts and graphs, images, video, audio and text.

Insert graphics

Graphics can be inserted into a presentation from ClipArt libraries or from image files. Once inserted in a presentation, graphics can be edited in a variety of ways (for example, see Figure 11.20).

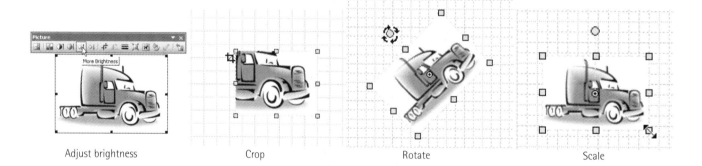

Adjust brightness   Crop   Rotate   Scale

Figure 11.20 Examples of graphic manipulations

Graphics can also be scanned directly into the presentation using scanning software.

Insert business data – charts etc.

Presentations are very often given to explain and distribute business information. This is often in the form of charts, graphics and organisational diagrams. These objects can be imported into a presentation from other applications, or they can be created using the tools available in the presentation application.

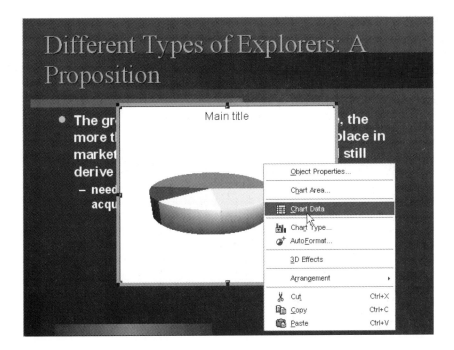

Figure 11.21 Creating business information with presentation tools – OpenOffice 1.1.3

Animation

All elements of the presentation can be animated in some way. A common animation applied to presentations is to have objects 'fly in' from outside the viewable area. All modern presentation applications have a large number of these animation effects which can be applied to objects in the presentation. In addition, many applications allow sounds to be attached to the animation.

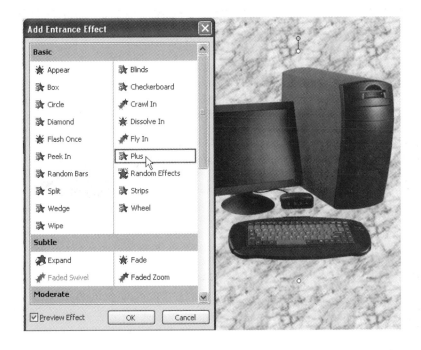

Figure 11.22 Adding animation effects – Microsoft PowerPoint 2003

More advanced presentation packages allow greater control of animation, such as allowing animations to follow predetermined paths around the slide using *animation to path* or shape-changing animations using *tweening* to allow animations to be created using key frames. In tweening, two key animation frames are created and the software constructs the animation frames 'between' the two key frames, hence 'tweening'.

Figure 11.23 An object animated to follow a motion path – Microsoft PowerPoint 2003

Action buttons/hyperlinks

Actions can be added to any object that is part of the presentation. When an object is selected, some kind of interactivity is initiated, such as the display of an animated object or branching to show a new slide.

An action button can be programmed using a scripting or macro language to carry out specific operations.

Hyperlinks can also be added to text and other objects in the presentation. When selected, the presentation software will try to load data from a URL. A URL (uniform resource locator) is the address of a resource, either on the local computer, the network to which the computer is connected or the Internet. If the presentation software cannot load the requested data, the default web browser will be loaded. This will then be used to display the document indicated by the URL.

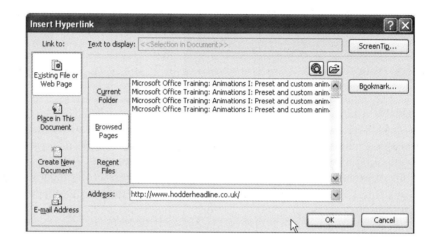

Figure 11.24 An object animated to follow a motion path – Microsoft PowerPoint 2003

Presentational style

There are some common rules to follow when creating presentations. These rules ensure that the presentations created by an organisation are clear, make good use of fonts and colour and are free from unnecessary material.

Formatting

Slides should be correctly sized for the target medium, i.e. screen, over-head transparency or projector. 'Breathing room' should be left around the border of the slide. This makes it easier to read.

Backgrounds

Similar backgrounds in a presentation give a presentation cohesiveness. Ensure the backgrounds are simple so they don't distract from important information. Also, ensure that there is sufficient difference between the foreground and background colours to ensure that text stands out.

Fonts

A relatively large size of type should be used in a font that is easy to read. A sans-serif font is normally less distracting than a serif font. All-capital text should be avoided if possible, because although it is eye-catching, it is difficult to read.

For transparencies and slides, headings should be 38–44 points, other text should be 28–32 points. Any type of less than 20 points should be avoided, because it is generally too small for an audience to read. When a smaller font cannot be avoided, bold text should be used to increase the general readability of the text. The colour of the foreground text should be sufficiently different from the background to ensure that the text can be clearly read.

Graphics

Ensure thick lines are used when creating line graphs and line drawings. Graphs and other objects imported from other applications should be checked for readability to ensure that the fonts and line widths are suitable for the presentation.

Slide content

For spoken presentations, the slide content should be structured to include only important points. The digital presentation should not include the whole spoken presentation.

Individual slides should not contain too much information because this is distracting for an audience.

Use colour wisely

Use colours that contrast so the distinction between colours is easily discernible. Remember that yellow is difficult to see on a white background. Red often signifies negative information such as decreased income, green often signifies positive information such as an increase in sales.

Web authoring

Web authoring software is available in a vast variety of styles. These range from text editors which allow hypertext markup language (HTML) to be constructed for web pages, to WYSIWYG (what you see is what you get) editors which allow web pages to be assembled using a visual editor, with little requirement to know or understand the markup language used to construct the page.

In addition to constructing HTML, modern web authoring tools may also include features to allow Java, JavaScript, Flash, VBScript, Dynamic HTML (DHTML), PHP, Perl and other server-side and client-side technologies to be created and edited, however the details of these technologies is beyond the scope of this course.

Create page

All web authoring tools have the capability to create new empty pages. Often applications will include a number of page templates or layouts which can be used to 'jump start' page development.

Site mapping

The more advanced web authoring applications include tools which allow a website to be created and/or managed using a graphic overview. This overview shows the links between pages and can be used to manage how the site is navigated (Figure 11.26).

Higher Information Systems

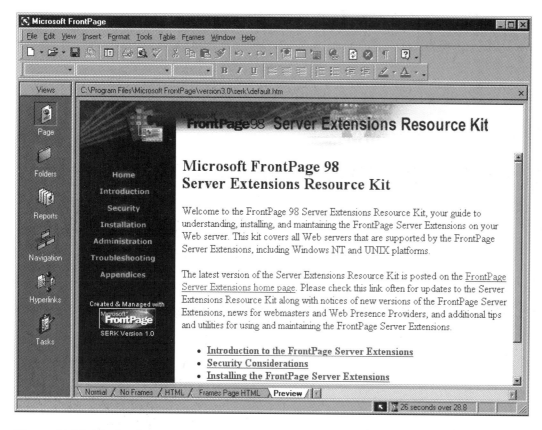

Figure 11.25 Microsoft FrontPage – A popular WYSIWYG web authoring application

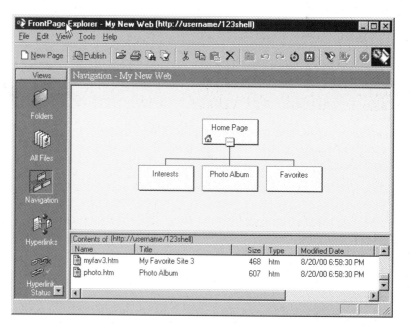

Figure 11.26 Website map in Microsoft FrontPage

Page structure

Web pages can have a wide variety of structures or layouts. These structures are generally based on frames or tables.

Frame-based web page layouts use a main page to establish a frame structure. This structure divides the web browser display area into two or more sections (frames). The contents of each frame are taken from a different web page. Frames provide great flexibility in designing web pages, but many designers avoid them because they are supported unevenly by current browsers.

Tables are now more commonly used to provide structure in web pages. The elements of a web page are entered into a table structure. This table structure ensures that pages are consistently displayed in the format which the web page designer intended.

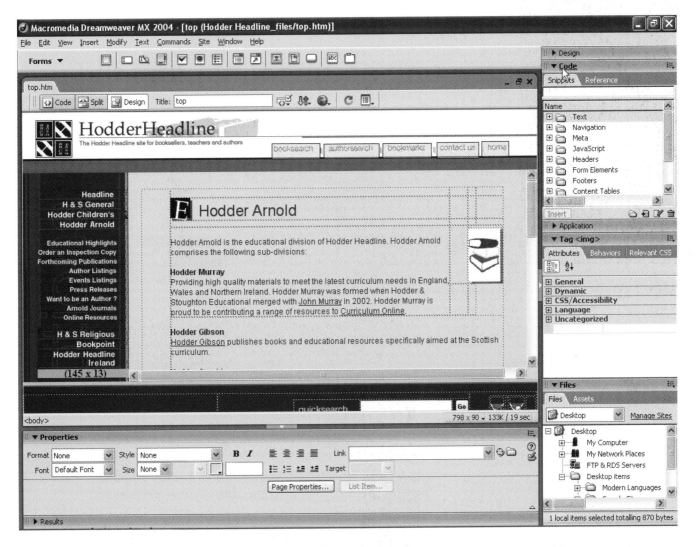

Figure 11.27 Table structure in Macromedia Dreamweaver

In addition to web page structures being based on frames or tables, there are other, more design-orientated structures which are commonly found in web pages.

Web pages will often include a header and a navigation menu. Corporate sites will often include information blocks down the sides of pages which will contain additional information.

Hyperlinks

A *hyperlink* is an element in an electronic document that links to another place in the same document or to an entirely different document. Typically, you click on the hyperlink to follow the link. The hyperlink is identified on screen using an anchor.

Static menu for navigation

Pull down menu

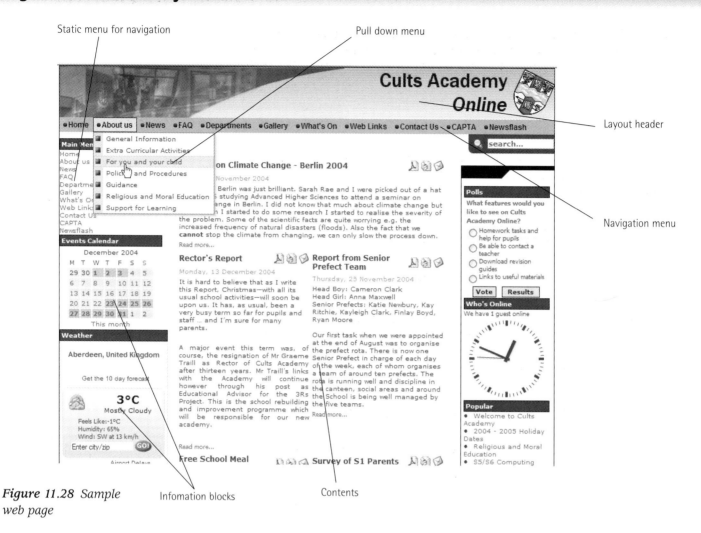

Layout header

Navigation menu

Infomation blocks

Contents

Figure 11.28 Sample web page

Web authoring applications allow hyperlinks to be added to documents in a number of ways:

- Text can be highlighted and turned into a hyperlink by allocating a URL. Normally, the hyperlink text will appear underlined and in a blue colour.

- Images can be selected and allocated a URL. When any part of the image is clicked by the user, the target document is loaded.

- Hotspots can be allocated to a number of areas within an image and a URL allocated to each hotspot. When the hotspot is clicked, the URL is activated and the target document loaded.

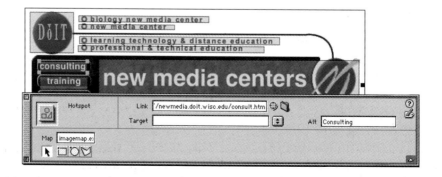

Figure 11.29 Creating image hotspots in Macromedia Dreamweaver

Hyperlinks can also appear within one document. When the text of a document does not all fit on one screen it is good design practice to include links to areas further down the page. These links use the same URL as the main document but have different *targets*, which are embedded destinations within the document.

Incorporating objects

Images and animations can be inserted into web pages relatively easily. Most web authoring applications have the facility to insert and then manipulate objects. For example, depending on the software being used, once an image has been inserted it can be scaled, turned into a hyperlink/have hotspots added, have its brightness/contrast adjusted, be optimised to reduce the time it takes to download it and be rotated.

These are only some of the possibilities; other objects that can be incorporated into a web page are videos, animations (such as those created by Macromedia Flash) and audio files (such as MP3).

Many advanced web authoring tools can create complex multimedia objects, such as navigation bars, pull-down menus and animated buttons. The user simply completes a dialogue box and the application creates the media object (Figure 11.30).

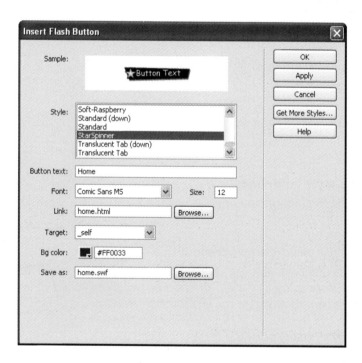

Figure 11.30 Creating an animated button in Macromedia Dreamweaver

Cascading style sheets (CSS)

Cascading style sheets are a feature of HTML that allows both website developers and users more control over the fonts, colours, layout, borders, etc. that go into each web page than can be provided by raw HTML. In fact, style sheets can control almost every aspect of the layout of a web page.

The cascading style sheet file is separate from the HTML files and can therefore be shared by multiple web pages to help provide a consistent look and feel across a website. By attaching different CSS files to a web page, a designer can experiment with different styles.

CSS technology is not yet fully supported by all browsers; however, newer versions of all popular browsers do provide some CSS support. CSS can be used to establish house styles and therefore develop a strong corporate identity using a consistent look and feel across all digital documents.

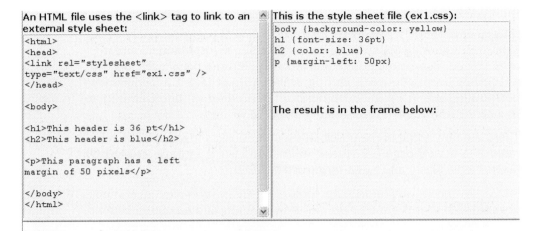

An HTML file uses the <link> tag to link to an external style sheet:

```
<html>
<head>
<link rel="stylesheet"
type="text/css" href="ex1.css" />
</head>

<body>

<h1>This header is 36 pt</h1>
<h2>This header is blue</h2>

<p>This paragraph has a left
margin of 50 pixels</p>

</body>
</html>
```

This is the style sheet file (ex1.css):

```
body {background-color: yellow}
h1 {font-size: 36pt}
h2 {color: blue}
p {margin-left: 50px}
```

The result is in the frame below:

This header is 36 pt

This header is blue

This paragraph has a left margin of 50 pixels

Figure 11.31 Example of a cascading style sheet

Web page style guidelines

There are several things to consider when constructing a website and web pages:

Follow a simple and consistent design

Complex designs can confuse users, so keep it simple. A consistent design will allow users to concentrate on content, without having to waste time figuring out how to navigate the site layout.

Don't use unnecessary graphics

It is important not to over-use graphics. Blinking text and other excessive decorations can be distracting; background colours and textures can affect download time. Think very carefully about the colours and textures you choose for backgrounds and the effect they have on the readability of the text.

Give people cross links

Visitors should be able to move from one major page to another on your site without having to go back to your home page. Put cross links to all your major pages at the bottom of all major pages.

Be careful about over-linking

While linking to other content in an organisation and throughout the world can help users, it can also lead to information overload. It is important to balance linking within page design. Too many links can be a visual eyesore on the page and detract from the main information.

Don't create dead-end links

Users can get discouraged from returning to a website if it contains pages which are filled with empty links.

Identify all pages

Place a standard paragraph of text at the bottom of all major pages. This should contain the name of the page owner, date of last update, organisation name, and an e-mail address for comments and reporting broken links.

Spreadsheet (data handling)

Spreadsheet applications are particularly useful for carrying out complex calculations and examining what-if scenarios.

What-if analysis

A basic spreadsheet uses a collection of text, values and formulae to complete calculations. Spreadsheet applications can quickly recalculate values when changes are made, so they allow you to do what accountants used to call 'working the numbers'.

Often, in financial, mathematical and engineering problem solving, we like to see the effect of changing some parameters on related parameters. In other words, we are interested in scenario changes. Such testing is called *What-if analysis*.

Example

Fred Smith runs a mobile phone shop and employs three sales people. Each mobile phone has a cost price of £10.00 and a sale price of £25.00. Fred is worried about the sales performance of one of his sales staff, Johnny Mitchell.

	A	B	C	D
1				
2		Oct	Nov	Dec
3	Charlie Burton	100	100	100
4	Johnny Mitchell	100	100	0
5	Tommy Kelly	200	200	100
6	Total Sales	400	400	200
7				
8		Quarterly Sales		1000
9		Fixed Costs		5000
10		Production cost/unit		10
11		Selling Price/unit		25
12		Profit		10000

Figure 11.32 What-if analysis, Part 1 – Open Office 1.1.3

How much more profit would Fred make if Johnny Mitchell performed as well in December as he had done in the previous months? The result can easily be computed manually, of course. But with a spreadsheet, such questions can be answered in a fraction of the time. The result of the query is shown in Figure 11.33.

	A	B	C	D
1				
2		Oct	Nov	Dec
3	Charlie Burton	100	100	100
4	Johnny Mitchell	100	100	100
5	Tommy Kelly	200	200	100
6	Total Sales	400	400	300
7				
8		Quarterly Sales		1100
9		Fixed Costs		5000
10		Production cost/unit		10
11		Selling Price/unit		25
12		Profit		11500

Figure 11.33 What-if analysis, Part 2 – Open Office 1.1.3

Goal seeking

Goal seeking is the opposite of what-if analysis. With a what-if analysis we amend the data to see what the result will be, as in the sales example above. With goal seeking, the required result is specified and the spreadsheet application is asked to calculated what the data values should be. The formulae required for goal seeking are more complex than those used in what-if analyses, and therefore require a greater understanding of the spreadsheet application's inbuilt functions.

For example, a function can be used to calculate the amount of money you would have after a period of years of investing a monthly amount at a particular interest rate. Then, using the goal-seek feature, you can see how much you would have to invest monthly to reach a particular goal. In the following example we will see how much money we need to invest each month to reach a goal of £100,000 for a child's university fund.

Example

First, a spreadsheet is created as if a what-if analysis were being carried out. An example payment amount of £100 monthly is entered, as is the predicted interest rate for the investment (10%), and the number of months for the payments to be made (assuming in this case that the fund is started when the child is born and runs until he or she is 18).

A spreadsheet function is now used to calculate the future value of the investment. This example is being created in Microsoft Excel, but the principles and functions used are available in most spreadsheet applications.

The Microsoft Excel function FV calculates the future value of an investment given the interest rate, number of payments and payment amount. In Figure 11.35 the Rate is divided by 12 because the payments are monthly but the interest rate is annual.

Once the function has been entered it is now time to use the goal-seeking tools. In Microsoft Excel this is selected from the **Tools** menu (Figure 11.36).

	A	B
1	University Fund	
2		
3	Payment Amount	-£ 166.51
4	Interest Rate	10%
5	Term (months)	216
6	**Final Amount**	

Figure 11.34 Goal seeking: setting up spreadsheet – Microsoft Excel

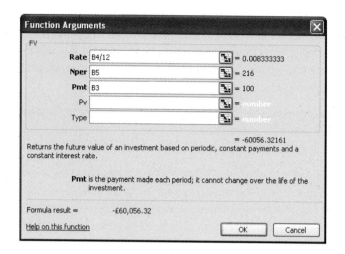

Figure 11.35 Goal seeking: inserting a function – Microsoft Excel

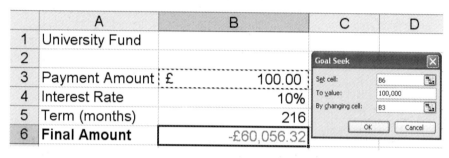

Figures 11.36 Goal seeking: goal-seek tool – Microsoft Excel

When **OK** is clicked the application calculates the *Payment Amount* required to generate £100,000.

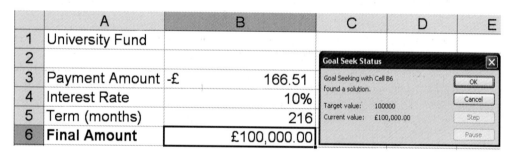

Figure 11.37 Goal seeking: goal-seek status– Microsoft Excel

The resulting *Payment Amount* is shown as a negative because you will be paying it *out* of your account.

Goal seeking is extremely useful for managers in organisations. It allows a manager to see what has to be done in order to meet a particular goal.

Forecasting

Spreadsheet applications can be used to forecast future trends and results based on historical data. Forecasts can be improved by using statistical tools to better understand the historical data.

Example

Fred Smith (from the earlier example) is still selling mobile phones. Business is good and he would like to forecast what sales will be like over the next few months if things continue as they are.

First of all Fred creates a spreadsheet which contains all his sales information for the last three years. He then tries to work out his average sales over a period of months so that he can use this *moving average* to calculate future sales, but there are problems. His sales go up and down through the year with people buying phones for Christmas presents or before they go on holiday.

In order to compensate for this he creates a formula for the moving average which averages the sales for 12 months and the sales for 13 months. But this still doesn't remove the seasonal nature of his sales data.

Fred now calculates a *seasonal index* that calculates how typical each month's sales are compared with the moving average. If the seasonal index is one then the moving average and the sales figure are identical and the sales for that month are typical for the company. If the seasonal index is less than one then the sales are less than the moving average and poorer than normal, and if the seasonal index is greater than one then the sales are better than the moving average. The seasonal index is created by a formula which divides the sales by the moving average (e.g. B7/C7). This seasonal index is calculated for as many months as possible and each month in the year is identified.

	A	B	C
1	Month	Sales	Moving Average
2	1	18,917	
3	2	19,043	
4	3	24,647	
5	4	24,811	
6	5	24,977	
7	6	19,556	24,476
8	7	19,686	24,835
9	8	33,973	24,987
10	9	34,199	25,158
11	10	34,427	25,098
12	11	20,216	25,252
13	12	20,351	25,978
14	13	20,487	26,164
15	14	20,623	26,400
16	15	26,693	26,036
17	16	26,871	26,225
18	17	27,050	26,366
19	18	21,179	26,507
20	19	21,320	26,897
21	20	36,792	27,061
22	21	37,038	27,246
23	22	37,285	27,181
24	23	21,894	27,348
25	24	22,040	28,134
26	25	22,187	28,335
27	26	22,335	28,591
28	27	28,908	28,197
29	28	29,101	
30	29	29,295	
31	30	22,937	
32	31	23,090	
33	32	39,846	
34	33	40,112	
35	34	40,379	
36	35	23,712	
37	36	23,870	

Figure 11.38 Forecasting: generating a moving average – Microsoft Excel

	A	B	C	D	E
1	Month	Sales	Moving Average	Month	Calculated Seasonal Index
2	1	18,917			
3	2	19,043			
4	3	24,647			
5	4	24,811			
6	5	24,977			
7	6	19,556	24,476	6	0.799
8	7	19,686	24,835	7	0.793
9	8	33,973	24,987	8	1.360
10	9	34,199	25,158	9	1.359
11	10	34,427	25,098	10	1.372
12	11	20,216	25,252	11	0.801
13	12	20,351	25,978	12	0.783
14	13	20,487	26,164	1	0.783
15	14	20,623	26,400	2	0.781
16	15	26,693	26,036	3	1.025
17	16	26,871	26,225	4	1.025
18	17	27,050	26,366	5	1.026
19	18	21,179	26,507	6	0.799
20	19	21,320	26,897	7	0.793
21	20	36,792	27,061	8	1.360
22	21	37,038	27,246	9	1.359
23	22	37,285	27,181	10	1.372
24	23	21,894	27,348	11	0.801
25	24	22,040	28,134	12	0.783
26	25	22,187	28,335	1	0.783
27	26	22,335	28,591	2	0.781
28	27	28,908	28,197	3	1.025
29	28	29,101			
30	29	29,295			
31	30	22,937			
32	31	23,090			
33	32	39,846			
34	33	40,112			
35	34	40,379			
36	35	23,712			
37	36	23,870			

Figure 11.39 Forecasting: generating a seasonal index – Microsoft Excel

You'll notice that the seasonal index for each Month 6 is different. In fact the seasonal index for each month in different years is never the same. Fred decides to use the seasonal index for the first complete 12-monthly period as the most reliable.

He can now use these figures to forecast sales with and without taking into account the seasonal nature of his business. His first task is to adjust his previous sales to take account of the seasonal changes. He does this using the seasonal index (Figure 11.40).

These seasonally adjusted sales make it easier to generate a forecast of future income because the seasonal peaks and lows of the business have been removed. A graph can now be created to illustrate the adjusted historical sales. Once this graph has been created a trend line can be added to it to show the best fit of the sales data.

Like any line on a chart, the trend line has an equation which can be used to forecast where the line would go if it were to continue across the graph.

	A	B	C	D
1	Month	Sales	Seasonal Index	Adjusted Sales
2	1	18,917	0.783	24,158
3	2	19,043	0.781	24,376
4	3	24,647	1.025	24,041
5	4	24,811	1.025	24,215
6	5	24,977	1.026	24,345
7	6	19,556	0.799	24,476
8	7	19,686	0.793	24,835
9	8	33,973	1.360	24,987
10	9	34,199	1.359	25,158
11	10	34,427	1.372	25,098
12	11	20,216	0.801	25,252
13	12	20,351	0.783	25,978
14	13	20,487	0.783	26,164
15	14	20,623	0.781	26,400
16	15	26,693	1.025	26,036
17	16	26,871	1.025	26,225
18	17	27,050	1.026	26,366
19	18	21,179	0.799	26,507
20	19	21,320	0.793	26,897
21	20	36,792	1.360	27,061
22	21	37,038	1.359	27,246
23	22	37,285	1.372	27,181
24	23	21,894	0.801	27,348
25	24	22,040	0.783	28,134
26	25	22,187	0.783	28,335
27	26	22,335	0.781	28,591
28	27	28,908	1.025	28,197
29	28	29,101	1.025	28,402
30	29	29,295	1.026	28,554
31	30	22,937	0.799	28,707
32	31	23,090	0.793	29,129
33	32	39,846	1.360	29,307
34	33	40,112	1.359	29,508
35	34	40,379	1.372	29,437
36	35	23,712	0.801	29,618
37	36	23,870	0.783	30,469

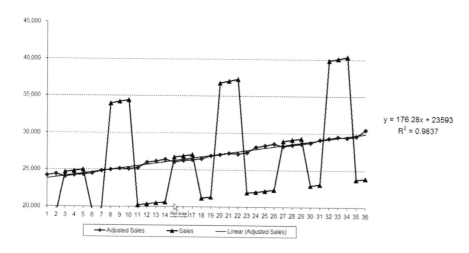

$$y = 176.28x + 23593$$
$$R^2 = 0.9837$$

Figure 11.41 Forecasting: graph of sales with trend line – Microsoft Excel

Figure 11.40 Forecasting: seasonal adjusted sales – Microsoft Excel

This formula ($y = 176.28x + 23593$) can be used to forecast the future values of seasonally adjusted sales. The formula is entered into the spreadsheet and the x value is replaced with the sales month value from the spreadsheet (i.e. for month 37 the cell reference would be A38).

Now that the seasonally adjust forecast is available (Figure 11.42), Fred can use these values, with his seasonal index, to forecast actual sales (Figure 11.43). To do this he creates a formula which multiples the adjusted forecast figure by the seasonal index.

Finally, Fred creates a graph to illustrate his current and future sales data. (Figure 11.44.)

This is only one example of how a spreadsheet can be used to forecast future data. There are many different way to generate forecasts.

Lookup tables

We use tables mainly so that we can find the information we need quickly. When we require a piece of information we can look it up, such as the time of the next train from a train timetable.

	A	B	C	D	E
1	Month	Sales	Seasonal Index	Adjusted Sales	Forecast Adjusted Sales
35	34	40,379	1.372	29,437	
36	35	23,712	0.801	29,618	
37	36	23,870	0.783	30,469	
38	37		0.783		30,115
39	38		0.781		30,292
40	39		1.025		30,468
41	40		1.025		30,644
42	41		1.026		30,820
43	42		0.799		30,997
44	43		0.793		31,173
45	44		1.360		31,349
46	45		1.359		31,526
47	46		1.372		31,702
48	47		0.801		31,878
49	48		0.783		32,054
50	49		0.783		32,231
51	50		0.781		32,407
52	51		1.025		32,583
53	52		1.025		32,760
54	53		1.026		32,936
55	54		0.799		33,112
56	55		0.793		33,288
57	56		1.360		33,465
58	57		1.359		33,641
59	58		1.372		33,817
60	59		0.801		33,994
61	60		0.783		34,170

Figure 11.42 Forecasting: seasonally adjusted forecast – Microsoft Excel

	A	B	C	D	E	F
1	Month	Sales	Seasonal Index	Adjusted Sales	Forecast Adjusted Sales	Forecast
35	34	40,379	1.372	29,437		
36	35	23,712	0.801	29,618		
37	36	23,870	0.783	30,469		
38	37		0.783		30,115	23,581
39	38		0.781		30,292	23,664
40	39		1.025		30,468	31,236
41	40		1.025		30,644	31,398
42	41		1.026		30,820	31,620
43	42		0.799		30,997	24,766
44	43		0.793		31,173	24,710
45	44		1.360		31,349	42,624
46	45		1.359		31,526	42,855
47	46		1.372		31,702	43,486
48	47		0.801		31,878	25,521
49	48		0.783		32,054	25,112
50	49		0.783		32,231	25,238
51	50		0.781		32,407	25,316
52	51		1.025		32,583	33,405
53	52		1.025		32,760	33,566
54	53		1.026		32,936	33,790
55	54		0.799		33,112	26,456
56	55		0.793		33,288	26,387
57	56		1.360		33,465	45,500
58	57		1.359		33,641	45,731
59	58		1.372		33,817	46,388
60	59		0.801		33,994	27,215
61	60		0.783		34,170	26,769

Figure 11.43 Forecasting: final forecast – Microsoft Excel

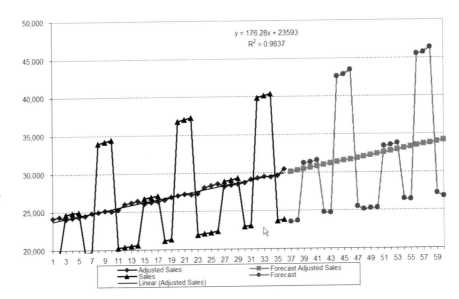

Figure 11.44 Forecasting: final forecast graph – Microsoft Excel

Spreadsheet applications can retrieve data from tables using lookup functions. The lookup table is placed on one spreadsheet and the spreadsheet software can retrieve data from it. This data can be inserted into the same spreadsheet or in another one.

This means, for example, that lookup functions on an invoice worksheet can handle the details of putting the unit price in the right place. When

=LOOKUP(A10,$F$5:$F$16,$G$5:$G$15)

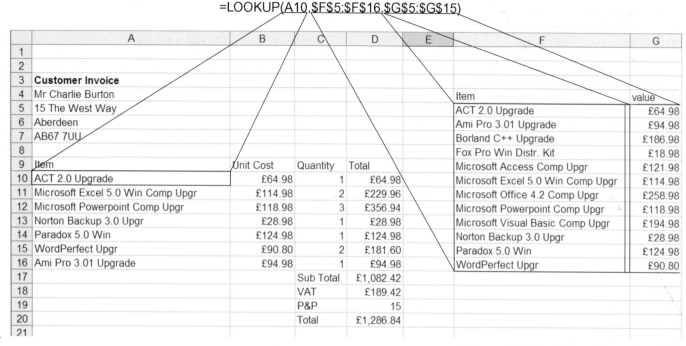

	A	B	C	D	E	F	G
1							
2							
3	**Customer Invoice**						
4	Mr Charlie Burton					Item	value
5	15 The West Way					ACT 2.0 Upgrade	£64.98
6	Aberdeen					Ami Pro 3.01 Upgrade	£94.98
7	AB67 7UU					Borland C++ Upgrade	£186.98
8						Fox Pro Win Distr. Kit	£18.98
9	Item	Unit Cost	Quantity	Total		Microsoft Access Comp Upgr	£121.98
10	ACT 2.0 Upgrade	£64.98	1	£64.98		Microsoft Excel 5.0 Win Comp Upgr	£114.98
11	Microsoft Excel 5.0 Win Comp Upgr	£114.98	2	£229.96		Microsoft Office 4.2 Comp Upgr	£258.98
12	Microsoft Powerpoint Comp Upgr	£118.98	3	£356.94		Microsoft Powerpoint Comp Upgr	£118.98
13	Norton Backup 3.0 Upgr	£28.98	1	£28.98		Microsoft Visual Basic Comp Upgr	£194.98
14	Paradox 5.0 Win	£124.98	1	£124.98		Norton Backup 3.0 Upgr	£28.98
15	WordPerfect Upgr	£90.80	2	£181.60		Paradox 5.0 Win	£124.98
16	Ami Pro 3.01 Upgrade	£94.98	1	£94.98		WordPerfect Upgr	£90.80
17			Sub Total	£1,082.42			
18			VAT	£189.42			
19			P&P	15			
20			Total	£1,286.84			
21							

Figure 11.45 Lookup table – Microsoft Excel

prices change, they only need to be changed in the lookup table, not in every individual invoice that is written. Lookup tables allow spreadsheets to make use of some of the advantages of relational databases, because values can be looked up using a 'find' value, which is essentially a key.

In Figure 11.45 the lookup formula for cell B10 is shown at the top of the figure. This formula searches for the value in A10 (the lookup value) in the range of cells $F$5:$F$16 (lookup vector). The $ signs signify that the range is an *absolute* cell range which will not change if the formula is replicated to other cells in the spreadsheet.

When a matching value is found in the lookup vector, the corresponding value in the result vector ($G$5:$G$16) is found and inserted into the cell containing the formula, in this case B10.

Charting

Charts transform data into graphics. The graphics are normally easier to understand than the raw figures on which they are based. Spreadsheet applications have a wide variety of charting tools which allow a range of

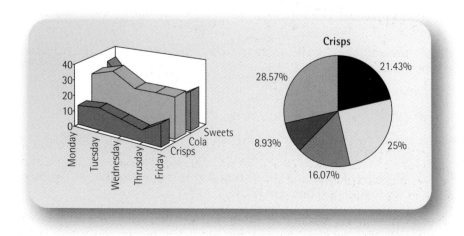

Figure 11.46 Example charts

different chart and graph types to be created and analysed. The trend tool, which was used in the forecasting illustration earlier, is an example of an analysis tool which can be used with a graph.

Advanced functions

As you have seen from earlier examples, spreadsheet applications can do much more than carry out the operations of a standard calculator! Below is a summary of the most commonly used advanced functions.

TODAY and NOW functions

The TODAY function returns only the current date. The NOW function returns the current date and time. This value will then be updated each time you recalculate the worksheet.

Within the spreadsheet, type in the following:

> = TODAY()
> = NOW()

AND or OR functions

The AND or OR function allows you to test up to 30 logical conditions and return a result of TRUE or FALSE depending on the result. The AND function returns a value of TRUE when all conditions are met and a value of FALSE if all conditions are not met. When using the OR function, a value of TRUE is returned if *any* of the arguments is true.

The syntax for the AND function is:

> = AND(logical condition, logical condition …)

The syntax for the OR function is:

> = OR(logical condition, logical condition …)

For example, you could use the AND function to determine if employees were eligible for benefits. Employees must work at least two years and be employed full-time before they are eligible for benefits. The function might look like this:

> = AND(B1 = "full-time",C1 > = 2)

If both these conditions were met, the spreadsheet application would return a result of TRUE. If one of these conditions was *not* met, the spreadsheet application would return a result of FALSE. We could then determine who was eligible for benefits.

IF function

The IF function returns one value if a condition you specify is TRUE and another value if it is FALSE.

The syntax for an IF function is:

> = IF(logical_test, value_if_true, value_if_false)

- The logical_test value in an IF function is a value or expression that can be either TRUE or FALSE. For example, B3 > = 60.
- The value_if_true part of the IF function is the value that is returned when the logical_test value is TRUE.
- The value_if_false part of the IF function is the value that is returned when the logical_test value is FALSE.

Imagine that you are a teacher and have a mark book containing overall term results for pupils. An IF function could be created that would state that if the overall mark is below 60, then return the value FAIL. If the overall mark is equal to or greater than 60, then return the value PASS. An example of this function is:

= IF(B3 > = 60, "PASS", "FAIL")

If you ever need to return a blank value for either the value_if_true or value_if_false portions of the formula, enter two double quotes ("") in the formula.

Nested IF functions

An IF function can be nested, which produces more complex formulae. For example, let's return to the mark book example above. In our spreadsheet, we want to return the value of A for each individual who has an overall mark of 89 or above; the value of B for everyone who has a 79 or above; the value of C for everyone that has a 69 and above; the value of D for everyone who has a 59 and above; and all others receive an F. This nested function would appear as follows:

= IF(F2 > 89,"A",IF(F2 > 79,"B",IF(F2 > 69,"C",IF(F2 > 59,"D","F"))))

Functions can become quite complex by nesting one function within another. For example, we will nest an AND function within an IF function. Going back to the benefit scenario mentioned earlier, if you wanted to calculate the amount of money each person would receive in benefits you could use the following function:

= IF(AND(B1 = "full-time",C1 > = 2),D1*.03,0)

This statement reads that if cell B1 states that an employee is full-time and employed for two or more years, then multiply their salary in cell D1 by .03. If these criteria are not met, then they receive no benefit and the amount would be zero.

COUNT function

The COUNT function counts the number of cells that contain numbers, or the number of cells which contain numbers from an argument list. If we wanted to count the number of pupils who scored 30, 29 or 28 in a test we would use the formula:

= COUNT(B1:B30, 30, 29, 28)

If we just wanted to count the pupils who had a mark for the test we would use:

= COUNT(B1:B30)

COUNTIF function

The COUNTIF function counts the number of cells within a range that meet the given criteria. The syntax for a COUNTIF function is:

= COUNTIF(range_of_cells_to_count, criteria)

An example of a COUNTIF function would be if you wanted to count the number of pupils who have the label PASS next to their name. The formula would be written as follows:

= COUNTIF(F2:F13, "PASS")

Macros

The purpose and use of macros in spreadsheet applications are identical to those in wordprocessing applications. Commonly used or complex sequences of operations can be simplified by recording them using a macro record or by programming them using a macro or scripting language.

When required, these macros can be run using a menu or by accessing a keyboard shortcut. In addition, in some applications it is possible to customise the user interface by adding a button to run the macro.

Project management

A project is any task which can be completed. A project can be anything from building a house to writing a computer program. Project management is the process of planning and controlling the project.

If time, money, or what your project could accomplish were unlimited, you wouldn't need to do project management. Unfortunately, most projects have a specific time limit, budget and scope.

The *budget* is the estimated cost of a project. The *schedule* is the timing and sequence of tasks within a project. The *scope* of a project defines what is to be achieved. It is this combination of elements – time (in terms of the project schedule), money and scope – that we refer to as the **project triangle**.

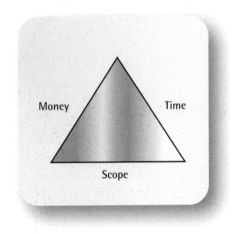

Figure 11.47 The project triangle

Understanding the project triangle will allow you to make better choices when you need to make trade-offs. If you adjust any one side of the triangle, the other two sides are affected. For example, if you decide to adjust the project plan to:

- finish earlier, you might end up with increased costs and less scope
- meet the project budget, the result might be a longer schedule and less scope
- increase scope, your project might take more time and cost more money in the form of resources such as workers.

Changes to your plan can affect the triangle in various ways, depending on your specific circumstances and the nature of your project. For example, in some instances, shortening your schedule might increase costs. In other instances, it might actually decrease costs.

Tasks are individual jobs which have to be completed as part of the project, e.g. reviewing the architect's plans when building a house. In project management, tasks are grouped together in logical blocks which contribute to project *milestones*. A milestone is a significant point in a project, e.g. foundations complete in a house building plan. Project management software allows time, scope and costs to be allocated to tasks.

Project management software greatly simplifies the management of projects. Money and time can be allocated and monitored as required to complete the project to scope, on time and within budget.

Timelining

Timelining is the process of allocating time and dates to project tasks and milestones. The first thing a project manager must do when using project management software is to specify the intended start of the project. From this, all other project dates can be calculated.

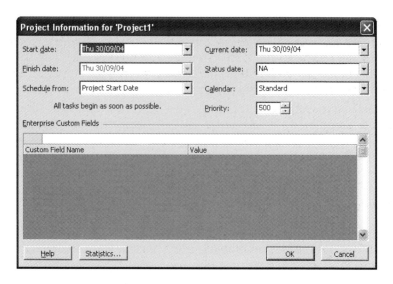

Figure 11.48 *Enter project information – Microsoft Project 2003*

The main screen of any project management software is a timeline screen. This displays a list of the tasks in the project and the time required to complete them.

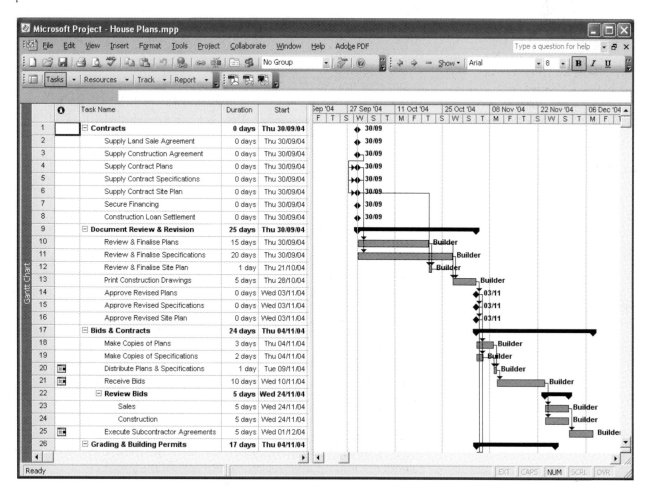

Figure 11.49 *Task view, Gantt chart – Microsoft Project 2003*

When a task is allocated to the timeline it is given a name and an expected duration. The task can also be given a priority to enable the project management software to prioritise tasks when there are insufficient resources or time available to complete them. The resources required for the task can also be added, as can any other associated costs. The project management software will create a list of all the resources used on the project.

255

Predecessor tasks are also indicated, if they exist. Predecessor tasks are those which must be completed before a new task can begin. For example, when building a house, the concrete cannot be poured for the foundations until the foundations have been excavated. In this case, 'excavate foundations' is the predecessor task for 'pour foundations'.

As more tasks are added to the timeline it becomes clear that some tasks must be completed in sequence and others can run concurrently. *Concurrent* tasks often have the same predecessor but are not dependent on each other. When concurrent tasks are present in a project then it is possible for each task to be worked on independently, subject to the availability of resources and budget.

Resource allocation

In order for a task to be completed it must have at least one resource allocated to it. This resource is most often someone to work on the task but can also be machinery, computer equipment, tools, subcontractors, in fact anything that allows the work to be completed.

Project management software allows resources to be used flexibly within the project. If someone is allocated to a task for 100 per cent of his or her time and is then pulled from the task for 50 per cent of the time to work on another task, the project management software will compensate for this change in working and increase the amount of time required to complete the first task. It is this adjustment and fine-tuning of time and resources that makes project management software so useful.

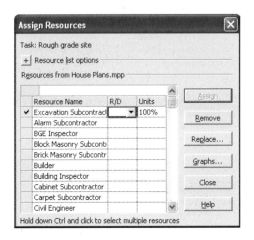

Figure 11.50 *Assign resources – Microsoft Project 2003*

Budget control

Each resource can be given a cost. These costs can be allocated on a per day, per hour or fixed cost basis. As resources are allocated to the project, the cost of the project can be calculated by the project management software (Figure 11.51). For example, a sub-contractor works for three days at a daily cost of £150. The software will work out the total cost for using the sub-contractor and allocate this to the cost of the project.

As the use of resources changes, the cost of the project will change. As the durations of the project tasks are changed, the costs will change accordingly.

Project management charts

Project management software can use a number of graphic representations to display information about a project and its progress.

	ⓘ	Resource Name	Type	Material Label	Initials	Group	Max. Units	Std. Rate	Ovt. Rate	Cost/Use	Accrue At
1		Sales Department	Work		S		100%	£0.00/hr	£0.00/hr	£0.00	Prorated
2		Construction Dept.	Work		C		100%	£0.00/hr	£0.00/hr	£0.00	Prorated
3		Sales Dept.	Work		S		100%	£0.00/hr	£0.00/hr	£0.00	Prorated
4		Client	Work		C		100%	£0.00/hr	£0.00/hr	£0.00	Prorated
5		County	Work		C		100%	£30.00/hr	£0.00/hr	£0.00	Prorated
6		County Sediment Control Inspector	Work		C		100%	£30.00/hr	£0.00/hr	£0.00	Prorated
7		Sediment Control Inspector	Work		S		100%	£25.00/hr	£0.00/hr	£0.00	Prorated
8		Department of Permits & Licenses	Work		D		100%	£30.00/hr	£0.00/hr	£0.00	Prorated
9		Building Inspector	Work		B		100%	£35.00/hr	£0.00/hr	£0.00	Prorated
10		Mason	Work		M		100%	£22.50/hr	£0.00/hr	£0.00	Prorated
11		Civil Engineer	Work		C		100%	£45.00/hr	£0.00/hr	£0.00	Prorated
12		Concrete Subcontractor	Work		C		100%	£0.00/hr	£0.00/hr	£150.00	Prorated
13		Concrete Subcontractor	Work		C		100%	£0.00/hr	£0.00/hr	£150.00	Prorated

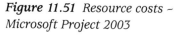

Figure 11.51 Resource costs – Microsoft Project 2003

Gantt charts

Gantt charts, sometimes called *project timelines*, are the most commonly used scheduling charts in business because they're easy to produce and easy to understand. Gantt charts have a timeline at the top and a list of tasks down the left side. Bars on the Gantt chart show the dates where tasks begin and end, based on precedence and duration.

The level of scheduling detail displayed in a Gantt chart can be determined by the time periods used for the timeline, i.e. hours, days, weeks or months. The time units used should be appropriate to the project.

Figure 11.52 Early start to early finish

Figure 11.53 Early start to late finish

Figure 11.54 Late start to late finish

We can show *float* on a Gantt chart. Float is the amount of time that a task may be delayed from its earliest start without affecting the project finish date. Float is a mathematical calculation and can change as the project progresses and changes are made to the project plan.

Figure 11.49 shows a Gantt chart for a house building project.

Network diagram

In a network diagram, tasks are represented by boxes and task dependencies are represented by lines connecting the boxes. Network diagrams are sometimes referred to as PERT charts.

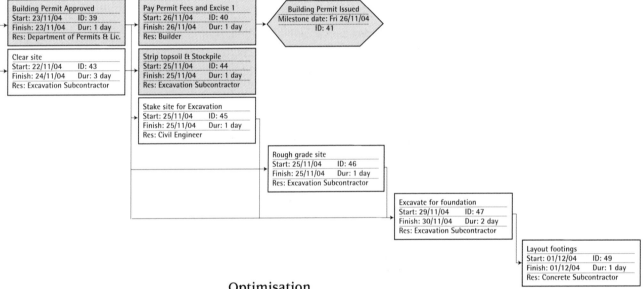

Figure 11.55 Example network diagram

Optimisation

Project plans can be optimised in three ways. They can be optimised to meet a time schedule, to meet a specific budget or to meet the requirements of the project scope.

Optimisation to meet schedule

Sometimes, when the project schedule is analysed, the project deadline cannot be met. There are several ways to adjust the length of a schedule to ensure that the deadline is achieved. The methods chosen depend on the limitations imposed on the project as a whole, such as budget, resource availability, scope, and the flexibility of the tasks.

The most efficient way to shorten the schedule is to change the tasks that lie on the *critical path*. The critical path is the series of tasks that must be completed on schedule for a project to finish on time. Each task on the critical path is a *critical task*.

The critical path is a series of dependent tasks whose last task finishes at the project end-date. If any of the tasks in this series move, the project end-date also moves. Modifying tasks that are not on the critical path may not affect the schedule. Possible actions are to:

- shorten the durations of tasks (usually a reflection of reduced scope or increased/more efficient resources)

- overlap tasks so that they can be worked on simultaneously

- remove tasks to meet the finish date (usually a reflection of reduced scope)

- assign additional resources
- decrease the amount of work assigned (usually a reflection of reduced scope or more efficient resources).

As you adjust the schedule, your costs might increase, resources might become over allocated, and your scope might have to change.

Optimisation to meet budget

If the project is over budget then adjustments must be made to reduce costs. Project costs are affected primarily by resources assigned to the tasks in the project. Therefore, to reduce costs, changes can be made to the project scope so that there are fewer tasks, or durations can be shortened for tasks that need resources.

As adjustments are made to the plan to meet the budget, the finish date might be extended, or the scope might decrease. For example, if the scope is cut to meet the budget, the finish date may actually occur sooner in the schedule.

Optimisation to meet scope

There are two aspects of scope to consider – *product scope* and *project scope*.

Product scope describes the final deliverables of the project, usually in great detail. Examples of product scope include product specifications or blueprints. Project managers normally have little control over product scope.

Project scope includes all of the project work done to produce the deliverables described by the product scope. A project manager has at very least some control over project scope.

Typically, the scope is adjusted when there is a problem with meeting the finish date or the budget for the project. The scope can be cut to bring in the finish date or cut costs. The scope can be increased if additional time or an increased budget becomes available.

Critical path analysis

Critical path analysis is the process of identifying the critical path in a project plan. The critical path consists of a series of tasks which begin when the project starts and finish when the project is completed. Any increase in the duration of any one of the tasks on the critical path will increase the total duration of the project.

The project management software can analyse the tasks in the project plan and highlight the critical path for the project manager.

Controlling projects with project management software

In addition to creating the project plan, project management software can be used to monitor and control the progress of the project. As work is completed on tasks this can be recorded as the 'percentage progress' for the task. If tasks are delayed because resources are not available or tasks have taken longer than expected to complete, then the project plan can be adapted to compensate.

Personal information management

Today, more people than ever are using software tools to deal with information. Personal information management (PIM) software allows a user to collect all their personal information in one integrated application. PIMs normally incorporate an address book or contacts database, calendar, task list and communication tools such as e-mail, fax and instant messaging. Common PIM applications are Microsoft Outlook, IBM Lotus Notes and Palm One Palm Desktop.

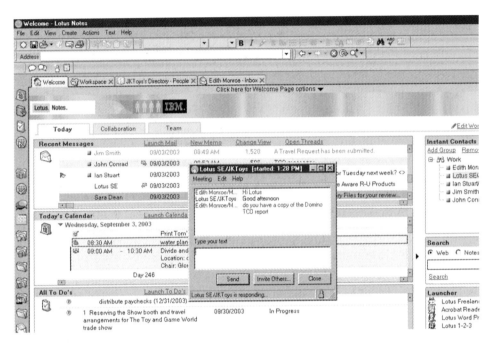

Figure 11.56 IBM Lotus Notes, Welcome screen. Courtesy of International Business Machines Corporation. Unauthorized use not permitted.

Communication

Communication is an essential part of any PIM. Most PIMs will include some kind of e-mail client (software which allows the user to send, receive and manage e-mail). E-mail can be organised into folders and flagged for various different responses. In addition to e-mail, other communication tools can be included or added by third party plug-in software. These additional tools might include fax, instant messaging and SMS text messaging.

Calendar

The calendar application in most PIMs allows the user to create appointments, add attendees to an appointment, specify the appointment location and set reminders for the appointment. The appointment will have a date, time and duration. It is normally possible to create a series of appointments, such as 'Meeting with Bill' every Tuesday at 10.30 am, 'Project team lunch' the first Wednesday of every month, or 'Vanessa's birthday' once a year.

Entries in the calendar can be amended or moved around the calendar. Clashes of event are normally shown in some way. The calendar can be shown in a number of views, such as 1 day, 5 days (working week), 7 days, 1 month and so on.

Some PIMs allow calendars to be shared on a network to allow appointments between work colleagues to be more easily made.

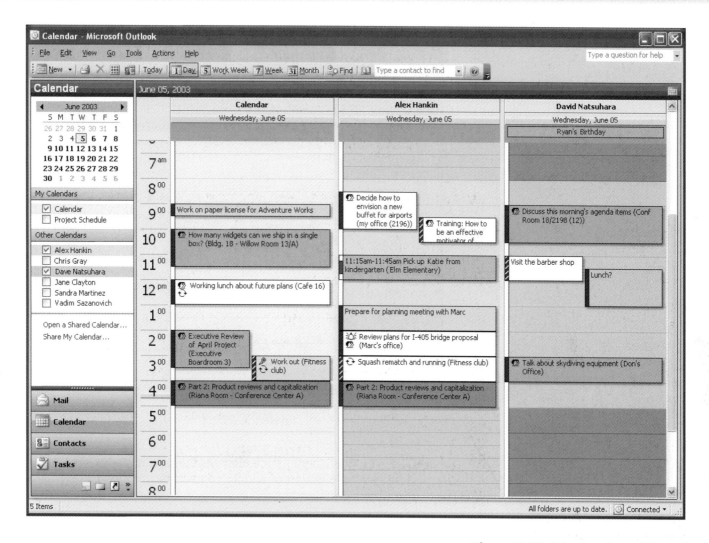

Figure 11.57 *Calendar view – Microsoft Outlook 2003*

Contacts

The contacts application of a PIM allows the user to store contacts details. These details include names, addresses, telephone numbers, mobile numbers, e-mail addresses, website URLs and so on. These contacts can be grouped logically into folders such as Friends, Work, etc. A contacts application is also sometimes referred to as an *Address Book*.

Tasks

Tasks are things that the user has to do. It is a 'to do' list. Details of each task are entered by the user; a due date can be set, a priority and a category (such as home, school, personal, etc.). Some PIMs provide tools to track the progress of each task by recording the percentage of the task complete and the total hours worked on the task. Other details can also be recorded with the task, such as who should be billed for it and the car mileage to be claimed against it.

Integration of PIM features

In high-end personal information managers all the main areas of the PIM are integrated together. If a context menu is opened when in the contacts application, the user will be given the option of arranging a new appointment with the contact, sending a message to the contact or creating a new task to be completed for the contact.

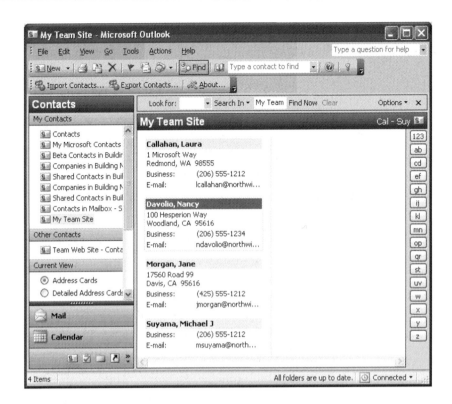

Figure 11.58 *Contacts – Microsoft Outlook 2003*

Similarly, if a context menu is opened over an existing appointment, the user will be given the option of adding contacts to the meeting, e-mailing the contacts who are attending the meeting, and so on.

Figure 11.59 *Integration of PIM services – Microsoft Outlook 2003*

Questions

1. What are the five classes of information management software?

2. Suggest a class of information management software for creating and managing each of these items:

a a diary for a head teacher

b a profit and-loss-account for a business

c a menu for a take-away restaurant

d a plan for a theatre production of Macbeth.

3. Perfect Manuscripts is a publishing company that employed a number of designers to produce a website to market the company's books.

a Identify **three** elements of a web page which may be affected by the application of a cascading style sheet.

b State **one** advantage of using a CSS file when a team is developing a website.

c The website team uses project management software to plan and control the progress of the website project. State **three** features of project management software which allow the team to do this.

d The team have used the project planning software to identify the critical path for the project. What is a critical path?

4. Jamie is creating a magazine for his school and has a number of photographs which he wishes to insert into the magazine.

a When Jamie imports a photograph into his magazine document it sits on top of the text he has typed, making the document unreadable.

Why is this and what can Jamie do to correct the problem?

b Jamie is using serif and sans-serif fonts in his magazine. Explain the difference between serif and sans-serif fonts.

c Jamie wants to create a table of contents for his magazine but is having some difficulty doing so. His friend Sally tells Jamie it is because he hasn't used any heading styles in his magazine.

i What are *styles* in relation to wordprocessing?

ii Explain why using styles would help Jamie create the table of contents.

d Jamie used wordprocessing software to create his magazine. Name and describe **three** features of desktop publishing software which would have made it easier for Jamie to create the magazine.

5. What is the purpose of a master slide in a presentation?

6. Holly is preparing a business presentation.

a She uses the outline view to enter the text of her presentation. Why does she do this?

b Holly inserts a number of business graphics using her presentation software. What are business graphics? Give an example.

c When her presentation is complete, Holly applies a number of different slide transitions to her presentation. What are slide transitions? Give **two** examples.

7. Simple animations can be created using presentation software.

a Give **two** examples of animation effects commonly applied to objects in a presentation.

b What is a motion path and how can it be used in a presentation?

8. The ladies at Greenways Golf Club have just completed two rounds of golf in a qualifying competition for the club championship. The four ladies with the lowest **gross** scores will play next week in the scratch championship semi-final.

	A	B	C	D
1	Greenways Golf Club			
2				
3		Round 1	Round 2	Gross Total
4	Joanne Smith	89	91	180
5	Mandy Clark	88	89	177
6	Alison Jones	99	91	190
7	Sarah Wilson	85	88	173
8	Jane Taylor	101	95	196
9	Mary Milne	82	84	166
10	Sheena Buchan	81	85	166

a The club secretary uses a spreadsheet to note the results. Describe how the *average score* has been calculated.

b The four leading ladies are to be seeded for the championship semi-final. If two players have the same gross score then the player with the better Round 2 score will go through. In golf, the lower the score, the better you have played.

i Describe how the package could produce a list sorted so that the top four seeds are shown first.

ii Describe how the use of macros could help the club secretary maintain the above spreadsheet.

9. Andrew is creating a web page using web authoring software.

a He creates his web page layout using tables. Why did he choose to use tables rather than frames?

b Andrew inserts an image into his page and adds hotspots to it. What are hotspots and what are they used for?

c Describe **two** features of good web page design.

10. Carol is the computing teacher at Blair Academy. She has been using spreadsheet software to record her spending of the budget for her department.

She's been told by a friend that she can use the software to forecast her future spending.

a What is meant by a forecast in this case?

b The spreadsheet makes use of *what-if analysis* and *goal seeking*. Explain each of these terms and give an example of each.

c Carol creates a complex spreadsheet which makes use of *nested IFs*. What are nested IFs? Give **one** example?

11. What are the three variables in any project plan? Why are these commonly referred to as 'the project triangle'?

12. Describe the layout of a typical Gantt chart and typical network diagram.

13. Ian is using a PIM to send and receive e-mail. His friend Paul tells him he could use the software to store details of his friends and family.

Name and describe two other features of personal information management software which Paul and Ian are unaware of.

Implications of Information and Communications Technology

The introduction of information systems, computing and communications technology has made a significant impact on the way we live our lives. This new technology has also required new legalisation to protect personal privacy and access to computer systems and data. Many organisations have adopted new technologies to gain competitive advantage over their rivals or to function more effectively. However, there are costs involved when installing and supporting information and communications technology (ICT), both financially and in terms of the impact it has on our lives.

Social implications of ICT

Since the early 1980s, ICT has had a significant impact on society. The way we work, communicate and our recreation have all been changed by new technology:

- we use mobile phones to be constantly available for communication
- we use e-mail instead of the standard postal service for written communications
- we use digital cameras instead of traditional film and video cameras.

All these changes increasingly affect the way we live our lives.

Mobile phones and other communications technologies mean that many of us are always available

Globalisation

Globalisation is a term commonly used to describe the impact of technological and business growth on global societies. Globalisation describes the increased pace of interconnection that has developed over recent years. It came about as a result of two factors. First, technological changes have enabled information and goods to travel much faster than before. Secondly, the end of the Cold War and the spread of a new political philosophy of liberalisation has led to the removal of trade barriers. As a result of globalisation, foreign trade and investment have grown dramatically.

The global development of communications technology has made the world a smaller place: for example, if you were to call a directory enquiries service for a telephone number you could be speaking to someone in Dundee or New Delhi, India. This is possible because the global telecommunications infrastructure is sufficiently developed to allow direct communication between almost any two points on the planet. This infrastructure is made up of hardware and software such as communications satellites, satellite dishes, ground-based transmitters, above and below ground cables, and wireless links.

The pioneering thinker on communications, Marshall McLuhan, coined the term, 'the global village' in the 1960s to express his belief that electronic communications would unite the world. The advent of the Internet has paralleled the emergence of **globalisation** as a concept. Proponents and critics of globalisation have very different perspectives on the Internet's role.

Global communications and technology – the positive view

Many within developing countries see the Internet as an opportunity to gain access to knowledge and services from around the world in a way that would have been previously unimaginable. Internet kiosks, which are often used for e-mail, are springing up in many parts of Africa.

The Internet can also facilitate opportunities for economic development in industries such as tourism. The Internet and technologies such as mobile communications allow developing countries to leapfrog steps in the development of the infrastructure. For example, in the Philippines a poor landline telephone system is being rapidly overtaken by the use of mobile phones with Internet access.

Globalisation has dramatically improved access for technological latecomers to advanced technologies and, to the extent that technological upgrading is important for development, it provides a unique opportunity for low-income countries to raise their population's income per head. Research shows that improved access to technology imports is increasing the demand for skilled labour in many low-income countries.

Global communications and technology – the negative view

Although the Internet started off as a communal medium for sharing information, principally among researchers and academics, it is increasingly becoming the tool of international corporations to market their products around the world.

Because rich countries generate most of the content on the Internet, the latter becomes a form of cultural imperialism, in which western values dominate. English is the language of the Internet, yet it is spoken, to some degree of competency, by only 20% of the world's population. Mandarin Chinese speakers account for more than twice that number.

The Internet is also creating new gaps between the rich and the poor. Rich countries have much greater access to the Internet and communications services generally. We are moving from an **industrial age**, in which wealth was created by manufacturing, to an **information age** in which wealth is created by the development of information goods and services, ranging from media, to education and software. Poor countries are not sufficiently involved in this information revolution and are falling further behind.

The social impact of globalisation

The impact of a global economy is viewed by many as a threat to our societies and national identities. Some think we are in danger of developing a global monoculture, feasting on corporate fast food and listening to rap music! Rather than globalisation, many consider this to be Americanisation because of the prevalence of American products and services within the global economy. The fact that American cultural products are so widespread in world markets is because of the success of the US economy and the strength of US businesses.

But it does not make sense to talk of a world of six billion people having a monoculture. The spread of globalisation will undoubtedly bring changes to the countries it reaches, but change is an essential part of life. It does not mean the abolition of traditional values. Indeed, new global media, such as the Internet, have proven a powerful means of projecting traditional culture.

A report by the UN Educational, Scientific & Cultural Organisation (UNESCO), showed that the world trade in goods with cultural content almost tripled between 1980 and 1991: from US$67 billion to US$200 billion. At the core of the entertainment industry – film, music, television and computer games – there is a growing dominance of US products. World Trade Organisation rules do not allow countries to block imports on cultural grounds. American culture is seen to be dominated by monetary relationships, with commercial values replacing traditional social relationships and family values.

The impact of globalisation on a business

The globalisation of a business can have a significant impact on the information systems it uses. The task of managing the information systems of a global organisation is complex, but the improvements gained, in terms of managing and controlling the business's operations, are significant.

When a business moves from being a national organisation to being a global one the complexity of its operations increases, as do the risks involved. To handle these challenges, a business will require faster communications and information processing. It will have to rely more on IT to assist with the management of the business across the world.

Corporate Internet presence

For many global businesses, a major part of their global presence is through their online website. A business website allows a company to increase international revenues, build a stronger global brand, enhance global customer relationships, establish an international online market share and reduce global operational costs.

An effective business website, designed to promote the company and meet the needs of consumers, can generate substantial income for the company and assist in expanding the company's operations into new markets.

Localisation

Often, however, a single global website is insufficient to meet the needs of the business and consumers. Global companies frequently localise their web content to conform to the language, cultural and legal norms of a particular area or country. This process often requires the services of language translators and cultural consultants with detailed knowledge of the target country or area.

E-commerce administration

The development of e-commerce has had significant impact on how international sales are managed. An online sales system should allow a user to make a purchase in his/her local currency, apply the correct taxes and tariffs due for purchase, calculate the shipping cost from the dispatch location to the customer and then allow payment to be made using one of a variety of recognised international payment methods.

Welcome to palmOne.

palmOne is a market leader in Palm OS handhelds, software and accessory solutions.
Create a mobile lifestyle with your palmOne handheld, powered by Palm OS.

Please **select a country or region below** to find information about palmOne, Inc.
(formerly Palm, Inc.) and about palmOne™ products and services.

Zire™ handhelds are simple, approachable and easy-to-use Palm Powered™ organizers for people balancing personal, professional or academic lives – or all of the above.

Tungsten™ handhelds pack advanced technologies into a pocketable expression of power, providing uniquely efficient Palm Powered™ handheld experiences for mobile professionals and serious business users.

Treo™ smartphones seamlessly combine a full-featured mobile phone and Palm Powered™ organizer with wireless communications including email, messaging and web browsing1, in a small, compact, yet easy-to-use device that simplifies both business and personal life.

Accessories for your Palm VII, Palm V, Palm III, or palmOne handheld can easily be customized to meet your needs. Add cases, expansion cards, keyboards, and more.

At **Software Connection,** you can download software from a selection of over 20,000 Palm OStitles. Organized into categories such as games, productivity, travel, and more, you'll easily find software for your palmOne device.

palmOne is the handheld market leader in areas such as **mobile business, healthcare, education and government** and will continue to extend that lead by delivering compelling business and enterprise mobile information-management solutions, business-focused hardware and software products, robust service and support, and innovative market-leading alliances with developers and solutions providers.

North America
- Canada
- United States

Asia Pacific
- Region
- Australia
- China
- Hong Kong-English
- Hong Kong-Chinese
- India
- Japan
- Malaysia
- New Zealand
- Philippines
- Singapore
- Taiwan
- Thailand

Europe
- Region
- Austria
- Belgium-English
- Belgium-French
- Denmark
- Eastern Europe
- Finland
- France
- Germany
- Ireland
- Italy
- Luxembourg
- Mediterranean
- The Netherlands
- Norway
- Spain
- Sweden
- Switzerland-French
- Switzerland-German
- UK

Latin America
- Region
- Argentina
- Brazil
- Chile
- Colombia
- Mexico
- Peru
- Venezuela

Africa
- Region

Middle East
- Region

1 An Internet service provider account, data service and carrier subscription may be required for Internet and email access. These services may need to be purchased separately.

Figure 12.1 Global homepage for palmOne Inc. Image provided by palmOne, Inc.

When a business operates in one country it requires knowledge of the laws, taxation and cultural expectations of only that country. When a business operates globally it requires detailed knowledge of each country in which it plans to offer goods and/or services.

Customer services

A truly global company must be able to respond to customer requests for information and assistance in a variety of languages and in a variety of locations. Businesses with global interests will require a workforce with a range of linguistic abilities and detailed knowledge of the products and services offered by the business.

Technology

Clearly a great deal of technology is required to operate information systems for any organisation on a global scale. Successful global companies such as Coca-Cola, eBay and Burger King have spent millions of pounds on information systems and communications technology.

The key factors for any global organisation are the telecommunications standards operated by the countries that host the organisation's operating centres (e.g. ADSL, ISDN and ISP availability), the reliability of the networks used by the organisation, the data-transfer speeds and the availability of qualified and competent support staff to maintain and develop the required systems.

Information poverty

In recent years, researchers have pointed out that there are huge differences in people's ability to obtain and act on information. This is causing concern, with experts arguing that a split is developing between the information 'haves' and 'have-nots' throughout the world. The **information-rich** have good access to information, especially online, but also through more traditional media such as newspapers, radio, television and books, and can plan their lives and react to changes in circumstances on the basis of what they know or can find out.

The **information-poor** don't have such access and are vulnerable to all kinds of pressures. Though the information-rich are mainly in the industrialised countries and the information-poor are mostly in the developing world, similar splits are obvious between prosperous and disadvantaged groups inside industrialised countries.

The Internet has ushered in the greatest period of wealth creation in history. It has had a major impact on how we communicate and do business. However, we often forget that perhaps as much as 80% of the world's population have no idea what a dial tone is, yet alone have access to the Internet. And this gap, the digital divide, between those with access to information, the information-rich, and those without, the information-poor, is widening as industrialised countries develop information services and access, while developing countries do not.

Information access

Information access requires four conditions:

- knowing that the information or information service is available
- owning or having access to the equipment necessary to connect to the information source (e.g. computer, television, telephone, software, modem)
- gaining access to the information service (e.g. afford access charges)
- knowing how to operate the necessary hardware and software (i.e. be 'computer literate').

A deficiency in any one of these areas reduces access. In other words, someone who cannot afford the right television or who does not know how to operate a computer may need information but cannot gain access to it. People without access represent one end of a social imbalance that is increasingly aggravated by technology: the gap between the information-poor and the information-rich.

Technology has created many millionaires in Silicon Valley (the part of California, USA where many computer companies are based) and has generated significant financial growth for the rest of the USA. However, not everyone has shared in this huge wealth. In the area of East Palo Alto, which borders on the high-tech Stanford University campus, at the heart of Silicon Valley, and the corporate headquarters of multi-billion dollar companies such as Yahoo and Oracle, more than 17% of the population lives in poverty and fewer than one in five families has a computer in the home.

Such low-income communities, even one like East Palo Alto, close to the heart of technological developments, may attract less investment in new telecommunications and connectivity, and in any case may lack populations with the education and motivation to take advantage of it. These places will experience the downside of the digital revolution.

This downside may result in urban areas of disinvestment, neglect and poverty, especially if these low-income communities turn out to be the last to have a digital telecommunications infrastructure and the skills to use it effectively.

Global perspective

There are an estimated 563 million people online globally, but even this staggering number is small when considered in context. For example, of those 563 million, fully 30% are in North America. Also, 563 million represents only 9% of the world's entire population.

The United States has more computers than the rest of the world combined. Even amongst highly developed nations, there exist vast differences in the availability of home Internet access. Sweden ranks as the nation with the highest percentage of home Internet connections at 85%; Brazil trails the list of developed nations with only 45% of its homes connected.

Proportion of population (%)* Country	Q4 2001	Q4 2002	Change
Spain	32	54	22
UK	62	68	6
Italy	50	56	6
Germany	59	63	4
USA	76	79	3
Netherlands	70	73	3
France	52	54	2
Brazil	43	45	2
Sweden	84	85	1
Hong Kong	73	70	-3
Australia	76	72	-4

*Among population aged 2+ in all households

Number of people (millions)* Country	Q4 2001	Q4 2002	Change
USA	158.9	168.6	9.7
Spain	10.1	17.0	6.9
Germany	38.7	41.8	3.1
UK	28.0	30.4	2.4
Italy	23.0	25.3	2.3
Brazil	17.6	19.7	2.1
France	21.9	23.0	1.1
Netherlands	8.7	9.2	0.5
Sweden	6.0	6.1	0.1
Hong Kong	4.1	4.0	-0.1
Australia	11.1	10.5	-0.6

*Among population aged 16+ in households with fixed line telephone(s), in millions

Figure 12.2 Number and percentage of people with current Internet access, any location. Source: Nielsen//NetRatings Global Internet Trends Q4 2002

UK perspective

In the second quarter of 2004, 52% of households in the UK (12.8 million people) could access the Internet from home, compared with just 9% (2.2 million) in the same quarter of 1998.

In July 2004, 58% of adults in Great Britain had used the Internet in the three previous months. The most common use of the Internet among these adults was for e-mail (85%) and finding information about goods or services (82%). The most frequent place of access was the person's own home (82%), followed by their workplace (42%).

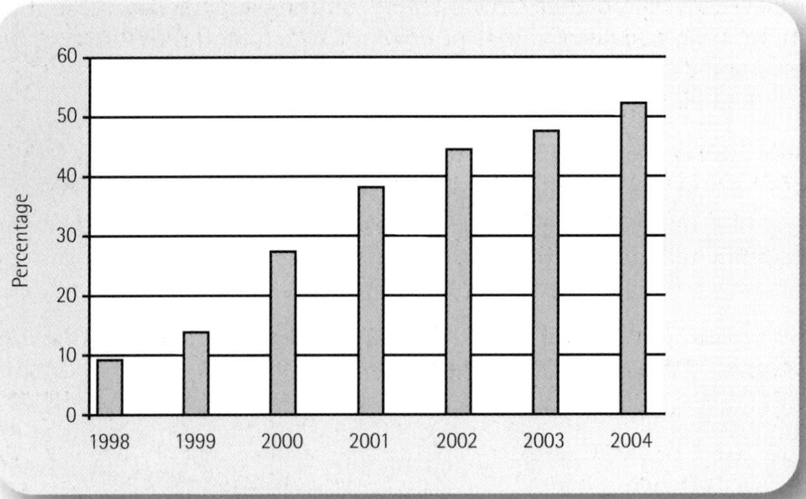

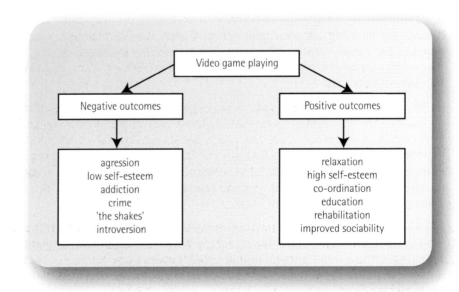

Figure 12.3 *UK households with home access to the Internet, 1998 to 2004*
Source: National Statistics website:
www.statistics.gov.uk
Crown copyright material is reproduced with the permission of the Controller of HMSO

In July 2004, 37% of adults had never used the Internet. Of these, 48% stated that they did not want to use, or had no need for, or no interest in the Internet; 37% had no Internet connection; and 32% felt they lacked knowledge or the confidence to use it. These adults were also asked which of four statements best described what they thought about using the Internet. Fifty-four per cent of non-users chose the statement 'I have not really considered using the Internet before and I am not likely to in the future'. This core group of non-Internet users represented 21% of all adults in the UK.

Effect of ICT on human relations

The homes of those who are fortunate enough to be information-rich contain an abundance of information technology. However, the use of computers, mobile telephones, personal digital assistants (PDAs), televisions, DVD players, games consoles and so on, reduces the amount of time that families spend together. This reduction in social interaction can have a negative effect on family relationships.

Figure 12.4 *Possible effects of video game playing*
Diagram reproduced from The effects of computer games on young children – a review of the research, *Jessica Harris, The Research, Development & Statistics Directorate, ISBN 1 84082 629*

In the workplace, the increase in digital communications can lead to workers feeling isolated because they no longer have the same level of contact with colleagues. This is especially true for teleworkers, who are based at a distance from main business operations, working from home or from a small regional office.

There is also some limited research that suggests that playing computer games may have both positive and negative effects on young people. These effects are often linked to other factors, such as an individual's self-esteem or lifestyle.

The impact on business organisations of an information-systems-driven business model

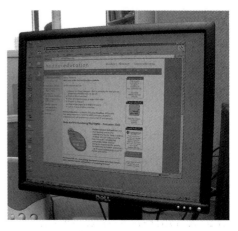

In the workplace many of us now spend many hours looking at screens; we tend to have less contact with colleagues

A business model essentially describes how a business functions. It will detail the flow of information (inputs, processes, outputs), the strategy for the business (what it aims to achieve), who is involved, what they do and how they work with others.

An information-systems-driven business model allows an organisation to plan and control its operations efficiently and effectively by using information systems to produce competitive advantage.

General advantages of an IS-driven business model

The use of information systems allows businesses to gain competitive advantage over others by organising and processing data in ways that are more efficient or effective than other computerised or manual systems. Data can be stored in a relational database, increasing the speed at which the data can be located and retrieved. Techniques such as data mining allow additional knowledge to be gathered from stored data. Examples of this include discovering trends in customer purchasing or in the costs of materials.

There are essentially two information-systems-driven business models: **centralised** and **decentralised** information systems.

Centralised IS business model

Centralised information systems take the main aspects of an organisation's IT business functions and centralise the data control. Individual business units within the company access this central store remotely and data can be processed using the central system. Centralised IS business models depend on the efficiency of the communications networks connecting business units to the central system and on the efficiency of the central data storage and processing.

Centralised systems have several advantages over decentralised systems. Senior and middle managers can access key business data within seconds. This means that essential business processes such as payroll, stock control, inventory and customer relationship management can all be controlled effectively. Key measurements of business productivity can be obtained at frequent intervals without a significant data collection effort by the company's staff.

The disadvantages of centralised systems are the significant costs of hardware, software and IT support required to control communications and the remote storage and processing of data. Such systems also leave a company vulnerable to system failure unless contingency plans, such as backup hardware, software and communications, are established.

Decentralised IS business model

A decentralised IS business model distributes the IT capabilities and data storage to business units. This allows these units to develop the flexibility to control and manage their data, but makes the administration and control of the business difficult for senior managers with overall responsibility for the whole business.

In decentralised models it is vital that managers in individual business units report back regularly to senior managers. This ensures that senior managers can effectively plan and control business activities based on feedback from the separate units. Decentralised systems require less complex hardware and software than centralised models, but communication between business units and managers is essential to ensure effective monitoring of the business.

E-commerce

E-commerce (electronic commerce) means conducting business communication and transactions over networks and through computers. It is the buying and selling of goods and services, and the transfer of funds, through digital communications, including buying and selling over the World Wide Web and the Internet, electronic funds transfer and all other methods of doing business over digital networks.

Figure 12.5 Amazon.co.uk – an e-commerce site

However, e-commerce also includes operations carried out between and within companies (such as marketing, finance, manufacturing, selling and negotiation) that enable commerce and use electronic mail, file transfer, fax, video conferencing, or interaction with a remote computer.

E-commerce – business to consumer

B2C (business-to-consumer) is the most common type of e-commerce. It is basically the concept of online marketing and distribution of products and services over the Internet and is a natural progression for many businesses that sell directly to consumers.

For the individual, it is relatively easy to appreciate the advantages that e-commerce brings. Why waste time fighting crowds in shops and supermarkets, when, from the comfort of home, one can shop online at any time in virtual Internet shopping stores and have the goods delivered directly to the home?

The advantages of e-commerce

The advantages of e-commerce are clear in today's business.

As the use of the Internet becomes more important in our everyday lives, it becomes essential for companies to use e-commerce. It is useful, not only to large worldwide companies, but it also enables small businesses to sell their goods and services to a wider range of people. E-commerce can also enable individuals to buy or sell something through online companies.

The role of e-commerce for everyday users

E-commerce provides easy ways for people to buy and sell through the use of several payment options. Although people usually pay by credit card they could also pay through PayPal® or a similar service, or through the mail, by cheque.

Online retailers frequently have a secure online shopping cart system where customers can add desired items to their cart, allowing them to shop quickly and efficiently.

Through e-commerce the user is more likely to find the best deals quickly, since a large number of retailers can be found with the click of a mouse. E-commerce comparison sites, such as http://www.kelkoo.co.uk and http://www.dealtime.co.uk, allow potential customers to compare prices

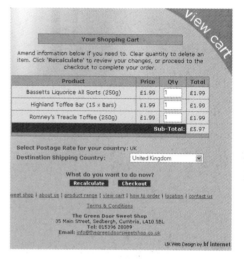

Figure 12.6 Sample shopping basket (cart) – http://www.thegreendoorsweet shop.co.uk

Figure 12.7 kelkoo.co.uk – a price comparison site

across multiple sites to find the cheapest price for an item and whether it is in stock. This saves time that might otherwise be spent sitting in traffic travelling from store to store, searching for the best deals.

So it is clear that e-commerce has advantages for customers. Through e-commerce users get easy access to a wide variety of products, hassle-free shopping, customised products and easy payment options. Any company trying to expand or simply give more users access to their products or services cannot afford to ignore the many advantages of e-commerce.

Business-to-business (B2B) e-commerce

Business-to-business electronic commerce, also known as e-business, is experiencing an explosive growth rate. Companies of all sizes and types are now buying and selling products and services via the Internet.

The first stage of e-commerce on the Internet comprised mainly business-to-consumer transactions. There is also a considerable growth in business-to-business activities (B2B), which involve a business purchasing material or services from another business via the Internet.

B2B e-commerce also offers benefits such as:

- reduced human involvement in the business process
- fewer overhead expenses
- a reduction in errors
- potentially improved advertising exposure, new markets and sales in additional regions of the country or world.
- both buyer and seller gain.

Currently there are two main areas of B2B e-commerce..

Supply-chain management

Supply-chain management is the management of the supply process, moving items for sale from supplier to seller often via warehouses. At its most efficient, supply-chain management operates on a **just-in-time** principle. In any business, the cost of storing stock and the cost of the stock itself is considerable. If a supply chain is managed correctly using a just-in-time method then new stock of a product will arrive just before existing stocks are used up. This minimises wasted space and storage costs.

Electronic procurement system

Electronic procurement is the process of purchasing any item for a business, including raw materials, stationery, software services and so on, via the Internet. This can produce significant cost savings for the buyer, because of the range of possible suppliers and the improved ability to source the best value. Sellers have the opportunity to expand to meet the needs of businesses on a country-wide, continental or global scale.

Case Study: Tesco – Supply chain management and electronic procurement*

* Extract from article 'Tesco in 2003', *Global CEO*, June 2003 by Padmini Maddali, Faculty Associate, ICFAI Knowledge Center

Until 1983, Tesco, the large retail chain, had its suppliers deliver many products for sale directly to stores. As volumes increased, this type of delivery scheme proved to be grossly inadequate. In addition, it did not facilitate standardisation and quality control. It was then that Tesco decided to switch to a centrally controlled distribution system, with warehouses carefully planned to match the retail network. These changes, combined with improvements in information systems, resulted in increased efficiencies in distribution. By 1989, Tesco had 42 warehouses.

During the 1980s, Tesco began to implement its automated sales-based ordering system (SBO), to link the sales and purchasing processes. By 1993, the company had built an electronic data interchange (EDI) network, the UK's largest electronic community, linking 1200 suppliers. This system facilitated ordering and replenishment by automatically calculating store needs based on sales, and generated orders for fulfilment in 24–48 hours.

In the 1990s, Tesco introduced 'composite distribution', which enabled fresh and chilled products to be distributed through a single vehicle and warehouse system. Eight such distribution centres, each serving 50 stores, were built, replacing the 26 used previously.

In the mid-1990s, Tesco revamped its distribution system. The firm's nine composite (variable temperature) distribution centres used a just-in-time system (known as pick-by-line or crossdocking). This meant that goods amounting to around 40% of total sales went straight to the stores within hours of arrival. Each day, the firm dispatched around 1000 lorry-loads of goods.

Figure 12.8 Tesco – Successful use of B2B e-commerce

Under the old system, where suppliers delivered directly to the stores in half-empty lorries, that figure was nine times higher. Constant replenishment allowed stores to carry less stock of each item, allowing more product lines to be squeezed into the same shelf space. Tesco also filled the gaps with new products, such as clothing and flowers. Just-in-time supply allowed Tesco to add 35 000 ft² (3255 m²) of sales space to its existing stores by cutting out stockrooms.

Tesco also opened a distribution centre in Southampton that incorporated a new automated order-picking system. In the Southampton depot, incoming goods pass on conveyor belts through a laser tunnel that reads the bar code on each case, directing it automatically to a cage or dolly where goods for each store are accumulated for loading on to temperature-controlled lorries for delivery to that store.

Electronic data interchange (EDI)

Electronic data interchange (EDI) is a technique for businesses to exchange information (usually commercially oriented data, as opposed to engineering data) in an electronic format, rather than via paper documents.

For example, suppose that Company A buys widgets from Company B. In a non-EDI setting:

- Company A's purchasing system prints a purchase order, which is mailed or faxed to Company B
- at Company B the purchase order is keyed into an order-entry system
- the order is processed, the item(s) shipped and B's accounts system prints an invoice
- the invoice is mailed to A, where it is entered into A's accounts system for processing.

Multiply this by hundreds or thousands of orders and a significant amount of printing, mailing and data entry takes place.

The idea behind EDI is that, since the order and invoice information exist in an electronic form, and the paper documents serve as a mechanism to transmit this data between the two companies, it would be much more efficient to transmit the data in electronic form, in such a way that the documents can be processed automatically. This would save the companies exchanging this information the overhead of printing, mailing and data entry. It would also reduce the possibility of data entry errors. It would also eliminate time delays that arise when order and instructions for shipping are sent by post.

EDI standards

For it to work EDI requires a number of standards to be established between trading partners. These standards are concerned with the structure of the data and how it is exchanged.

Data structures

All organisations have their own internal standards for data transfer, but these standards differ widely between organisations. EDI requires a set of data standards be defined to allow data to be transferred from one business to another. You could think of this data standard as a common language which all trading partners speak (in addition to their own internal language).

When data is sent from one company to another, the data is first converted to the structure defined for EDI transfers. This is done with computer software which converts data from a company's internal database into a file that conforms to the EDI data standards.

When this file is received by the trading partner, it is translated (again by software) from the EDI data standard into the internal standard for the receiving trading partner.

EDI provides trading partners with a means of streamlining business processes, saving time and resources for all involved.

Online identities

Anyone who uses the Internet regularly has an online identity defining him or her to the rest of the online community. This identity could be in any form, for use in forums, chatrooms, reviews of products on websites or for online gaming.

These online identities are different from users' real identities because they are usually based solely on online activities. The online identity of a person develops as they use the Internet. They could sign up for a free e-mail account, such as Hotmail or Yahoo! Mail. These accounts provide access to instant chat services which tell friends when the user is online and allow instant communication via the user's desktop. E-mail posts to newsgroups about hobbies and interests, for example, will further circulate the user's e-mail address and the content of the messages will reflect his or her personality and opinions. A user might also make purchases from online shops and leave reviews for use by other customers.

Within a relatively short space of time, a user can develop a significant presence in the online world.

Ways to develop an online identity

Online identities can be developed in a number of ways. A quick way to establish an online presence with friends and family is to sign up for one of the instant messenger services such as MSN Messenger, AOL Instant Messenger or Yahoo! Messenger.

Profiles and avatars

In addition to allowing web-based e-mail and instant messaging, these services allow the user to create a profile which contains information describing him or her. These profiles can contain photographs but many users prefer to create an avatar. An avatar is a graphical representation that users create to represent themselves; it can look like a person, an object, or an animal. Since an avatar may look nothing like the user, people tend to create avatars which represent the way they would like to be seen by other people online.

Figure 12.9 Yahoo! avatars.
Reproduced with permission of Yahoo! Inc. by 2005 by Yahoo! Inc. YAHOO! and the YAHOO! logo are trademarks of Yahoo! Inc.

This online image of a person can often include references to hobbies and interests. A user's mood can also be indicated by the facial expression of the avatar.

People need to be careful when creating an online profile. The information in a profile is often available for others to view and can be used to send junk e-mail or to otherwise invade privacy.

Blogging

Another way to convey information about you and declare your online identity is to maintain a **blog**. A blog is basically a diary that is available on the web. The activity of updating a blog is **blogging** and someone who keeps a blog is a **blogger**.

Blogs are typically updated daily using software that allows people with little or no technical background to update and maintain the blog. Postings on a blog are almost always arranged in chronological order, with the most recent additions featured most prominently. Bloggers use their blogs to inform others of what they have been doing, their opinions about a variety of topics and so on. Anything can be discussed in a blog. Bloggers should be careful only to disclose information about themselves that they are happy to have in the public domain.

The problems with online identities

One of the problems with online identities is truthfulness. Which users have an identity that is truthful and accurate and which are embellishing their own personality to impress or attract others? When you communicate with someone online, there are major trust issues in ensuring their identity: how can you be sure that they are who they say they are?

Chatrooms require users to create an online identity by choosing a nickname when they first log on. It is very easy to lie online and online identities can be created and embellished for the user's benefit and choice. For security and safety on the Internet it is very important that users should never supply personal information, especially in chatrooms, where it is very common for people to pretend to be someone they are not!

Real identities are masked by online identities on the Internet for obvious security reasons and also for the entertainment value of posing as the identity you would like to be.

Who can have an online identity?

Absolutely anyone with access to the Internet can have an online identity. With no registration or membership required, users can simply log into a chatroom and sign up with a virtual nickname. They can then develop an online identity to suit the situation. The advantage of identities is that users can change them whenever they feel the need or desire to assume a different persona.

Privacy online

Concerns about privacy are not new. But the computer's ability to gather and sort vast amounts of data, and the Internet's ability to distribute it globally, magnifies concerns. Online advertisers and marketers, in particular, want to know as much about you and your buying habits as possible.

Companies use this information to target sales of products and services to your interests and lifestyle, delivering, for example, tailored news, information on bargain travel, or the latest book on your favourite subject. That may be good news for some, but what if you don't want your personal information shared or sold for marketing purposes?

Mining the clickstream

The address of each document or other resource on the World Wide Web is given by its **uniform resource locator** (URL). With these URLs, various tracking tools (including web browser **cookies**) can mine and manipulate your online data trail (called a **clickstream**) to build a detailed database of personal information without your knowledge or consent. This database can reveal the locations that an individual visits on the Internet, who they associate with (via list-servers, chatrooms and newsgroups), and how they engage in political activities and social behaviour.

Some steps to protect your privacy

Users can protect their privacy online and prevent the vast majority of online tracking by following a few simple steps.

1. Look for privacy policies on websites

Websites can collect a lot of information about your visit, what computer you use, what type of hardware and software you have, what websites you have visited. Websites that ask you to provide even a small amount of personal information can tie the data you provide to your browsing habits. An increasing number of websites have begun to provide privacy policies that detail the sites' information practices. Look for these policies and read them carefully. While privacy statements are not the only answer to online privacy risks, the effort should be encouraged and commended.

2. Never give out personal information online

Giving out personal information online means, potentially, giving that information to strangers. All Internet users should protect their privacy by disclosing information only that is truly required by others, such as that used for online shopping deliveries, etc. Information used for online transactions within the UK and the European Union is protected by data protection laws and European directives.

3. Clear your memory cache after browsing

After browsing the World Wide Web, copies of all accessed pages and images are saved on your computer's hard disk. While these copies make subsequent visits to the same sites faster, the browsing record provides others with a complete history of the sites you have visited. This has implications for personal privacy, particularly if you share a computer with others. To protect their privacy, users should delete these caches of files every time they finish browsing.

4. Make sure that online forms are secure

If a form is not encrypted, the data within the form can be read as it travels between computers. Online forms should be encrypted so that only the intended recipients can readily translate the information.

You can check whether a form is encrypted by looking for the commonly used graphics: a key, which is broken if the page is insecure, and a lock (locked is secure and unlocked is not secure). The graphic appears in the corner of the browser screen; clicking on the lock or the key will inform you of additional security information about the page. You should not input sensitive personal information about yourself (such as financial or medical data) on web pages that are not secure.

5. Reject unnecessary cookies

Cookies enable websites to store information about your visit on your own hard drive. Cookies inform site operators if you have visited the site and, if you have obtained a username and password, cookies remember that information for you. Many of the 'personalised' search engines use cookies to deliver news topics that users select; sites often use these same preferences to target advertisements. Furthermore, cookies can be used to track you online and enable the creation of a profile without you realising it. Newer web browsers allow you to recognise sites that send you cookies and reject them outright. Browsers also allow you to delete cookies if you choose to.

6. Keep your e-mail private, use encryption

E-mail is not as secure a medium as many believe. E-mail can be easily rerouted and read by unintended third parties and messages are often saved on e-mail servers for indefinite periods of time. Encryption technology allows users to protect e-mail messages by encrypting them. Even if an e-mail is intercepted it cannot be read without the correct encryption keys.

7. Be aware of clickstream tracking

From the moment you type in a web address, a log is kept with information about your visit. When you visit a website the following is typical of information that is logged automatically by the web server about your visit:

> 212.227.118.102 – - [03/Dec/2004:15:20:06 -0800] 'GET /book.htm HTTP/1.0' 200 8788 'http://www.perfectpapers.net/' 'MSIE 6.0; Windows NT 5.1; SV1'.

Figure 12.10 Server log entry

This information can be analysed by a computer system using the following meanings.

Server Log Info	Component name	Meaning
212.227.118.102	remotehost	Name of the computer requesting the web page.
–	rfc931	The name of the remote user. This field is usually blank.
–	authuser	Login of the remote user. This is also usually blank.
[03/Dec/2004:15:20:06 -0800]	date	Date and time of the request.
'GET /book.htm HTTP/1.0'	request	URL of the file requested. This is noted exactly as the user requested it.
200	status	Error or status code generated by the request.
8788	bytes	Size (in bytes) of the document returned to the client.
http://www.perfectpapers.net/	referrer	The URL the visitor came from immediately before they requested the file.
'MSIE 6.0; Windows NT 5.1; SV1'	agent	Records the visitor's browser and operating system.

Figure 12.11 Log component meanings

This information can be processed by web log analyser software and, together with other website information such as cookies and online logins, be used to build a significant profile of your activities online.

8. Opt out of third-party information sharing

All European Union online companies must provide you with the option to not receive further information from a company. In addition, these companies must ask your permission to share your personal information with others. If you opt not to share information, the company is not allowed to share information about you with others.

Protect your privacy online

Our privacy can be invaded in many different ways. We can be sent unsolicited e-mail (called **SPAM**), have our online activity monitored and have our information harvested by **web spiders** (programs which extract contact and other information from websites, newsgroups, etc., and add it to contact lists).

Every day, most of us walk down the street without being recognised or followed. While anonymity is often taken for granted in the real world, such a luxury is not available online. This means that we all need to take great care when online to protect our identity and our privacy.

Current legislation

There are a number of laws that apply to information systems. These impact on how data is stored, transmitted and made available for others, and on how intellectual property is protected.

Data Protection Act

The Data Protection Act 1998 governs the processing of personal data in the United Kingdom. The earlier Data Protection Act 1984 was revised in 1998 and brought into effect on 1st March 2000. It sets rules for processing personal information and applies to some paper records as well as those held on computers. The Data Protection Act works in two ways. It gives you certain rights. It also states that those who record and use personal information must be open about how the information is used and must follow the eight principles of 'good information handling'.

The previous Data Protection Act 1984 was limited to computerised data and storage systems, whereas the 1998 act deals with all data in paper and electronic format. The first act was created before the widespread adoption of the Internet and, therefore, did not deal with the export of data from one country to another. The Data Protection Act 1998 now bans cross-border data flows unless the target country has an adequate level of protection for the rights and freedoms of data subjects via its own laws.

Protecting personal data

Many people and organisations (**data controllers**) have details about us (**data subjects**) on computer or in paper files. This growth in the use of personal information (data) has many benefits, such as improved medical care or helping fight crime. There are also some possible problems. You could have problems if your information is entered wrongly, is out of date, or is confused with someone else's. You could be unfairly refused jobs, housing, benefits, credit or a place at college. You could be overcharged for goods or services. You might even find yourself wrongly arrested just because there is a mistake in the information held about you.

Personal information is becoming increasingly valuable. Think before you supply it. Always ask why an organisation is asking for information about you. They may ask about your income, hobbies, interests, or family life. Do they need this information? You may not have to provide it. If someone wants to use your information for another purpose, for example direct marketing, you should be told about it and given a choice. Of course, there will be times when you will need to give your personal information for legal reasons. If this is the case, this should be clearly explained.

The eight principles of good information handling

The eight principles were put in place to make sure that your information is handled properly. They say that data must be:

1 fairly and lawfully processed

2 processed for limited purposes

3 adequate, relevant and not excessive

4 accurate

5 not kept for longer than is necessary

6 processed in line with your rights

7 secure

8 not transferred to other countries without adequate protection.

By law, data controllers have to keep to these principles.

How can I find out what is held about me?

The Data Protection Act allows you to find out what information about you is held on computer and in some paper records. This is known as the 'right of subject access'. If you want to know whether information is held about you and if so what, you will need to write to the person or organisation you believe holds the information. You should ask for a copy of all the information held about you to which the Data Protection Act applies.

You are generally entitled to receive a reply within 40 days so long as you have paid any necessary fee (not more than £10).

The data controller will send you a copy of the information they have about you. You should also receive a description of why your information is processed; anyone it may be passed to or seen by; and the logic involved in any automated decisions. The information may be sent as a computer printout, in a letter, or on a form. However, it should be easy to understand, and any codes should be explained.

However, there are some exceptions. For example, information can be refused if providing you with that information would be likely to affect:

- the way crime is detected or prevented

- catching or prosecuting offenders, or

- assessing or collecting taxes or duty.

In some cases your right to see certain health and social work details may also be limited.

The register of data controllers

The register of data controllers contains the names and addresses of all data controllers who have told the Commissioner that they process personal information. It also includes broad details of the data they process in terms of type, purpose, the people that they may want to give the information to, and whether the data may be transferred to any countries or territories outside the European Union. All companies which hold personal data are required to register.

The Information Commissioner

If you believe that one of the principles has been broken (or any other requirements of the act) and you are unable to sort the problem out yourself, you can ask the Information Commissioner to assess whether the requirements of the Data Protection Act have been met. The commissioner may take enforcement action against a data controller who breaks the requirements of the act and this may eventually lead to prosecution.

Compensation

You are entitled to claim compensation through the courts if damage has been caused as a result of a data controller not meeting any requirements of the Data Protection Act. If damage is proven, the court can also order compensation for any associated distress. You can only claim compensation for distress alone in very limited circumstances.

Harmonisation of European Union data protection legislation

In 1995, the European Union formally adopted the Directive on the Protection of Personal Data. The directive granted data subjects a number of important rights including:

- the right of access to personal data
- the right to know where the data originated (if such information is available)
- the right to have inaccurate data corrected
- the right of recourse in the event of unlawful processing
- the right to withhold permission to use data in certain circumstances; for example, individuals have the right to opt out free of charge from being sent direct marketing material.

In July 2002, the EU adopted a directive translating the principles of the 1995 directive into specific rules for telecommunications and other electronic communications, addressing privacy and security, marketing, cookies, data retention, etc.

Copyright, Designs & Patents Act

The Copyright, Designs & Patents Act 1988 includes the copyright of software. An offence is committed under this act if you make unauthorised copies of a software package, whether for personal use or for sale.

This act provides legal protection for original literary, dramatic, musical and artistic works, for films, sound recordings, broadcasts and cable programmes, and for typographical arrangements of published editions, in addition to computer software.

Anyone convicted of an offence under this act can expect a fine of unlimited amount plus a prison sentence ranging up to a maximum of two years.

Software licences

Software is generally not sold outright to the purchaser. Instead the purchaser is granted the right to use it as laid down in the user licence. It is normally expected that only one person at a time will have access to and use the software concerned. A network licence can often be purchased, normally at a reduced rate, for a defined number of users. A site licence might be available to cover an unlimited number of users within one set of premises.

It is, therefore, illegal to make copies of software without the copyright owner's consent, or to duplicate software loaded on a hard disk for use on any other personal computer unless allowed for under the licence.

Computer databases

All computer databases are copyright within the European Union due to the 'Database Directive', a piece of European Union legislation that grants copyright protection to database creators for 'selecting and arranging' the information contained in a database, even if the creator does not hold the copyrights on the collected information.

This directive has been used several times in legal decisions, particular decisions which have been concerned with 'deep linking'. Deep linking involves creating a link which points directly to a web page or other content within another site, usually bypassing advertising at the site opening page or other identifying pages.

The directive also protects against the 'unfair extraction' of materials contained in a database, specifically mentioning downloading or hyperlinking as examples of prohibited extraction methods. This makes it illegal to link to content within a website which is generated by a database.

Web content and digital media

All web content is copyright to the site owner (unless otherwise stated). It is illegal to download and use website graphics, text and other material without the permission of the site owner.

DVDs, Multimedia CD-ROMs and all other digital media are also included in the Copyright, Designs & Patents Act and unauthorised use and copying of such material is illegal.

Software piracy

Software is one of the most valuable technologies of the information age, running everything from PCs to the Internet. Unfortunately, because software is so valuable, and because computers make it easy to create an exact copy of a program in seconds, software piracy is widespread. From individual computer users to professionals who deal wholesale in stolen software, piracy exists in homes, schools, businesses and government. Software pirates not only steal from the companies that make the software, but with less money available for research and development of new software, all users are hurt. As the number of PCs and Internet use grow, the incidence of software piracy is growing, too.

There are five common types of software piracy.

End-user piracy

End-user piracy occurs when a company employee reproduces copies of software without authorisation. End-user piracy can take the following forms:

- using one licensed copy to install a program on multiple computers
- copying disks for installation and distribution
- taking advantage of upgrade offers without having a legal copy of the version to be upgraded
- acquiring academic or other restricted or non-retail software without a licence for commercial use
- swapping disks in or outside the workplace.

Client–server overuse

This type of piracy occurs when too many employees on a network are using a central copy of a program at the same time. If you have a local-area network and install programs on a server for several people to use, you have to be sure that your licence entitles you to do so. If you have more users than allowed by the licence, that's 'overuse'.

Internet piracy

With Internet piracy, software is downloaded illegally from the Internet. The same purchasing rules should apply to online software purchase as for software bought in traditional ways. Internet piracy can take the following forms:

- pirate websites that make software available for free download or in exchange for uploaded programs
- Internet auction sites that offer counterfeit, out-of-channel, infringing copyright software
- peer-to-peer networks that enable unauthorised transfer of copyrighted programs.

Hard-disk loading

Hard-disk loading is where a business that sells new computers loads illegal copies of software onto the hard disks to make the purchase of the machines more attractive. The same concerns and issues apply to value added resellers (VAR) that sell or install new software onto computers in the workplace.

Software counterfeiting

Software counterfeiting is the illegal duplication and sale of copyrighted material with the intent of directly imitating the copyrighted product. With packaged software, it is common to find counterfeit copies of the CDs or diskettes incorporating the software programs, as well as related packaging, manuals, licence agreements, labels, registration cards and security features.

Regulation of Investigatory Powers Act

The Regulation of Investigatory Powers Act 2000 (RIP) is a law covering the interception of communications. It was introduced to take account of technological change such as the growth of the Internet and strong encryption. It also establishes the legal techniques for intercepting and monitoring electronic communications.

A quote from the bill:

> *Make provision for and about the interception of, communications, the acquisition and disclosure of data relating to communications, the carrying out of surveillance, the use of covert human intelligence sources and the acquisition of the means by which electronic data protected by encryption or passwords may be decrypted or accessed; to provide for the establishment of a tribunal with jurisdiction in relation to those matters, to entries on and interferences with property or with wireless telegraphy and to the carrying out of their functions by the Security Service, the Secret Intelligence Service and the Government Communications Headquarters; and for connected purposes.*

The act gives government agencies wide powers and has numerous critics, most regarding the regulations as dangerously excessive and a threat to civil liberties. Critics claim that the issues of internet crime and terrorism were used to push the act through and there was little substantive debate in the House of Commons.

Especially contentious is a requirement to supply a **cryptographic key** to access data to a duly authorised person on request. Failing to provide the key is a criminal offence, with a maximum penalty of two years in jail. The accused must prove that they do not have the key but claiming to have mislaid or forgotten it might not be accepted as a defence. Both the innocent and the guilty are caught in that condition, the guilty because they would rather serve two years than ten or more. Additionally those under investigation may not tell anyone except their attorney that they are being investigated, under threat of five years imprisonment. This last item is the newly coined offence of 'tipping off'.

Another concern is that the act requires UK Internet service providers to install systems to track all subscribers' communications traffic and log this, possibly in perpetuity. This must occur at the ISPs' expense rather than the government's.

RIP can be invoked by any government official on the grounds of national security; preventing or detecting crime; preventing disorder; public safety; protecting public health; and in the interests of the economic well-being of the United Kingdom.

Lawful Business Practice Regulations

The RIP Act governs the interception by employers of communications made over a private telecommunication system, i.e. telephone, e-mail and Internet, and makes such interception unlawful except where an employer has lawful authority. The Lawful Business Practice Regulations clarify where an employer does have lawful authority under the RIP Act. Businesses are given wide powers to monitor or keep a record of e-mails in various situations in the workplace, including where they need to provide evidence of a communication to establish facts, ascertain compliance with regulatory practices or procedures, investigate or detect unauthorised use of the system, prevent or detect crime, or ensure the effective operation of the system. Companies can also monitor, but not record, communications in order to establish whether they are communications that are relevant to the company's business.

This would mean that in principle employers can monitor e-mail use to make sure that employees are following company procedures, for example protocols governing the way that customers are dealt with. It also means that employers can monitor where they suspect that an employee is breaching an equal opportunities policy by harassing another employee, or indeed where it is suspected that an employee is accessing illegal material from the Internet. Monitoring for the purpose of seeing whether e-mails are relevant to the business or are private is also permitted.

Although wide powers are granted, employers have to bear in mind that such monitoring and recording is only authorised where the employer has made all reasonable efforts to inform the users of the system that e-mails may be intercepted. This highlights the need for an e-mail/Internet use policy which is distributed to all staff and makes clear that e-mail and Internet use will be monitored. The policy should also set out permitted and prohibited uses and what the penalties are for misuse of the system. Simply circulating the policy will not be enough – employees need to be educated about the potential risks arising from e-mail and Internet use and about what is and is not acceptable behaviour.

Freedom of Information Act (Scotland) 2002

The Freedom of Information Act (Scotland) 2002 enables any person to obtain information from Scottish public authorities. This is a legal right and ensures that all people get information to which they are entitled. This legal right of access includes all types of 'recorded' information of any date held by Scottish public authorities. Since 1st January 2005 any person who makes a request for information must be provided with it, subject to certain conditions.

The act is promoted and enforced by the Scottish Information Commissioner. The Commissioner is Scotland's independent enforcer of freedom of information with legal powers to ensure the public's right of freedom of information is upheld.

Organisations covered by the act

- All Scottish public authorities including the Scottish Executive and its agencies
- the Scottish Parliament
- local authorities (including schools)
- NHS Scotland
- universities and further education colleges
- the police.

Right of access to information

Every individual has a general right to apply to a Scottish public authority for information. The act places an obligation on all Scottish public authorities to adopt and maintain a publication scheme. This scheme sets out: the categories of information the authorities publish; the manner in which it is published; and details of any charges for receiving the information.

The public authorities have to allow access to the following information: the provision, cost and standard of their service; factual information or decision-making; and the reasons for decisions made by them.

Exemptions

There are some exemptions to the act. Information which comes under the coverage of the exemptions need not be disclosed by the public body. The exemptions are information relating to national security and defence, police investigations, and the formulation or development of government policy.

If a public authority decides not to release information, as it considers it exempt, it must give reasons for its decision. This refusal notice allows the applicant to request a review of the decision, and then to seek a ruling from the Scottish Information Commissioner.

Other information may be exempt as it is already 'published' and is therefore easily accessible.

Computer Misuse Act (1990)

The Computer Misuse Act (1990) was introduced to deal with the issue of computer hacking and other unauthorised access to computer systems and unauthorised modification of computer data.

The act defines three offences in each of its three sections:

- *Section 1:* unauthorised access to computer material
- *Section 2:* unauthorised access with intent to commit or facilitate commission of further offences
- *Section 3:* unauthorised modification of computer material.

Unauthorised access to computer material

It is an offence to gain unauthorised access to a computer system. This includes causing a computer to perform a function with intent to secure access to any program or data, knowing that the access is unauthorised. This is an offence regardless of whether the motives for access were well-meaning or malicious. Access to any program or data held in a computer system is a wide definition and includes altering/erasing the program or data, copying it, moving it, using it and having it output from the computer in which it is held.

Examples of such offences could include unauthorised use of another person's username and password, persistently trying to guess a username and password, and laying a trap to obtain a password or password file (possibly using a Trojan or a virus).

Unauthorised access with intent to commit or facilitate commission of further offences

It is an offence to gain access with the intent to commit another crime, for example, gaining access to a person's online bank account with the intention of stealing their money.

Unauthorised modification of computer material

The final offence is to cause unauthorised modification of computer material. The act states that a person found guilty of this offence is liable on conviction to a maximum prison sentence of five years or an unlimited fine or both.

Examples of offences under this section would be deleting another user's file, modifying system files, the introduction of viruses, or deliberately generating information to cause a complete system malfunction.

The act also states that on a charge of attempting to commit an offence as outlined above, it is immaterial where the attempt to gain unauthorised access was made so a hacker from outwith the UK could be prosecuted. There have been several successful prosecutions of computer virus writers and hackers using this law.

Health and safety regulations

There are a number of health and safety regulations which are specific to the IT sector and computer use. All businesses in the information technology and telecommunications sector must comply with legislation designed to protect customers and staff. Health and safety legislation requires employers to:

- make the workplace safe and without risks to health
- make sure that machinery is safe
- make sure that safe working practices are set and followed.

The Health & Safety Executive (HSE) has responsibility for regulating all aspects of health and safety in Britain.

The Health & Safety (Display Screen Equipment) Regulations

The Health & Safety (Display Screen Equipment) Regulations 1992 detail requirements placed on employers with regard to their employees and the use of computer equipment and workstations.

Where display screen equipment is used, each workstation has to be assessed with regard to the health and safety of the user. The findings of the assessment should be used to reduce the risks identified. The workstation is the area where the employee works and the equipment that he/she uses.

The minimum requirements of the workstation (i.e. display equipment, keyboard, software, accessories, disk drives, telephone, modem, printer, document holder, work chair, work surface or desk, etc. when provided are laid down in the schedule at the end of the regulations.

If possible, employers should organise the work of users so that work on the display screen equipment is periodically interrupted by breaks or changes of activity.

Before a person is employed as a user, that person has a right to have an appropriate eye and eyesight test carried out by a competent person. Such tests should be available to users at regular intervals.

Before any person becomes a user he should be provided with appropriate health and safety training in the use of any workstation on which he is to work. Users are to be given information on the measures being taken to comply with the regulations insofar as they relate to the user.

Seating and posture for office tasks

For office tasks, the following are needed:

1 an adjustable back rest on the seat
2 good back/lumbar support
3 height adjustability on seat. Arms should be horizontal to the table.
4 thighs not exposed to excess pressure

Figure 12.12 Seating and posture for office tasks

5   footrest/support if the feet are not flat on floor; this reduces pressure on the backs of the legs

6   clear space around the desk for postural changes and movement

7   a mouse and keyboard within easy reach; arms should be at right angles and not outstretched.

8   minimum wrist movement

9   adjustable screen height and angle to align eyes with the top of the screen

10 space on the desk to rest wrists during breaks in typing.

Portable appliance testing (PAT)

PAT is an important part of complying with electrical health and safety legislation. Regular PAT testing should be done where electrical equipment is used by employees. PAT testing should also be carried out after a piece of equipment has been serviced or repaired. PAT testing ensures that an item is free from electrical fault.

Electricity in the workplace

As well as general health and safety legislation, electrical safety in the workplace is covered by the Electricity at Work Regulations 1989. These regulations require that employers take steps to limit the risk of injury from electricity to people working on or near to electrical systems.

Economic implications of ICT

The main driving force in the development of ICT has been the benefits this new hardware and software bring to business. The possibilities to expand to global markets and streamline complex manual processes through computerisation have exciting possibilities for businesses and other organisations.

Competitive advantage

Businesses can improve their efficiency and effectiveness by applying ICT and information systems to those areas of the organisation where it will improve service delivery, production, information gathering, processing and analysis, and where it can effectively improve the communication between the business, its customers and its suppliers. In this way ICT can help businesses to maintain and increase their competitive advantage over competitors.

A business has a **competitive advantage** when it can make greater profits selling its products or services than its competitors. This happens when a company can charge a premium because its product or service is more valuable, or because it can sell its product or service for less than its competitors because it is a more efficient producer.

The benefits of ICT for competitive advantage

In order to gain or increase this competitive advantage, a business can use the benefits provided by ICT and information systems. Businesses operating in a very competitive environment can obtain cost advantages by using ICT to, for example,

- sell products online
- keep potential and actual customers informed about product information through the company website
- keep electronic records of financial and customer information and use a system that records sales information electronically
- by linking sales information to a stock control and reporting system, know when to purchase new supplies and/or increase production.

If the IT system has been designed properly and the operators trained in using the system, the information provided is likely to be up-to-date, accurate and relevant. This means that managers can use this information to make more informed decisions than if the information came from a manual system, where it is unlikely to be up-to-the-minute. Having the latest information is vital for business decision-making, especially when decisions concern future actions, or the pricing and purchasing of products.

If a business has a website, customers can also be kept informed. Information about products and product details and the facility to make online purchases brings significant advantages to both the customer and the business. The fact that the World Wide Web operates 24 hours a day allows businesses to communicate with customers around the world and enter foreign markets without the cost of establishing a physical presence. The World Wide Web offers 24-hour global trading without the traditional costs related to a global enterprise.

Business costs

However, there are costs involved in developing the systems to gain and maintain this competitive advantage. These costs include the initial setup of the system, the running costs and the investment costs. Taken together these individual costs contribute to the total cost of ownership for the system.

- *Initial setup:* the initial cost to design, develop and install the system. This will include the cost of the systems analysis and design to produce the system and specialist installation and configuration services for hardware and software.

- *Running:* the cost of operating and maintaining the system. Running costs include the cost of electricity, data connections provided by telecommunications companies (such as ADSL), salaries of support staff, cost of consumables such as paper, printer suppliers and so on.

- *Investment cost:* the cost of supporting the system in terms of capital investment in hardware and software.

Total cost of ownership

The **total cost of ownership** (TCO) is the total cost of an information system throughout its lifecycle, from acquisition to disposal. The aim of TCO analysis is to identify, quantify and, ultimately, reduce the overall costs associated with ownership of networked assets.

The TCO is the combined hard and soft costs of owning a networked information system. 'Hard' costs include items such as the purchase price of the information system, implementation fees, upgrades, maintenance contracts, support contracts and disposal costs. These costs are considered 'hard costs' because they are tangible and easily accounted for. Hard costs are the capital investment required to produce the system.

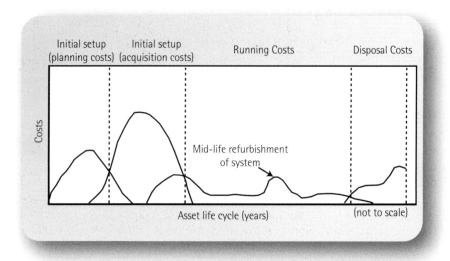

Figure 12.13 Phases in the TCO of an information system

Even more significant in most environments, however, are the 'soft' costs related to management, support, training, hidden costs and downtime. Because they don't occur at acquisition time, these costs are frequently overlooked in budgets, often leading to unexpected increases, or, worse, a transfer of management and support responsibility to end users.

TCO helps to avoid 'apples vs. oranges' comparisons (where it is difficult to make comparisons because the items being compared are not very similar) among alternatives competing for the same limited budget. For example, a company might be considering the alternative of buying a used ink-jet printer or a new laser printer. The ink-jet printer will be considerably cheaper than the laser printer, but the repair costs and consumable costs of the ink-jet printer will be much higher than those of the laser printer: all of these need to be taken into account when considering a purchase.

The TCO has to be compared to the total benefits of ownership (TBO) to determine the true viability of an information system.

Ethical implications of ICT

Ethics refers to well based standards of right and wrong that prescribe what humans ought to do, usually in terms of rights, obligations, benefits to society, fairness and specific virtues. Ethics, for example, refers to those standards that prohibit us from stealing, murder, assault, slander and fraud, and encourage us to be honest, compassionate and loyal. Ethical standards also include rights, such as the right to life, the right to freedom from injury, the right to choose, the right to privacy, and the right to freedom of speech and expression.

ICT ethics are not very different from general ethics. In a world where information and communications technology has come to define how people live and work, and has critically affected culture and values, it is important for us to review ethical issues and the standards that we apply to our use of information systems.

Figure 12.14 Dilbert's boss asks him to do something unethical

General issues

Analysing and evaluating the impact of a technology such as ICT can be very difficult. ICT does not only involve technological aspects but also the use of data, information and knowledge. ICT assists and extends the ability of mankind to capture, store, process, understand, use, create and transmit information at a speed and scale which had never been thought possible before. Some of the impact and changes brought about by ICT are obvious, but many are subtle. Some of the main ethical implications and considerations are detailed below with some examples.

- *Unemployment:* The automation of work has caused creative destruction by eliminating some jobs and creating new ones. How does this affect the employment or unemployment of the workforce?

- *Crime:* For example, stolen and counterfeit ATM cards are used to steal millions of pounds each year. The relative anonymity of such machines and computer systems makes some crimes easier and creates many new types of crimes.

- *Errors:* Data input is prone to human and device error. Computer programs that process information might contain thousands of errors. These errors can create wrong and misleading information about individuals and organisations. Information and program errors might result in financial loss, or even the loss of lives.

- *Intellectual property:* Millions of pounds of software is illegally copied each year all over the world via CD, DVD and online piracy. This phenomenon has a great impact on the software industry across the world. Software developers need consumer support from all over the world to maintain the progress of technology.

- *Digital divide:* How does ICT affect local community life? The increasing use of computers has increased the separation of rich and poor, creating a digital divide between the information 'haves' and 'have-nots'.

- *Professional ethics:* How well trained and ethical are our ICT professionals? Faulty and useless systems that cause disasters and problems for users might be built by incompetent ICT professionals.

Censorship and freedom of speech

The range of content on the Internet means that there is much material that different sections of society may find offensive or disturbing. Many sections of society are pressing for censorship of the Internet. Around the world some governments restrict access to the web and limit the sites available to prevent their populations accessing offensive material or material relating to free speech and democracy.

Censorship

China, for example, is seeking to control all incoming traffic from the Internet through the implementation of various restrictions. The reasoning is to stop any action initiated on the net that 'hinders public order'. Among other actions, Internet service providers must register with the authorities.

Around the Middle East similar attitudes exist. The first priority seems to be to restrict sexual content on the net. Secondly, political and religious information is monitored, or outright censored. Saudi Arabia states that all communication is subject to inspection. The official policy is to protect people from the harmful effects of pornographic material and whatever other harmful items are on the Net.

In the UK there are no explicit Internet laws, as yet. The UK is using previously written obscenity laws to enforce respectable Internet publishing. Various UK organisations are attempting to initiate voluntary regulation of content on the Internet. The belief is that the only alternative to self-regulation is eventual government control.

This self-regulation is the method that freedom of speech proponents are promoting as the answer. It satisfies the legal 'good faith' effort to restrict undesirable ('indecent') sites from being accessed by children and it meets the 'least restrictive means possible' clause without needlessly treading on 'decent' sites. The introduction of a self-rating system, such as the platform for Internet content selection (PICS), developed by the World Wide Web Consortium, is leading the development of this self-regulation approach.

Freedom of speech

Freedom of speech is one of the most revered human rights in democratic societies. It is fiercely protected in the courts that rule on its behalf. However, it does have limits. As has been noted repeatedly and wisely, freedom of expression is not an absolute right. There are limits, both moral and legal, to which we must adhere.

The Internet has opened doors to freedom of speech that have never been accessible before. The ideal of free speech has never really been achieved in the past because the control of communications media has always been in the hands of a few people. Most people's free speech was limited to small rooms, discussion amongst family, friends and maybe neighbours, but often only to their diaries! Certainly such a grand scale of many speaking to many has never been achieved before with such success. The

Internet allows the least privileged people to enter and take part in discussions on any subject of their choosing with many of the most privileged members of society.

Privacy and encryption

Maintaining privacy in our personal communications is something everyone needs. Encryption is a means to achieve that privacy. It was invented for that very purpose. That makes encryption a good idea? But encryption, like most things, can be used for good or evil. And the debate over how to harness this powerful tool rages on as people on both sides see that there are no easy answers.

Encryption is the process of scrambling a message so that only the intended recipient can read it. The actual cryptographic process is generally a complicated mathematical formulation, the more complex, the more difficult to break. A **key** is supplied to the recipient so that they can then decipher the message. Keys for encryption algorithms are described in terms of the number of bits. The higher the number of bits, the more difficult that cryptosystem should be to break.

The need for encryption

As more and more information is stored on computers or communicated via computers, it becomes more important to ensure that this information is invulnerable to investigation and/or tampering. Think about your own personal information (e.g. medical records, school records, employment history, etc.) and you will quickly think of areas where you want, need or expect privacy.

Encryption is seen by many people as a necessary step for commerce on the Internet to succeed. Users are unwilling to trust a site enough to make a purchase unless they are confident that the site is secure. Encryption provides consumers with the confidence they need to do Internet business.

Encryption can also provide a means of 'message authentication'. The *PGP* (Pretty Good Privacy) *User's Guide* explains, 'The sender's own secret key can be used to encrypt a message thereby signing it. This creates a digital signature of a message which proves that the sender was the true originator of the message, and that the message has not been subsequently altered by anyone else, because the sender alone possesses the secret key that made that signature.' This prevents forgery of that signed message and prevents the sender from denying the signature.

Insecure communications

E-mail and most other Internet communications are certainly not secure. While you may believe that the use of a password makes your communications private, you should be aware that sending information without encryption is like sending postcards through the mail. Your data is totally open to interception by anyone along the way. You may believe that your personal communications are not incriminating and do not contain content that you must keep secret and you may be right. But there are many common situations, where users have a legitimate need for security, both to protect information and to ensure that information is not amended.

Users placing orders with credit cards via the Internet, doctors protecting patient files, businesses sending trading information, etc. all need encryption for communication.

Global citizenship

We live in a world that is getting smaller, a world with a global focus, rather than a national focus, where people travel the world for work and holidays, and where communications can travel round the globe in seconds. Many of us have family origins or family members in other countries. We live, work and study alongside people from all over the world. All forms of culture are shaped by global influences. Each decision we make as people can have an impact on global society.

We are all global citizens and, as such, must take responsibility for the world around us, consider 'global issues' and how we can support others around the globe. As our world develops, we must learn to respond to the issues that arise. The analysis of future trends from current research into the global economy has revealed that:

- the economic gap between the richest and the poorest within countries will widen significantly, and poverty will increase
- information technologies will reduce hugely the privacy of individuals
- inequalities between those who have access to information technologies and those who do not will increase dramatically
- conflicts of interest between developed and developing countries will increase
- the cost of obtaining adequate water will increase due to population growth, deforestation and environmental deterioration
- migration flows from poor to rich areas within and between countries will have an impact on security and social order
- increased use of genetic engineering will create more complex ethical questions
- economic growth will be fuelled by knowledge (ideas, innovations and inventions) more than natural resources.

Other undesirable but less probable areas have also been identified (increased regulation and control by governments; a decline in people's sense of community and social responsibility; increased consumerism; a rise in drug-related crime). An effective global citizen will be able to respond to these changes because of their abilities:

- to conceive of problems in global as well as local terms
- to work with others in a cooperative way and take responsibility
- to understand, accept, appreciate and tolerate cultural differences
- to think in a critical and systematic way
- to resolve conflict in a non-violent manner
- to participate in politics at local, national and international levels
- to change lifestyle and consumption habits to protect the environment
- to be sensitive towards and defend human rights.

The global dimension to citizenship is more than learning about global issues such as sustainable development or international trade, as important as these are. It is also about understanding the global factors to local issues which are present in all our lives, localities and communities.

As global citizens and users of ICT we have a responsibility to use hardware, software and communications technology appropriately with due consideration for others.

Questions

1. Give **three** advantages and **three** disadvantages of globalisation.

2. Describe **two** examples of the impact of globalisation on business.

3. Explain the difference between 'information rich' and 'information poor'.
   What are the disadvantages of being 'information poor'?

4. Explain the term *digital divide* using an example.

5. Give **two** advantages and **two** disadvantages of e-commerce for the consumer.

6. Big Toys Inc. is a global company specialising in the sale of children's toys. The company has spent a considerable amount of money developing a global infrastructure to support a centralised IS business model which makes use of MIS, DSS and EIS.

   a Explain why a centralised IS business model is the most appropriate model for a company which makes use of MIS, DSS and EIS.

   b The company make use of a complex supply-chain management system.
   Explain **two** benefits for the company of such a system.

   c What is *electronic procurement* and what are the advantages of using this in business?

7. EDI is a tool for exchanging business data.

   a Explain why EDI was developed for communication of data between businesses.

   b Explain the need for *data standards* in EDI and how these standards would be used.

8. What precautions should users take when creating an online identity?

9. What is an avatar and how can it be used?

10. Our privacy is increasingly being invaded by companies and individuals using ICT.

    a Describe **two** ways that a user can protect his/her privacy online.

    b Describe the process of *mining the clickstream*.

11. An organisation is likely to hold a lot of information about its employees. Employers must comply with the Data Protection Act 1998.

    a What steps must an organisation take to ensure that it is operating within the rules of the Data Protection Act?

    b Explain your rights under the Data Protection Act 1998.

12. Explain the implications of the European 'Database Directive' for web designers.

13. Software piracy is an offence under the Copyright, Designs & Patents Act 1988.

  a Describe **three** types of software piracy.

  b Software piracy has negative effects on the producers of software and the end users. Describe **one** negative effect for:

  i producers

  ii end users.

14. What is the purpose of the Regulation of Investigatory Powers Act?

15. Discuss the possible positive and negative implications for employees of a company that monitors their communications.

16. a Briefly outline your rights as defined by the Freedom of Information Act (Scotland) 2002.

  b What steps must an organisation take to ensure that it is operating within the rules of the Data Protection Act?

17. Businesses have a duty of care for their employees. State **three** requirements that employers must adhere to in relation to health and safety.

18. Explain the term *competitive advantage* and give **three** examples of how ICT can be used to gain competitive advantage.

19. Explain the concept of *total cost of ownership* (TCO).

20. Azak uses his computer to complete his work for college. His work involves using the World Wide Web to search for details of the Iraq War.
Azak knows that some of his lecturers are concerned about the ethics of using the World Wide Web to research for coursework. Describe **one** other ethical issue that might arise from the use of a computer system with access to the Internet.

21. Big Solutions PLC is a firm selling complete software solutions to large commercial and governmental organisations.
One of the employees is found using the internal e-mail system to try to sell toiletries from a company called SmellyGood to other workers in the firm.
Comment on the legality and ethics of doing this.

22. Censorship of Internet content is commonplace in a number of countries around the world.

  a Explain why some countries censor or prohibit access to the Internet.

  b Explain why censorship of the Internet may sometimes be required to protect individuals, such as children.

23. Explain why encryption is needed to protect individual privacy.

24. In our ever more complex world it is important that we understand our positions as global citizens.

  a Describe some of the responsibilities of a *global citizen*.

  b How should a global citizen use ICT?

Index